When You
Are the
Headline

MANAGING
A MAJOR
NEWS STORY

When You Are the Headline

MANAGING A MAJOR NEWS STORY

Robert B. Irvine

DOW JONES-IRWIN
Homewood, Illinois   60430

This publication is designed to provide accurate and
authoritative information in regard to the subject matter
covered. It is sold with the understanding that the
publisher is not engaged in rendering legal, accounting, or
other professional service. If legal advice or other expert
assistance is required, the services of a competent
professional person should be sought.

*From a Declaration of Principles jointly adopted by a Committee
of the American Bar Association and a Committee of Publishers.*

ISBN 0-87094-926-8

Library of Congress Catalog Card No. 87–70394

Printed in the United States of America

2 3 4 5 6 7 8 9 0 BC 4 3 2 1 0 9 8 7

To Ann and Eddie

The Eye of the Beholder

It's 4:30 A.M. and CBS News is on the phone. They want to talk to somebody about an accident in Bhopal. Ed Van Den Ameele, Union Carbide's media relations manager, suddenly was wide awake. "They had a wire service report out of India that said there was a gas leak and a few people had been killed," he recalled. "At the time the guy said 30 to 35. He started giving me all of the details, including the cows that were lying dead in the streets. As I talked to him, he kept getting more reports. By the time I got off the phone the death count he had was up to 200 to 300 people."[1]

Union Carbide was no different than the hundreds of companies and organizations each year that traditionally have avoided publicity and maintained a low profile, but are suddenly thrust into the glare of the news media spotlight when they find themselves in the midst of a major story. The exposure that began for Carbide with that first phone call would continue for more than a year. The resulting coverage in the print and broadcast news media would be closely followed by the financial and investment communities, plaintiff's attorneys, government officials, employees, community leaders, and other influential groups whose primary information and perceptions of the company would be gleaned from those news reports. The actions of those publics, based on the media coverage, would give the company far more to think about than the accident itself.

You're staring into the monitor in the control room at the Kennedy Space Center, watching what looks like a perfect lift-off of the Challenger space shuttle. Mission Control reports in a technological litany to a worldwide audience of millions as the shuttle and its booster rockets thunder upward through the cold, clear January sky—for 73 seconds. A spurt of flame, a violent, fiery explosion, and Challenger is gone. The data on the control room computers suddenly disappear and are replaced by the same straight lines you see on a cardiac monitor when a patient has died.

Shirley Green, NASA's newly appointed director of public affairs, sits in stunned silence with everyone else in the control room. As emergency procedures go into effect, she carries out her first duty by calling the administrator's office in Washington and then starts thinking about the statement that has to be made to the public. After all, the entire world saw the explosion, and NASA has a public affairs contingency plan for accidents. NASA's management is out of town or tied up implementing its contingency plan for accidents. The top executive for the Office of Space Flight at the Kennedy Space Center that day says he'll talk with reporters, but he keeps being pulled into meetings and saying it will be a few more minutes. Meanwhile every phone in the NASA press center is ringing, and reporters are milling around wanting details, pictures, information, interviews—anything.

A press briefing is scheduled and then repeatedly postponed. White House Press Secretary Larry Speakes is calling, wanting to know when NASA is going to say something. He keeps getting the same answer—in a few more minutes. More hours pass. By the time a briefing is held, the die has been cast. What went on in those four and half hours so tainted NASA's relations with the news media that neither Shirley Green nor anyone else could reverse the situation in the following months.

The phone rings on Thanksgiving afternoon. The quiet Rocky Mountain monotone of Dr. DeVries catches your attention in a hurry. Bill Schroeder's heart is giving out, and we may have to push up the operation to this weekend. How close are you to being ready to announce? We're okay . All I need to do is finish the release and brief the family on what will happen when the announcement is made. "Good," he says. "See you on rounds tomorrow." Turkey and football are forgotten. Phone calls have to be made.

What will you do if your organization is going to be in the midst of a major news story? Hopefully, you won't be faced with a catastrophe of the magnitude of Bhopal or with such an agonizing, public tragedy as the explosion of Challenger. But magnitude is meaningless when it comes to news coverage, and there doesn't have to be loss of life or extensive damage for the media to head your way. If you're a prison warden somewhere in the Southwest, the manager of an industrial facility outside of Chicago, a mine supervisor in West Virginia, or a hospital administrator in a small town, a dozen reporters and television cameras will be the same for you as the 1,500 newspeople were for NASA after the Challenger accident.

You quickly find that *When You Are the Headline*, there's much more at stake than how the story is reported. The integrity of your organization and your personal and professional reputation will be on the line in every statement you make. What you say and how you respond to the news media influences your organization and the perceptions it conveys to the diverse publics it deals with in the course of its business. Warren Anderson, chairman and CEO of Union Carbide, observed, "You have so many audiences it's difficult to be responsive to one audience without concerning yourself with the others. We had to be thinking about congressional hearings as well as press conferences. The questions are simple. How you respond to them can get complicated, and it's in 'the eye of the beholder.' You can respond in a way that will insure the shareholder feels comfortable and really mess yourself up with another constituency."[2]

An onslaught from the press is never easy. It's more sudden, more aggressive, more incessant than anybody can imagine. Shirley Green at NASA recalled that after the Challenger accident, never in her life had she seen so many people descend on such a small space so fast and with so much intensity. "I don't know how that many people could have appeared from almost nowhere in so short a time," she said. "We had 400 to 500 newspeople credentialed for the launch, and most of those were photographers. By nightfall 800 more had come. By the next day we had 1,400 to 1,500 members of the press. It was wall-to-wall people."[3]

If you've never dealt with the national news media before, you'll find the majority of the journalists to be smart, hard working, and highly reputable. They will report the story, but their news organizations also will editorialize. That's the nature of their business. The story itself may be a straight news report, but the wording of headlines and photo captions—which is all that many people will read—will depend in part on how you and your organization respond in those first few hours of the media disclosure.

Suddenly you're a public figure. Reporters will want to interview you, and you'll be invited to be a guest by producers of the network morning shows and evening news shows and late-night shows and weekend news shows. It may seem like the chance of a lifetime, but you won't know the "rules" until you appear on the set—and find out you're appearing alone or with your worst critics from some other city via satellite. Nor can you anticipate the questions or comments that may be fired at you. When it's live TV, each response has to be your best, and you will have to make those decisions on the spot and all by yourself.

Every journalist has the instincts of an investigative reporter; it becomes ingrained in them throughout their professional training and experience. It is reinforced by their editors or news directors in much the same way IRS supervisors train the agents assigned to audit your tax form. They know you're not telling them everything, and they're going to be looking for any hole, any discrepancy or inconsistency that will unlock the door to what you have chosen not to disclose.

If it's a national story and the initial probing gives any indication there's more to it than has been reported, you're likely to meet the journalistic gunslingers—the reporters, researchers, and freelancers who ride into town with one intent—to dig up the startling or juicy details. They usually know little or nothing about the subject when they arrive, and they will be very friendly in seeking out your help. Then tough, incisive questions will be asked and you quickly find they are very adept at coming up with sources to give them the details you are not willing to provide.

A breaking news story is no place for foxhole mentality. That approach will not succeed with the news media any more than if your competition wants the lion's share of your business and you decide to do nothing about it. The media is looking for someone who will be direct, straightforward, and honest. If you tell them what you don't know and what you do know, if you promise to get back to them with a statement—if you stick to your word and return their phone calls— the odds are that even if you can't give reporters exactly what they want, you will survive the onslaught intact.

In making those choices you create a prism through which you and your organization are going to be perceived by the media, by all of your constituencies, and by the general public. To change the shape of the prism and alter the way your organization is perceived after those critical first hours will be much harder than anybody can imagine. Consider the job that faced NASA after the Challenger accident.

You, as an executive or as the person responding to the news media, suddenly will become essential to the future of your organization. Its perceived value will be determined primarily by whatever information you convey to its board members, investors, customers, government officials, employees, and other publics via the news media. Your statements will spill over and affect your entire industry, a point that Warren Anderson of Union Carbide made about Bhopal when he said that the accident "raised an issue that's worldwide, that goes far beyond what Union Carbide did at Bhopal. It's an issue of how you cope with new products, new plants. . . the health and safety of individuals."[4]

The same applies if it's not a disaster but an important new development in medical science. The artificial heart has been far more than a story about Dr. DeVries' experiment with Barney Clark, Bill Schroeder, and the others who volunteered to live out their lives with a mechanical pump for a heart. In many ways it symbolizes the revolution that is reshaping our health care delivery system and changing its priorities. The government, the American people, and the news media have begun looking at health care in an entirely new way over the past five years. There's still the same strong interest in medical breakthroughs, but we no longer live in a "Yes Doctor" society. People are questioning what the medical community is doing, and the news media has mirrored that change in attitude by exploring the social, ethical, and financial implications of the artificial heart as well as reporting on the experiment itself.

The big question in everyone's mind will be what long-term impact the news story will have on your organization. Nobody really knows in those first few days; but the news media will editorialize, and your publics will draw conclusions according to how you and your organization are perceived through the media prism. Organizations often talk about their profit centers. You—who determine how your different publics will perceive the value of the organization during a major news story—will become its "value center."

How your organization responds to the media can have a greater effect on its value than virtually any business decision it makes. The members of top management who are involved will determine whether it's to be a hostile media siege that can tear the organization apart or a planned, well-managed working relationship with the press that actually strengthens the organization while making sure the accurate story is told.

When You Are the Headline was written to show how you can protect and perhaps even enhance your organization's value when it's in a major news story. Most people assume that involves some type of crisis management, and it's true that many major news stories emanate from disasters like Bhopal or the Challenger accident. But Bill Schroeder's story wasn't a crisis. Bill's operation and early recovery was an exhilarating experience for the participants, the press, and the public relations staff who were brought together by a remarkable man who chose to live out his life with a mechanical heart rather than to die, and who thus caught the imagination of the world.

Recall the round-the-world nonstop flight of the Voyager for a moment. That wasn't a crisis, but like the artificial heart, it fascinated all of us. For one week Voyager was a major news story for a small, entrepreneurial company whose briefing center was in a hangar on the Mojave Desert. It's management team found responding to the media deluge as exciting and exhausting as the flight was for the two pilots in that strange looking airplane.

You'll find no fancy formulas in the chapters that follow. The approach I'm advocating, and the one urged by the media, is common sense communications that can be employed by any organization, large or small, for any type of news story, whether it's in your local community or worldwide. The basic principles are the same for the worst possible disaster for a major corporation, as in the case of Union Carbide after Bhopal, or a medical experiment where the human interest is as great as the scientific significance, as with Bill Schroeder. They are based on being responsive but having a disclosure strategy that's realistic considering the situation and the nature of your organization. You can't transform the personality of your institution or its corporate culture just because a major news story is about to break. But you can be pragmatic in developing a strategy for disclosing what has happened and for providing background information and visuals, updating the news media, and protecting the privacy of the participants from the reporters and television crews who will be at your front door within minutes of the first news bulletin. That's what this book will describe.

When You Are the Headline is for people whose jobs involve working with the news media. It's also for senior executives who've never had any experience with "those people" but who know they will have that responsibility if their organization finds itself in the midst of a newsworthy situation. It is for every executive because it demonstrates (1) just how a new "value center" will emerge and (2) the permanent effect your decisions regarding media relations can have on how the organization is perceived and on the way it will operate in the future. Essentially, *When You Are the Headline* is for anyone who may someday be forced to direct his or her organization through a major news story. Considering the growing pervasiveness of news coverage, that description fits most executives today, regardless of the organization they manage.

THE ORIGINS OF THIS BOOK

When You Are the Headline had its origins before dawn one morning in December 1984 outside the hospital room of artificial heart patient Bill Schroeder. Dr. William C. DeVries, the surgeon who had implanted Schroeder's mechanical heart, had given me the details for the overnight medical update on his patient's condition, which would be distributed to the media as soon as I got downtown to the briefing center. He leaned against the wall for a few moments and then quietly asked if I had a personal record of what we had been going through with the media. I had been keeping a log. Often it was the only way I could drain my mind after being pulverized in our endless workdays, which always seemed to start and end in the darkness of night.

When You Are the Headline originally was to be based on our experiences with the artificial heart. However, from the initial research and interviews with both journalists and spokespersons, it became apparent that the media's approach in covering a major story is basically the same, regardless of whether it's medical or nonmedical. At that point, the scope of the book was expanded to include news events outside of the medical arena to make it more useful to a broader cross section of readers who someday might find themselves or their organizations in the headlines.

By June 1985, when I left Humana to begin work on this project, Dr. DeVries had implanted artificial hearts in three patients. We had gone through all of the major milestones in the ensuing news coverage at least once. Bill Schroeder had provided the media with an 18-day news bonanza until his first stroke impaired his ability to speak and changed the tenor of the media's relationship with Humana. Still, in April, Schroeder became the first artificial heart patient to be discharged from the hospital when he was moved to a transition apartment across the street. Murray Haydon, a private person by nature, suffered respiratory damage after his artificial heart operation and chose not to be interviewed by the news media.[5] Jack Burcham suffered kidney failure and died just 10 days after his JARVIK-7 was implanted. Burcham's death provided our initial experience with the news disclosure that we knew would happen at some point but dreaded all the same.

Murray Haydon died on June 19, 1986, after living 488 days with a mechanical heart, and Bill Schroeder lived until August 6, 1986, a record 620 days with an artificial heart. They had been insulated from most of the news media coverage during their last months of life, but Dr. DeVries still has had to contend with the critics and nay-sayers who feel the artificial heart experiment should be terminated because it cannot sustain an acceptable quality of life.

If the clinical trial could have proceeded without the extensive media coverage, I believe that by now Dr. DeVries would have completed the initial series of seven permanent artificial heart implants authorized by the FDA and the data would be undergoing review. Instead only four have been done. Dr. DeVries deserves the chance to complete the initial experiment so the FDA and the medical community, not the media, can determine whether the mechanical heart is viable for human use and how to improve it so that patients can enjoy a quality of life similar to what they now have with pacemakers.

I could not have been an employee of Humana and provided an objective assessment of our experiences with the news media. Nor could the news media have been as candid in their observations as they have been for this book. At the same time, a closeness with Humana has remained and has contributed significantly to the information in the following chapters. George Atkins and the Humana public affairs staff as well as Dr. DeVries, Dr. Lansing, and the other physicians, nurses, and staff at Humana Hospital-Audubon have provided many invaluable insights in the hope that others will understand what it's like *When You Are the Headline*.

The same holds true for the other spokespersons, participants, and members of the news media listed in the back of this book whose perspectives significantly expanded its scope. In fact, I had remarkable cooperation and support from everyone—except the Russians. My phone call to the Soviet Embassy in Washington requesting an interview regarding the media coverage of the Chernobyl nuclear power plant accident lasted less than one minute.

When You Are the Headline was written by one person, but it really is an anthology of information from hundreds of people who have been involved in major news events. While many are quoted, many others provided ideas that have profoundly influenced my thinking and writing, and their contributions are equally appreciated.

Bill Birnes at Shadowlawn Press has been a mentor to this novice author and an immense help in organizing my many ideas and initial drafts into what follows. The panel of public relations professionals and members of the news media who reviewed the early drafts provided many excellent ideas, but also the encouragement to keep me going on a writing project that often seemed like *War and Peace*.[6] My partner, Jack Guthrie, and our staff at Jack Guthrie and Associates have my gratitude for their endless patience, support, and for filling in for me. And finally to Becky, and our wonderful family— thanks for saying "I love you" so often with your endless understanding and help during these past two years.

This book belongs to us all.

Robert B. Irvine

CONTENTS

CHAPTER ONE

You May Not Have Time for This Book

By the time you get through this chapter, the Channel 4 "Action News" van could be pulling into your parking lot, while your office is frantically trying to contact you. They have NBC on one line and your boss on the other, wanting to see you right away. Scores of reporters and camera crews could be in your lobby before you can draft one paragraph of a press release, much less find out for yourself what has happened. The University of Arizona Medical Center in Tucson had that experience in 1985, when an artificial heart had to be flown in and implanted to keep Thomas Creighton alive on the operating table, and it undoubtedly will happen again.

How much time will you have to get ready? If "Action News" is on its way and the phones are ringing, you'd better skim through Chapter 2 to familiarize yourself with The 60-Minute Game Plan—and then get going. On the other hand, if you're not facing an imminent onslaught of the news media, I'll take you through what it will be like and then discuss what your organization needs to do to prepare itself and the people who will be involved, including yourself.

You know your organization and its top management. How prepared are they to cope with thousands of phone calls from the press, TV trucks in the parking lot and camera crews in the hall, a barrage of diverse questions from reporters, the intensity of the TV cameras and lights, and microphones thrust under their noses? Do they know who will be the spokespersons for the organization during a breaking news story? Do the key members of top management understand the impact a media onslaught can have on your organization, its people, its extended family, and its future? Do they appreciate how a major news story can affect the perceived public value and the actual dollar value of your corporation? This book addresses these issues.

You think your odds of getting involved in a major news event are almost nonexistent. Perhaps, but consider the major news stories of this past year and think about how the people at the center of those stories reacted. How many corporate, nonprofit, and government organizations have suddenly found themselves in the glare of the news spotlight? Imagine what your counterparts in each of these institutions went through when the cameras were suddenly turned on them. And think about what impact the favorable or unfavorable publicity is still having on their normal business activities.

The worst approach by far is to wait for the news story to break before getting ready, but it's one that top executives and their public relations people seem to take all too often.[7] Getting ready for the possibilities of being involved in a news story can begin now and should be one of your top priorities. As the case studies in this book will demonstrate, media onslaughts are never easy—but they can be managed.

Everyone starts off as a novice when a major news story breaks, regardless of how much media relations experience they've had. Many executives and public relations professionals have done extremely well in responding to news media onslaughts, while others have made horrendous mistakes.

Your success will be determined more by how well organized you are, your skill in providing useful information and visuals, and your choice of spokespersons than by your "media relations" skills. Ultimately what makes the difference will be your honesty and integrity, your ability to be flexible, your basic management skills, and your endurance in working in a stressful situation where both the participants and the press will be making unreasonable demands on you during workdays that never seem to end.

A QUICK INTRODUCTION TO THE NEWS MEDIA

The case studies that follow may cause you to think ill of the media. This is not my intent. The fact is that most members of the news media are people whom you can work with and respect. Journalists have been through this business of a breaking news story many times.

They see more personal tragedy and loss of life in a year than we probably will be exposed to in a lifetime. Their only reason for being sent there is to report on what's happening, not to attack the organization involved. You may have negative experiences, but they will be with those few newspeople who don't handle themselves in a professional or tasteful way, which may occur in any business or professional group, including your own.

Reporters have learned to work in a world of ducking and weaving, deliberate delays, stonewalling tactics, and outright lying by people who fear the consequences of giving bad news to the press. They have seen every conceivable move of politicians, physicians, personalities, and public relations people trying to accentuate the positive, eliminate the negative, and not mess with anything in between. And they know how to work around lawyers who feel there are legitimate reasons for not making any comments to the media at all and who will advise their clients to remain silent "so all the facts can be brought out in court, where they can be judged fairly and equitably."

The major problem the news media has to contend with is the phenomena of "pack journalism." When your organization is the subject of a media onslaught, this will be your problem as well. The term was coined by Sigma Delta Chi, the Society of Professional Journalists, to describe the change that occurs in reporters and their news-gathering techniques when they must compete for information and visuals with other local and national news organizations. Ed Yeates, a veteran journalist for KSL-TV who covered both Barney Clark's and Bill Schroeder's artificial heart operations, described it well. "We didn't know what to expect when we arrived in Louisville, but being in an alien market, you don't take chances on missing out on something. Well, that's the way pack journalism operates. The more media that come around, the more their curiosity and excitement build. It gets to the point where it can become a circus."[8]

In this competitive environment, the media seems to move at the speed of light in covering a major story. CBS News called Ira Furman, chief spokesperson for the National Transportation Safety Board, about the crash of Delta Flight 191 before he could be alerted by the NTSB operations center. Bob Henrie, spokesperson for the Emery Mining company during the Wilburg Mine fire, reached Huntington, Utah, the small town nearest the mine, following a crash landing at the town's airstrip after a 22-inch blizzard. At least 20 news organizations somehow traveled over an 8,800-foot mountain pass during the storm and were already there when he stumbled into the company office. Even though Humana provided no names, ABC News located and interviewed the young girl who kissed Bill Schroeder when he ventured out of the hospital for the first time on an impromptu wheelchair ride. That was at 4:30 P.M. The young girl's comment, "It was like talking to history," was part of the nationwide "ABC Evening News" broadcast at 6:00 P.M.

Journalism is a self-righteous profession that has established high, albeit unenforceable, ethical standards to justify its protection under the Constitution. Nobody is arguing with the importance of the First Amendment. It is a load-bearing wall in the structure of our democracy. Yet there have to be some practical limits to the freedom of the press, especially when that basic right begins to conflict with an individual's right to personal privacy—which also happens to be protected by the Constitution..

And lest we forget, the news business is just that—a business. "The news" is not a public service, and it's not a money-losing proposition; it is a commercial product that is gathered, packaged, and sold by the media. Journalists do satisfy the public's interest in having the latest news, but in the process they also satisfy their employers' financial interests, as well as their own career objectives.

During a conference of physicians, journalists, and public relations professionals, Jerry Bishop of *The Wall Street Journal* pointed out that most of the reporters who covered the artificial heart operations work for corporations that own newspapers, television stations, and networks, and that none of their employers had been obligated to cover the medical news story. "Newspapers make money by selling information. Some newspapers make it by selling very accurate, well-reported information. Others do it by selling very sensationalized information," Bishop observed. "That's the name of the game, that's the way it operates. Now some of us may think we have a higher role, but this is the way the press operates. We were there in Salt Lake City and Louisville, writing about these stories, because we felt that this is information that our readers would be willing to pay for. They pay for it so I don't think the press can plead any altruistic, or overall higher motives than that."[9]

Journalists cannot and will not control each other. They are not licensed and have no universally accepted code of ethics. There are no guidelines, no policies for media coverage other than to use good professional judgment. Most of the time they will make the right decisions, but the problems often occur miles away when the newsroom editors or rewrite people make interpretative decisions based on rationale that they alone understand at the time. That's when you find out that the news business is no different than your own and that they can foul things up just as badly. The problem is that when they do, the public gets the wrong impression about your organization, not theirs.

Many onslaughts could have been used as case studies in this book. Some, like Johnson & Johnson's handling of the two Tylenol poisoning crises, were not included because the companies have done an excellent job of explaining to others how they dealt with the media.[10] The news stories profiled in *When You Are the Headline* were all major media events that received worldwide coverage from the press. They are important for our purposes because by examining them we can see the different interactions that occurred among the journalists, the stories' participants, the public relations people, and management and how the coverage of each event was shaped by these interactions.

EVENTS AND DEVELOPMENTS

The stories fall into two basic categories. Several were disasters that became news "events" with the worldwide media coverage prompted by the public's interest in knowing what had happened to those involved and the reasons for the tragedy. In seeking the answers, journalists invariably revealed questionable actions or deficiencies among the people involved, pointing out their frailties and those of the organization itself. In other instances the news media reported on a medical experiment in response to the public's fascination with any bold new step that might turn out to be a lifesaving development for thousands. Part of the story, as it has been since the days of Pasteur, revolved around the efficacy and ethics of the experiment, with physicians, philosophers, and politicians using the news media to question whether it was appropriate for humans, the quality of life it would provide, and if it could be afforded by society.

Each story began as a media onslaught. Several became drawnout sieges in which the patience and stamina of people on all sides were stretched to the limit. Each represents a type of news media onslaught that is likely to occur again and provides insights into specific facets of the news story to help those who will be involved the next time. Specifically, tne case studies are:

Dr. Barney Clark's Artificial Heart

The immense news coverage of history's first permanent artificial heart patient virtually ended the traditional privacy between doctors and their patients involved in a medical experiment. For the first time the mass news media, particularly television, brought the world in on the ground floor of a clinical trial of a new medical device without having to wait for the results to be published in a medical journal.

The University of Utah expected the national news media to cover Barney Clark's surgery and the first few days of his recovery before moving on to other news stories. In fact, more then 300 newspeople showed up on December 1, 1982, during a snowstorm to cover the 10-hour operation. But then they didn't leave! For 112 days the media could be found in the hospital cafeteria, providing an incessant stream of news reports on Dr. Clark's crises and recoveries. After his death the coverage continued for more than a year as the media dug into questions of medical ethics, social implications, and financial considerations regarding the artificial heart program. The publicity also focused on the principal investigator, Dr. William C. DeVries and his running battle with the hospital's institutional review board to get approval to do a second artificial heart implant.

The extent of the checkbook journalism was surprising but set a precedent that would be seen again with Baby Fae and Bill Schroeder. *Stern*, the German magazine, paid for rights to show photos of Barney Clark's surgery, but the deal fell through when Dr. DeVries refused to release a photo showing Dr. Clark's diseased heart hanging from a forceps, dripping blood. The *Reader's Digest* signed a contract with Barney Clark's family for a book and assigned two writers who worked on the project for more than a year. The book has never been published, and Mrs. Clark filed suit seeking the unpaid part of the agreement. *Life* was willing to pay a University of Utah photographer $50,000 for one picture from the artificial heart operation, and Dr. Jarvik has said he was offered $1 million by the *National Enquirer* for exclusive rights to the artificial heart story.

As the artificial heart story evolved in the general news media, Dr. DeVries was portrayed as a surgical folk hero with a new device that could save thousands of patients dying from heart disease. That created problems for the clinical investigation and for DeVries himself. The lanky surgeon, a cross between Hollywood's Gary Cooper and Melville's Billy Budd, could handle the international renown in his own down-to-earth way, but he found it difficult dealing with the petty jealousies and politics at the University of Utah, as they are in any teaching institution. No matter that DeVries had brought immense worldwide recognition to the University of Utah. Many of his colleagues felt their own clinical research projects were more important but might lose out in the awarding of grants because of the publicity the artificial heart was receiving.

More than a year of meetings were required before approval was given by the Medical Center for a second artificial heart operation. In the meantime, he was passed over in the hospital's search for a new chief of cardiac surgery. DeVries' medical practice dwindled as referrals of open heart surgery cases declined sharply. His subsequent decision to leave the University of Utah was viewed with anger by many in Utah who thought he had sold out his allegiance to Humana. Others were angry because they respected him and understood his frustrations. Then there were those at the medical school and hospital who were relieved that DeVries and the artificial heart program had gone elsewhere.

Bill Schroeder's Artificial Heart

Humana had an immense public relations "problem/opportunity" when Dr. DeVries agreed to join the newly formed Humana Heart Institute International at Humana Hospital-Audubon in Louisville, Kentucky, its headquarters city. The artificial heart was a potential bonanza of favorable exposure for the $3 billion hospital and health care services corporation, but we also knew it would be viewed by the media as the proverbial fox in the henhouse. Here was a for-profit hospital company, one of those high-flying darlings of Wall Street frequently attacked by the *New England Journal of Medicine* and other critics, suddenly agreeing to underwrite the most famous clinical trial in history. The potential story ideas on Humana's ulterior motives were obvious and endless.

Bill Schroeder's surgery and remarkable recovery during the first 18 days provided the media with an abundance of medical news stories, which abruptly dried up when he suffered his first stroke.

Schroeder had thrived on the publicity. Even after the stroke he still enjoyed having photographs taken of him having Christmas dinner with his family, giving his "Rocky" salute on an exercycle, and eating pizza with his new dentures. However, with his speech impaired by the stroke, Schroeder no longer could carry on a conversation and didn't want to be interviewed. Consequently, the media suddenly found that the seemingly endless flow of upbeat news on Schroeder was replaced by weekly medical updates on his slow progress in recovering from the stroke. They had praised Humana's openness with the news media during Schroeder's surgery and initial recovery but now began to criticize the company for not providing the same access to Schroeder, his family, and the medical team that had been provided before the stroke. Meanwhile, the American Medical Association blasted Humana's artificial heart program as a medical experiment in a "circuslike atmosphere."

Bill Schroeder contended with strokes and other medical problems during his 620 days of life with an artificial heart. When he died, the media acknowledged his remarkable contribution to medical science, but the brunt of the coverage focused on whether the artificial heart was a viable alternative for patients with end stage heart disease. The debate still continues, with one of the major elements being whether the Humana media relations program was appropriate for the level of integrity the Humana Heart Institute International sought to maintain and whether this public relations program itself violated medical ethics and the privacy of its patients.

The Wilberg Mine

The 28 miners on second shift were unaware of the blizzard raging through the Utah mountains on Wednesday night, December 19, 1984. Their long wall mining machines had been churning through the coal so easily that by 9:30 P.M. the Wilberg Mine was closing in on a production record for tonnage in a 24-hour period. Then came the scream, "Fire in the intake." Only one miner managed to get into another passageway and crawl through the smoke to the entrance. Several others started out with him but became separated in the smoke and fire. Wilberg was to become one of the worst mining accidents in America in recent history.

Mine disasters are nothing new; but when one occurs during the Christmas season and the fate of 27 miners is not known for three days, the story takes on an entirely different significance for the news media. Even with the 22-inch snowstorm, more then 200 newspeople descended on Huntington, Utah, the small town nearest the Wilberg Mine, to cover a 72-hour drama focusing on whether the 27 trapped miners were still alive and how the rescue teams were risking their own lives in an underground inferno while trying to find and bring out their trapped comrades.

The Wilberg Mine fire proved to be a difficult story for the media to cover. The road up to the mine was closed to all except vehicles and personnel involved in the rescue operation. The response of several news organizations was to charter helicopters and fly into the narrow canyon to get close-ups of the smoke and fire pouring from the mine entrance. One helicopter just missed hitting the high-voltage lines supplying electrical power to huge fans ventilating the mine while rescue crews were underground, groping through the smoke and fire in search of survivors.

With access to the mine and its rescuers shut off, the media had to rely on details phoned down from the mine entrance to the mining company office in Huntington, which wasn't enough for their many editors and news directors in newsrooms hundreds of miles from the scene. The life-and-death drama in the Wilberg Mine had caught the attention of the world at Christmastime. Needing more to report and photograph, the media also turned its attention on the mining community and its families for human interest stories.

At first the 2,800 residents of Huntington welcomed the press and were awed by the satellite dish that was suddenly set up on their main street. Then the tightly knit community began to see insensitive, almost ghoulish reporting tactics as the reporters and camera crews pursued the miners' families on the street and at home, and the community's grief turned to rage. Media vehicles were pelted with beer and snowballs when they drove through town. The situation deteriorated and grew uglier as the full extent of the tragedy finally became known. Several photographers and TV camera operators were shoved, punched and kicked when they attempted to interview and photograph miners' families.

The rescue efforts and news media coverage continued around the clock for three days. By Saturday night the bodies of 25 miners had been located, and the remaining two miners were presumed buried in a caved-in section or consumed by the fire. Efforts to remove the dead suddenly had to be abandoned when the still-raging fire broke through near the main entrance, nearly cutting off the rescue teams. With the fire again out of control, and no survivors, the mine was sealed to cut the air supply feeding the inferno. Months later, the miners' bodies were finally brought out. By that time, it had become a local news item.

"Baby Fae"

An anonymous infant lived for 20 days with the heart of a baboon in a surgical experiment that caught the imagination of the world but startled the normally conservative medical community and ignited hostile reactions from the news media trying to report the story. The experimental operation on October 26, 1984, had an immediate front-page appeal because xenography, cross-species transplantation, had never been attempted on an infant before Dr. Leonard Bailey performed the surgery at Loma Linda University Medical Center near Los Angeles on the premature baby dying of a congenital heart defect. Baby Fae died three weeks later of complications related to the rejection of the walnut-sized baboon heart.

In many respects Loma Linda's dilemma in deciding how to relate to the news media was typical of many medical institutions that have never sought out the media spotlight and are not sure what to do or how to respond when the glare suddenly hits them. Here a traditionally conservative medical school affiliated with the Seventh Day Adventist Church, which had always kept a low profile, was suddenly spotlighted. The few times Loma Linda University Medical Center had sought out the Los Angeles news media, little interest had been shown. Why should a reporter drive all the way to the edge of the Mojave Desert for a story when the likes of the UCLA Medical Center and other medical institutions were nearby?

Even before the surgery was announced, Loma Linda seemed to be preparing for a siege. Vacations for all security personnel were canceled, and they began working 16-hour shifts. Locks on strategic doors were changed, electronic surveillance was increased, and the institution's police dog units went on call around the clock. The Medical Center's primary concern was the possible reaction of animal rights groups to the experimental surgery, but they also had no idea how the press would react and thus did not intend to tell the news media about Baby Fae's operation until after it was completed and the baby's condition had stabilized.

The plan was to perform the surgery on Friday morning and to deliver press kits on Saturday morning to the major news outlets in Los Angeles, announcing that Loma Linda Medical Center had transplanted a baboon heart into an infant. The plan went awry, however, when the newspaper in Barstow, California, where the mother lived, found out and interviewed her on the day before the operation. Another nearby newspaper in San Bernardino found out through a leak and almost broke the story on the morning of the operation. The first disclosure came from a Los Angeles television station on Friday afternoon, which was then picked up by the wire services. The onslaught was on!

Within hours the press coverage began to turn negative when the media learned that no effort had been made to seek out a human heart transplant for Baby Fae before proceeding with the surgical procedure to transplant the baboon heart. An infant donor heart became available 12 hours after the procedure, leading to accusations in the press and by others who read the news reports that Loma Linda had known of the availability of a human heart but had ignored it so the experiment could proceed. Some information provided by the Medical Center, including the age of the baby and whether she had previously been discharged from the hospital, turned out to be untrue when checked out by the media. Loma Linda's rationale was that they were trying to protect the anonymity of the baby's and parent's names, but the result was charges that Loma Linda was deliberately lying to the news media. This further damaged the credibility of the institution and caused many reporters to question the experiment as well as the integrity of Dr. Bailey and the Medical Center.

Dr. Bailey, after appearing at an initial press briefing, refused to clarify the many questions and issues raised by his statements about xenograph research grant applications that had been turned down or his scientific articles on the subject that had been rejected. This just added fuel to the fire caused by the misstatements made by the several medical spokespersons who briefed the press on different occasions. On one occasion a surgeon on the Loma Linda medical faculty opened a news conference by saying he had just seen Baby Fae being nursed by her mother. In fact, Baby Fae was not nursed. Lawrence K. Altman, M.D., the highly regarded medical writer for the *New York Times*, spoke for the media when he observed, "When researchers like Dr. Bailey decline to talk directly to the press and delegate that task to others who do not know the facts and who answer questions by guessing at the answers or by making factual mistakes, then the absent principal investigators are responsible for the resulting mistakes and distortion, if not sensationalism, that result."[11]

Loma Linda expected to gain significant recognition from the Baby Fae experiment and from the news media's perspective. That certainly has happened. "It would be hard to find a more flagrant example of what not to do than the Loma Linda model. From start to finish it stands as a worst-case scenario in terms of mismanagement of information, misunderstanding of the role of the press, and possibly miscarriage of research."[12]

The Challenger Shuttle Explosion

The unthinkable came at 73 seconds into the 25th space shuttle mission, with America's first teacher-astronaut aboard and with millions of school children across the country watching for the first "lesson from space." After a seemingly flawless launch on January 28, 1986, Challenger suddenly disappeared in a fiery explosion of orange and yellow and red flames that engulfed the spacecraft, spewing fragments across the sky amidst tentacles of vaporizing rocket propellant. Veterans at NASA, including its public affairs staff, knew within moments that there was no hope for the crew. They waited in vain for Challenger to break out of the fiery white cloud and begin its glide back toward the Cape Kennedy runway, which was to be the emergency procedure if a major problem occurred during launch. But nothing intact emerged from the fireball. Only the two solid rocket boosters veered away, one with a strange plume pouring from its side. And the downlink was lost: the spacecraft had stopped sending telemetry and radio signals.

Hugh Harris, NASA's chief of public information at the Kennedy Space Center, handled the public narration during the countdown and lift-off before routinely switching the commentary to Mission Control in Houston when the Challenger cleared the tower and headed toward space. Harris had seen rockets explode, as had most of the people in the control room, yet he could only watch the TV screen in stunned, incredulous, horrified silence.

NASA has had a public affairs contingency plan for shuttle accidents since 1983. Statements under Public Affairs Responsibilities clearly establish NASA's intentions in an emergency. Specifically:

> Declaration of an emergency or the occurrence of a catastrophic mission failure underlies the continuing responsibility to maintain a full flow of accurate, timely, and factual information to the news media.
>
> In the event of an emergency involving crew injury or fatality, the fact will be apparent to radio listeners and TV viewers, as well as observers at the launch and landing sites.
>
> Delay by NASA in confirming such information serves no useful purpose.
>
> Status of the crew will be the prime public consideration under any emergency situation. Consequently the facts, once confirmed, should be announced as quickly as possible. No longer than 20 minutes should elapse before an announcement is made.[13]

In line with NASA's public affairs contingency plan, Shirley Green began trying to line up Jesse Moore, associate administrator for spaceflight, to talk to the press at the briefing center, a half mile from the control room. That didn't work either. Dr. William R. Graham, acting director of NASA, had called from Washington immediately after the accident and had placed Moore in charge of an interim review board, which began meeting to determine how the data from the mission could be saved and collected while rescue and recovery were underway. With Moore tied up, and the acting director elsewhere, Green had no senior official who could speak for NASA.

It would be nearly five hours before Moore would brief the media, only to provide little new information on the accident. In the interim, Harris drafted written statements regarding the few facts they had at the time and providing details on the search and rescue efforts underway. He was not allowed to release anything. NASA's well-oiled media relations capabilities—until then one of the best in the field—had failed at the critical time when it was most needed.

The same basic failure of management to understand priorities would be cited later by the Rogers Commission as a basic cause of the Challenger disaster itself. In its report to the president, the commission even referred to NASA's failure to be forthright with the public: "For the first several days after the accident—possibly because of the trauma resulting from the accident—NASA appeared to be withholding information about the accident from the public. After the commission began its work, and at its suggestion, NASA began releasing a great deal of information that helped reassure the public that all aspects of the accident were being investigated and that the full story was being told in an orderly and thorough manner."[14]

It only took a few hours, but NASA's management myopia and subsequent siege mentality regarding the news media seriously damaged a highly effective press relations program that had been developed and refined over a quarter century of space flight. It also turned the media against NASA in an attack that would continue unabated for six months. In the process the image of an organization that represented the best of American know-how and technology would come to be perceived as a bureaucracy whose inept management decisions had cost the lives of the seven astronauts.

Delta Air Lines Flight 191

"Pull up! . . . Pull up! . . . Pull Up!" "Delta! Go around!" The two warnings came within seconds of each other at Dallas-Fort Worth International Airport on August 2, 1985. One was an electronic voice from the ground proximity alarm in the cockpit of Delta Flight 191. The other came from a controller in the control tower who saw the L1011 break out of a thunderstorm on its final approach, but off course and much too low. By that point the plane was doomed, caught in the grip of a wind shear, a sudden wind shift or downdraft during thunderstorms that can cause a plane to stall or drive it into the earth. The plane hit the ground 2,000 feet short of the runway and skidded across a peripheral highway, crushing a car and killing its driver before slamming into two water tanks and exploding in flames. One hundred thirty-six passengers and crew died in the accident. Of the 31 who survived, most were in the tail section, which broke away in the impact.

The crash at approximately 7 P.M. triggered two separate public relations responses. For Jim Ewing and Bill Berry at Delta Air Lines, it was based on Delta's 24-page procedures manual for handling aircraft accidents. For Ira J. Furman of the National Transportation Safety Board, it was based on his press relations experience at numerous disasters, which started with keeping a suitcase half packed at home. Furman would add either winter or summer suits when he knew where the NTSB "Go Team" was headed.

Furman's Delta 191 assignment began later that night at the crash site, walking just inside the cordoned-off area to let the news media know that he would be representing the NTSB. He then set up a briefing area in a nearby hotel for the daily news media briefing, which would begin the next night after the Go Team had finished working. Furman would spend most of the next three days at the crash scene, responding to reporters who braved daytime temperatures approaching 120 degrees and stomached the sight and smells of burnt-out wreckage and charred materials to get the technical information for their stories.

Lines of responsibility for responding to the press following an aircraft accident are clearly defined. The NTSB focuses on details regarding the accident and has responsibility for any information or visuals coming from the crash scene. The airline's responsibility is to provide information on the fate of the passengers and crew. "The actions Delta had to take within that first 24-hour period will affect its image within the entire transportation industry—and the bottom line—for months. One wrong move could have given them a real black eye," said Brian Scruby, a retired public relations vice president at American Airlines who handled the DC-10 crash at Chicago, which took 273 lives.[15]

Delta Air Lines' effectiveness was a reflection of its corporate philosophy of being open with the public, the press, and its own people. It also was due to the top-down management adherence to the procedures in its Standard Practices manuals. The SP for aircraft accidents had been ready for 12 years even though Delta had not needed it. It also is the basis for Delta's *Public Relations Incident Emergency Procedures Handbook*, which is in use throughout the airline's network of cities on a daily basis in handling minor incidents and emergencies.

In contrast to the aftermath of the Challenger explosion, Ewing briefed the media one hour after he arrived at Delta's headquarters in Atlanta. The intervening time had been spent assigning responsibilities to the public relations department staff as they arrived. He then headed to Delta's flight control center to get what few details could be confirmed at that point. Ewing would make five trips down to Delta's training center that night to brief the media or provide them with updates as more information became available from the crash site.

Matt Guilfoil had transferred from New York to become Delta's marketing manager three weeks before the Delta 191 crash and while he knew very little about the Dallas-Fort Worth press, he was familiar with the guidelines in the incident emergency procedures handbook, which designates the marketing manager as the Delta spokesperson in the locality where an emergency occurs. Guilfoil learned press relations in a hurry that night. The first TV crew got to the arrival gate for Flight 191 at DFW airport 35 minutes after the crash. The rest of the local and national news media poured in over the next few hours, until Guilfoil was facing more than 100 journalists and 17 television cameras when he provided the casualty figures to the news media late that night. Novice or not, Guilfoil proved to be a highly credible spokesperson for Delta and has been singled out by several members of the press for his effectiveness in responding to the media directly and over the phone. "We knew what the media's intentions were, and we opened our hearts to them. It's proven to be the only way to do business with the press," said Ewing. "If anyone needs a lesson in crisis management, number one would be to give the press all you can as soon as you can. But I hope as an employee I'll never have to go through anything like that again. It was dreadful."[16]

Dallas-Fort Worth was the intermediate stop for Flight 191, which had originated in Fort Lauderdale and was enroute to Los Angeles. For Delta, that meant that both press relations and public relations were needed immediately in all three cities since most of the victims or their families and friends would be from those areas. The marketing and operations managers in the three cities coordinated the efforts, with the assistance of company volunteers who carried out Delta's policy of personally notifying the next of kin for each passenger and then arranging for their needs in traveling to Dallas. Many of the Delta people developed close personal ties with the families in the grim days that followed and have maintained them since then. Several have since had to have psychological counseling.

Ironically, rather than being applauded, Delta received considerable negative publicity because the compassionate actions of its employees apparently reduced the number of lawsuits filed against the company by the victims' families. *The Wall Street Journal* referred to it as "'The Delta Plan,' a state-of-the-art blueprint for insurance companies to follow in the event of a disaster."[17] Plaintiff's attorney Richard Brown, a partner in Melvin Belli's San Francisco law firm, contended in the Chicago *Sun-Times* that "although Delta did give special treatment to victims' families, the motivation was to save money. 'They save themselves literally millions and millions of dollars when they do this. That's the name of the game here,' he said. 'They [families] go through one of the worst emotional things in their life and who's holding their hand? The person they have to turn around and sue.'"[18]

Bhopal

A neutron bomb seemed to have been dropped on Bhopal, India, the morning of December 3, 1984. Buildings were intact, but the bodies of more than 1,000 people lay sprawled among the carcasses of dogs, cows, buffalo, and other animals. As many as 200,000 other people were staggering through the streets, blinded, coughing, and screaming from exposure to a highly toxic chemical, methyl isocyanate (MIC). More than five tons had vaporized into a white gas that drifted into the city's low-lying slum areas around 2 A.M. after leaking from a storage tank at the Union Carbide plant. "The effects of the chemical on human beings resemble those of nerve gas. When inhaled, it reacts with water in the lungs, often choking the victim to death instantaneously. It can be just as lethal when absorbed through the skin."[19]

Union Carbide had a written crisis management plan, but Bhopal wasn't a crisis—it was a disaster for which few executives in any corporation would dare suggest a contingency plan. More than 2,500 people would die and as many as 100,000 would be maimed after being exposed to MIC in what has become the worst industrial accident in history. Even if there had been a media relations plan for disasters, such a plan would have been difficult or impossible to implement with Bhopal. The company was besieged immediately by the media but found itself hamstrung in trying to respond since it had no information on the accident. Only two phones lines were open between Bombay and Bhopal. Worse yet, the chemical plant's management had been arrested by Indian government officials who refused to let them talk. The only information Union Carbide could get was secondhand reports from its office in Bombay, which relayed bulletins broadcast by the national news service in India. Still, Carbide held an initial news briefing for the media less than 12 hours after the first word of the accident.

Union Carbide's subsequent response was equally intelligent. Warren Anderson shrugged off the immense legal liability potential of the Bhopal accident and stated that Carbide assumed the moral responsibility. Since Carbide could not determine what the situation was from its corporate headquarters, Anderson then led a team directly to Bhopal to assess the magnitude of the tragedy and to bring Carbide's resources to bear on helping the victims and rectifying the damage. The action was applauded by the American business community and particularly by the chemical industry. However, despite assurances to the contrary, Anderson and his party were met at the Bhopal airport by Indian officials and were confronted with an arrest warrant charging them with seven offenses including culpable homicide not constituting murder and causing death by negligence. After being detained for six hours, with negotiations involving the U.S. and Indian governments, Anderson was flown out in a government plane and ordered to leave the country immediately for his own safety. Only then were Union Carbide scientists allowed into the chemical plant to assess what had happened. Anderson's trip was perceived as a bold, symbolic gesture of the company's concern.

Carbide's subsequent press relations were not expansive because the company tried to strike a balance between human compassion, informing the media, and corporate survival. They were an integral part of the contingency plan that was quickly drafted to deal expressly with the Bhopal tragedy, and they became the operating guidelines for the Bhopal Team, a management task force that worked full time on the problem, with Anderson as its head.

Union Carbide's interaction with the news media has been compared and contrasted with Johnson & Johnson's handling of the Tylenol poisonings. This comparison is hard to understand. With Tylenol, eight people died, and it was proven that the cause was deliberate product tampering. With Bhopal, the deaths were in the thousands, the disaster occurred in a foreign country that refused to disclose important details regarding the accident, and the exact cause is still unknown.

Considering the magnitude of the tragedy and the fact that it had traditionally been a conservative, low-key organization, Carbide has been quite successful in its media relations activities regarding Bhopal. Anderson became the personification of Union Carbide and conveyed the impression of the personal concern of this chemical company for the tragic accident. Despite liability suits seeking more than $15 billion in damages, a subsequent gas leak at its Institute, West Virginia, plant, and a hostile takeover bid by GAF, Union

Carbide was able to withstand the pressure and to pursue an orderly transition to the next generation of company management when Warren Anderson retired in November 1986. Although still involved in litigation as a result of the accident, Carbide nevertheless is an excellent example of how a low profile organization, with a well-planned and well-managed crisis communications program can navigate through a media onslaught and emerge intact.

APPLYING THE CASE STUDIES

You will find that there are no heroes or villains in this book. We all made our share of well meaning but regrettable mistakes because of inexperience, sheer fatigue, communications breakdowns, and the extreme pressure that news media coverage adds to an already stressful situation. Those errors and shortcomings, as well as admirable decisions, will be pointed out among the press, public relations people, and participants—not to throw bouquets or brickbats, but in the hope that you will learn from our wrong decisions as well as the right.

All the participants in these case studies agree that onslaughts are never easy, but they can be managed. It all depends on your knowing how far to go with the journalists and then anticipating what the media will need to cover the story. The participants and the press will make unrealistic demands, and you will find it will be an exhilarating, exhausting experience. You'll be working in a communications minefield, but you can get through it if you step carefully and keep thinking ahead, even if "ahead" is only a few minutes away.

They're in the Lobby and on the Phone

If a major news story has just broken and the media already knows, you have no way to know how extensive the news coverage will be, what direction it will take, or how long it will last. Regardless of what the story is, your most important job will be to communicate the facts and to minimize the disruption for those involved. Your success will depend on how well you can manage the media's coverage of the situation. That doesn't mean press censorship or restriction. We're talking about providing the media with what it needs to get its job done, but on your terms, not theirs.

You will need time and information to get control of the situation. Likewise for the media. They move awfully fast but still will need to get ready to cover the story. So the first step will be to get control of the time while you find out what's going on and prepare to discuss it with the press.

THE 60-MINUTE GAME PLAN

You'd like all the time you can get, but if the media has the story, we're talking minutes, not days or weeks. Those reporters will want to know what's happened so they can file their initial news reports, but they also want to know what to tell their editors or news directors who will make the decisions about how their news organizations will cover the story. How long will it take you to get the basic facts on what has happened—preferably in person, not over the phone? Take that time and add 60 minutes. You'll need that hour to summarize the situation and reach the top people in your organization to discuss what you think should be disclosed. That's your working window to help you estimate when the first briefing can be held.

Get the Phones under Control

If the media has the story, every phone in your office sounds like it has short circuited with its ringer on, and the main switchboard is being flooded with calls that can't get through to you. Everyone involved wants to know what to tell the media—and any other callers trying to find out more about what has happened. The answer needs to be simple and straightforward. It also must reduce the pressure and buy you the time needed to get the situation under control. *The response from your office and from the operators on the switchboard needs to be exactly the same.* It should be used as a mantra, a statement that can be repeated as often as needed to reduce the stress that will build as the media calls and pressure steadily increases.

> We are aware that there have been reports of a (situation) and are currently getting the details. Any information we can provide will be disclosed at a briefing that is tentatively scheduled for approximately (time). You will be directed to the briefing site when you arrive.

Have your assistants repeat it to the press and to themselves. They should not vary from this statement no matter how intense the phone calls get. Despite the apparent hostility from a network television news producer who's pressuring to get through to anyone who will make someone available for a live interview, they should stick to the mantra statement.

The phone calls should be handled by secretaries, operators, and anyone else you can round up to help out—except the public relations staff, if you have one, and yourself. Many of the callers will press for more information, but nothing should be confirmed by those answering the phones. Their response should be your mantra statement and that's all. Changing one detail will give the press the edge it needs to call about inconsistencies in your organization's statements.

You may know some members of the local media. All of a sudden they will be your closest friends and will want to talk to you directly. The same will apply to any of your public relations people whom they've known in the past. Don't pick up your phone unless someone has screened the call and tells you who's on the line. The only calls you should be taking now are from anyone who may have information on what's happened. The response regarding your whereabouts should not be that "they're in a meeting." That trite turnoff frustrates the caller but also conveys the idea you're trying to figure out what to say. Your people can be more helpful: "(<u>name</u>) and the rest of the department are out getting information for the (<u>time</u>) briefing."

Get Your Team Together

Ideally, you're not a one-person show, because you're going to need at least four people who aren't answering phones to help you in preparing for the media. The people who can help most are those who know about your facilities, your business, your employees, and the ins and outs of your organization. If you are part of a bigger organization, how fast can you pull in the corporate office public relations people, the university's public information office, communicators from other departments, or anyone with a communications background who can be relied on to do double duty?

What you won't need is anyone who tends to get hyper in a pressure cooker situation. In the next hour they're going to have to work with the quiet speed and efficiency of an EMS crew at a major accident. Get them together for a five-minute meeting. Take them into your confidence by telling them what you know thus far and then put them to work.

Your own job in the next hour will be to get whatever facts you can and then to figure out what will be disclosed to the media at the specified time. While you're doing your job, someone else needs to concentrate on the logistical details. The third assignment will be to anticipate what the media will want to know in covering the story.

The Place and Space People

Logistical details may seem like they should be last on your list, and indeed they are often overlooked or given low priority in planning for the media. But how well they are handled will determine how well you control the situation when the participants are face to face with the reporters. One person who's good at organizing meetings, parties, and functions should get the assignment of making arrangements for media briefings. He or she should concentrate on finding a suitable place for media briefings. He or she should concentrate on finding a suitable place for the first encounter with the press, while also scouting out the options for the best long-term solution. Have the person skim Chapter 6 to learn what is needed in a briefing center before getting started. It will take a few minutes but may later save many hours of false starts and blind alleys.

The War Room

The job for the rest of your people in the next 60 minutes will be to pull together whatever information and materials your organization has on hand and to anticipate what the media will need as the story unfolds. Someone who knows your public relations files can gather any relevant background information, photos, and other materials for your review. Don't worry about your media mailing lists, if you have them. You won't have any time or need for mailing press releases. All it takes is two phone calls to unleash an onslaught.

If someone in the office has a radio, they should have it on while the information and materials are being pulled together to pick up bulletins and newscasts. If you have more than one, tune them in to different stations, preferably the ones that carry network radio newscasts to determine what is being said about the situation and whether the story has been moved to the national level. If someone has a portable stereo or "boom box," they may be able to record the broadcasts. Otherwise they can turn on a tape recorder beside the radio or take notes on what is being reported by the different stations.

Your experienced public relations people, as well as any cynics or incisive thinkers on hand, should be assigned to come up with the questions that may be asked at that first briefing. They also can define the types of information, photos, graphics and illustrations, video clips, and other materials that can be provided within the next few hours to supply the news media with useful background materials for their coverage of the story. Agree to meet in 60 minutes and get going.

Get the Facts

You may be able to confirm what has happened just by looking out the window and seeing the flashing lights of emergency vehicles. Or, it may take one phone call to someone in your organization who knows what is going on. But that's not enough. You will need all the details you can get to determine what should be disclosed.

With the pressure building up by the minute, the best thing to do is get as close to the situation as possible. Go to the scene and find out what's been happening from someone who's been watching the situation. Start with the essential details first:

- When did it happen?
- Who is involved in the situation?
- Who is in charge from your organization?
- What is going on at the present time?
- What will be the most likely next steps?

Some questions undoubtedly will be asked by the media that cannot—or should not—be answered yet. Don't hesitate to ask these questions so you have the information to work with and can provide an informed response to the question when it is raised:

1. What caused the situation?
2. How many people have been directly affected? Where are their families, and have they been notified?
3. What is the likely outcome? When will it occur?
4. Is there any risk to others than those involved?
5. When will someone who is involved in the situation be able to meet with the press to bring them up to date on what has happened?
6. What are the biggest problems, questions, and concerns at the present time, and what's being done to resolve them?

Resist the urge to get whatever information you can as quickly as possible and get back to your office. You've got one hour. The longer you can stay where the action is, the better prepared you will be for dealing with the media later on. And who knows, you might get lucky and talk with one of the people who's directly involved.

If you find yourself with no more questions and just waiting for something else to happen, give the people in your office a call and bring them up to date. They can use any information you have in developing appropriate responses to likely questions as well as in anticipating what will be needed later in responding to the media. They may also have a number of good questions you overlooked in the intensity of the situation.

You can also take advantage of any slow time to go over your notes and get them organized into a rough statement. Review your ideas with the people you've been talking to in order to be sure of the details. They probably will have some valuable suggestions. The more you include them in what you are doing now, the more you'll be able to check with them in the future.

Your presence at the scene, or the fact that you're asking questions and taking notes, may well result in a confrontation with whoever is in charge, considering the tension that person's under. Don't be surprised if you find yourself responding to:"Who authorized you to be here? What do you plan to do with this information? The last thing we're going to do is say anything to the media." You needn't be defensive. Just point out that there's one problem with the situation here and another rapidly growing problem with the news media converging on your facility to cover the story. All you are going to do is get that situation under control in the way he wants to get his problem in hand.

Don't get into a long discussion. He won't have time for that, and neither will you. Show him your notes or the rough statement you've drafted and get any suggestions he might have. Make sure he realizes that you'll be checking with the appropriate people before anything is released. He may want to review any information before it goes out. That could be a legitimate request or a power play, depending on the individual. Since you will need him later on, tell him you'll call him before anything is disclosed to the public. Make it a point to do that and also to get a copy of the statement to him for any of the participants.

THE DISCLOSURE PLAN

The hour is up, and it's time to pull your team together for a quick meeting. Fill them in on what you've learned and find out what has been accomplished:

1. Where will the first briefing be held? Subsequent briefings?
2. How many media calls have you had, and what are they asking?
3. What's being reported by the local radio stations?
4. What background information and materials can be quickly duplicated for the media?
5. What are the questions the media is most likely to ask?

You should be able to get a sense of these things fairly quickly and come up with a game plan for the first media briefing. Anticipating the questions also will help in refining the information in the statement.

Concentrate on the facts and details that have been confirmed— the time the situation began, what happened, and who from your organization is involved. Keep in mind, however, that this will be the first of many briefings. Its purpose should be to confirm what has happened so the media can make its initial reports and begin to decide how much coverage the story will receive. Their biggest concerns will be the facts that are known now and what the prospects appear to be for additional news. Keep the briefing just that—brief. There will be plenty of opportunities for elaboration later when the participants are available and the situation has been more clearly defined.

Read the statement and get everyone's suggestions. Then get it duplicated so it can be typed up while you're reviewing it with your management. Don't just pick up the phone, though. Take a few minutes to think through what it will take to get the other members of management to understand and support your game plan for dealing with the media.

Getting Management on Your Side

A plant manager can be just as important in your life, and just as tough to deal with, as the chairman of a major corporation a dozen notches further up your organization's ladder. Regardless of whether its your immediate boss, the general manager, or the chairman of the board, you probably know enough about the CEO to anticipate his reaction when he finds out that the national media is moving in and will be covering what's happened. The big question is what it will take to get his support and approval for your game plan, especially that initial media briefing.

He undoubtedly knows about the situation and may even have heard that TV crews are prowling around outside the facilities, which undoubtedly has spiked his blood pressure beyond its already elevated level. What he's not likely to know is the extent of the news media's interest in what's happened. That's the reason for your phone call or visit to his office if he's in the same facility. Have your ideas outlined on a notepad so you can make your case as quickly and cleanly as possible.

There's no foolproof method of selling the CEO on having the organization get involved with the media under normal circumstances, much less when it may be the focus of national news coverage. There are, however, some do's and don'ts for your discussion with him:

1. There will be enough tension already, so don't add to it. Remember that the last thing he needs in addition to his present concerns is word that a mob of people from the news media will be descending on his facility. Think of it from his perspective and consider the insights of Warren Anderson, himself a CEO. "What is absolutely essential in any of these cases is to calm things down," Anderson said. "You need someone who is not frantic and who is a doer—who motivates himself."[20] Focus on the facts and present them calmly.

2. Give him your assessment of the news potential, based on having been at the scene and on the interest the press has shown thus far. Tick off the number of media calls you've had already and prominent examples of the media who've been in touch. Give him an idea of the type of news reports that already are being carried by your local news stations, especially any inaccurate information.

3. This is no time to push. You need to build confidence that you can handle the media and minimize the disruption of the organization that the news media can cause. Walk him through your game plan for dealing with the media. What is needed now is quiet confidence, even if your stomach is churning.

4. Your most important point is that you've already told the media there will be an initial briefing at approximately (time). Don't hide it until the end. You're better off playing it matter-of-factly as you walk through the game plan. If the reaction is "Who authorized you to tell them that?" your response should be that they will either get the information from his spokesperson or they are going to get it from bystanders as well as from rumormongers, relatives, and disgruntled employees who will become instant authorities. You'd rather the news media got the facts you want them to have instead of gossip and secondhand opinions.

5. The CEO needs to understand that the purpose of the initial briefing is to buy time and reduce the pressure from the news media until the situation is more clearly understood. It also will establish the organization as the primary source of information for the media. If he still has doubts, mention the damage done to NASA's excellent working relationship with the media when it waited nearly five hours before disclosing anything to the press about the Challenger shuttle explosion. Contrast that to the results of Delta Airlines briefing the media within one hour. Then read the statement and get his reaction.

If you're lucky, you'll get a nod of approval and be told to get going. But don't count on it. Siege mentality may have set in, just as it did at Cape Kennedy after the Challenger accident. The prospects of dozens of news media outside the building can be downright frightening to any executive who has seen *The China Syndrome* or similar Hollywood portrayals of the press. You may be told to check with the legal department, the corporate headquarters, or anyone else he turns to when he's faced with a thorny problem. You know whom he wants you to consult with, and you may have talked to them, which will be a point in your favor. If you haven't, perhaps they can help in providing a second opinion on your game plan and statement. The problem is that you don't have a lot of time to take people through the hoops you've already cleared. It's also tough for them to make good battlefield decisions when they're sitting in the Pentagon. The CEO needs to know:

1. You and he have the same goal—that the news event will be covered accurately and in the most favorable light under the circumstances. Having that first briefing get off on the right foot will be essential if the organization is to maintain a good working relationship with the media as the news coverage progresses.

2. You are the one who knows the details of what's happened and you also know how to deal with the media who are moving in to cover the story. Your lawyers and the people in a corporate office don't have that advantage.

3. This is no time for an organizational gym meet. If the news media get the impression your organization will not deal with them honestly and openly, they are not going to waste time, and will start using other sources to get the details. They have deadlines and will meet them with or without your help.

4. The last thing the CEO should have to be concerned about—in addition to the situation itself—is phone calls from his power sources prompted by rumors, innuendos, and inaccurate stories in the news media. The chances of that occurring will be less if the organization takes the initiative with an initial briefing of the media to give them the facts as they are known now.

5. Nobody is an expert, but you know how to work with reporters better than anyone else on the scene. He is going to have to trust your judgment because you're the best person at this point to handle the press. If he wants to put someone else in charge for the long term, that's his decision. In the meantime you want to get control of the media coverage. This means taking the initiative and providing the facts that can be confirmed before the situation gets out of hand.

When you get back to your office, call the field boss to go over what you'll be disclosing in the statement and to get any last-minute developments that may affect what you'll say. Then head for the briefing room. However, if the CEO refuses to let anything be done without a management meeting to decide what your approach should be in dealing with the media, you'll be in the same position as the NASA press relations staff during those five hours after the Challenger explosion. "You quickly learn what it's like to be mugged."

THE INITIAL BRIEFING

It's going to be unnerving when you approach the room where the briefing will be held and see the glare of TV lights ahead. The trick is not to go to the podium right away. Take a minute to get used to your surroundings and adjust to the light. Get an update from one of your people who has been with the media to find out who's in the room, what information they have picked up from other sources, and what they have been asking about.

Then get the right expression on your face. Regardless of how good or bad the situation is, you need to look calm, relaxed, and confident when you walk in front of those cameras. This may be one of the most unnerving experiences in your career, but the public needs to get the impression through the media coverage that everything is under control. Don't rush. Take a few moments to get your notes in order and then to size up the audience. Then give them a quiet, confident smile when you begin your remarks.

Start off by introducing yourself, giving your position with the organization, and thanking the media for responding so quickly. Then set the limits for the briefing—you will provide a statement, which includes the information that can be confirmed at this point. You know they have questions, but you will only respond to those where the factual information has been confirmed. Any questions that cannot be answered will be taken down, and responses will be provided as soon as you have checked with the participants and have the answer.

Then get into the statement: "This is what we can confirm at this point . . .". Read it slowly, carefully, and with the assurance that these are the facts. Make it a point to pause briefly between paragraphs and look up at the reporters so they get the impression you're speaking to them and not just reading a canned statement.

The barrage of questions will start the moment you have finished the statement. Don't feel you have to rush into responding. Take your time. The media will wait, and even if they don't, you need to maintain control of the briefing. Start with reporters who have raised their hands. Some may be difficult to see in the glare of the TV lights, but it's important to respond to the questioners on your terms, not theirs. A good suggestion from the White House press office is to have someone spot the questioners in the audience for you if the glare is too much, so you don't have to worry about which question is next and can just concentrate on the answer.

Make it a point to repeat every question you are asked. That gives anyone who will be transcribing the briefing a chance to get the question through your microphone and not from a barely audible voice in the crowd. It also makes sure that you've correctly interpreted the question—the reporter is likely to rephrase it if he thinks you misunderstood what he was asking. And finally, you can size up the question as you repeat it so that you will be in a better position to know how to respond.

It seems to be human nature to respond to someone's question, even if we don't have all the information for a good answer. We also think if we talk long enough we'll give enough information for the questioner to piece together an answer from what we've said. That may be OK for a casual conversation, but it can be catastrophic at a news briefing. The longer you take in responding to a question the more likely you will later regret something you said.

If there is one thing that every spokesperson in this book can agree on it is this: Don't speculate. If you are not absolutely certain of the answer, don't even try to guess. Simply smile and indicate you don't have the facts to respond to that question, and you are not going to speculate.

Many questions will be time oriented. "When will they know if . . .?", "When will you have a chance to . . .?", "How soon will the participants . . .?", "When will it be over?", etc. Details on time are an important part of any news story and also help the media in scheduling its coverage. But they are among the most difficult questions to answer accurately. Again, don't speculate, not even a little. *Guesses don't count when you're dealing with reporters.* They will be sizing you up during that first briefing, and your working relationship with them will be determined by how much they can count on you for information that will hold up after they develop and file their stories.

Keep the question period relatively short and under your control. When you're ready to break it off, indicate "I'll take two more questions, then I want to get back to see what's happening." Wrap up the briefing by indicating when the next update will be held. Take the news media's deadlines into consideration in scheduling the next update. It may be impossible to predict how soon the situation will be resolved or when the participants will be able to discuss what has happened. The media will understand that. But they also would appreciate an update of what has happened since the last briefing as their deadlines approach so they can include the latest information in the story.

Set a tentative time and place for the next briefing. Think in terms of Eastern standard time, regardless of where you are, because that's the universal time zone for the TV and radio networks and wire services. The optimum times for your next briefing would be 7–8 A.M., 2–3 P.M., or 7–9 P.M. EST, depending on when the story has broken. Indicate that if anything develops in the meantime, everyone in the room will be advised, and the wire services will be asked to alert the other media of the new time for the update. Otherwise you'll see them at the designated time.

The briefing will end with someone wanting to know "What about photos?" or "When can we talk to the family?" They'll also want to get you aside when you leave the podium for specific questions or a one-on-one interview. Be friendly and polite but also indicate that you have to get back to find out what has been going on. Let them know you'll be happy to talk to them later, when there's a lull.

MAINTAIN CONTACT WITH THE NEWS MEDIA

You need to get back in touch with what is happening at the scene of the news event, but it's equally important that one of your public relations people and a secretary stay in the area where the next news briefing will be held. Select people who are mature, relate easily to newcomers, and are not going to be overwhelmed when they suddenly find themselves talking with a producer from "CBS Evening News" or a correspondent from *Time* who has just climbed off a plane and needs to find out what's going on.

Their primary job will to register any media as they arrive and provide them with background information and available photos. They will likely be working with the media on a variety of needs, ranging from hotel rooms and extension cords to parking space for the satellite transmission truck. While helping the media get organized to do its job, they'll also be establishing a working relationship that may prove invaluable to both the participants and the press in the days ahead.

A pile of phone messages will be waiting when you get back to your office, but resist the temptation to wade into them. Your first call should be to one of the participants at the scene to find out if anything has happened that might require an update sooner than you had planned. Your second should be to your CEO to brief him on how the media has reacted thus far. Then it's time to brief working on those call slips from the news media.

Sort through the messages and divide them up. You take the national news media and other calls with interview requests or specific questions. Any members of your staff can make the other calls and use the statement you provided at the briefing. Don't, however, let them make the mistake that occurred at Loma Linda. Some people who answered phone calls from the news media after the Baby Fae disclosure provided information based on what they thought was correct, and in some instances they were wrong. That just reinforced the media's negative reactions and accusations about lying when they learned of other misinformation coming from the Loma Linda Medical Center. If the reporter wants additional information, their response should be that you are the only person who can elaborate beyond the statement and that you'll have to return the call. They also can suggest that the reporter keep an eye on the wire services for additional information from the Q-and-A session.

You'll also be tempted to get a smidgen of satisfaction as you return each call by wadding up the phone message slip. A better approach is to make brief notes on the back about the conversation and how it will be used. Stack them up and, when there is a lull, one of your secretaries should begin typing up a phone call log with each reporter's name, news organization, phone number, and the gist of the call.

This will be just the beginning of a nonstop workday that will continue until the situation is resolved and the media interest abates. Months later you will look back and see that by moving quickly in briefing the press, your organization took the important first step in gaining control, which can make all the difference in how the public will see the situation through the eyes of the news media.

Circle the Wagons

Perhaps you know your organization *will* be engulfed in a news story which, luckily, hasn't happened yet. That's when the classic defensive technique in an impending battle can be adapted to help you in preparing for the media onslaught. It applies if you're likely to be immersed in a major celebration, a scandal, or any announcement that will generate intense public interest. You need to rally your forces, take stock of the information and visuals that will be your ammunition, and decide where the engagement is to take place.

GETTING THE LAY OF THE LAND

Start off by doing as much intelligence gathering as you can in a short period of time. You can learn a lot from others who have gone through the same experience you're facing. Look at some recent issues of *Time* or *Newsweek* to see what organizations have suddenly found themselves in the news and who the spokespersons were. Make some phone calls and take careful notes, because they undoubtedly will have some insights, observations, and war stories to tell you. If you have time to visit the sites of their onslaughts, take advantage of the opportunity. The three days I spent in Salt Lake City immediately after Dr. DeVries announced he would be coming to Humana provided the insights and background information that became the basis for Humana's artificial heart media relations plan.

You may also want to use some of the electronic news libraries to see how the media has covered similar stories. Humana used the

Mead Data NEXIS computer system to determine what had been written by the news media about the artificial heart and by whom. That search provided more than 200 articles as well as a good perspective on how the coverage evolved during the artificial heart implant and after the death of Barney Clark. As the weeks had worn on, the ethical questions and issues had become much more prominent in the media's coverage of this medical experiment. A year later a similar NEXIS inquiry disclosed that 992 news stories then existed on the artificial heart, and the coverage had followed the same reporting pattern.[21]

We also used Hill & Knowlton, a public relations consulting firm, in our research efforts. In addition to reviewing our plans for announcing Humana's first artificial heart patient and the public relations support that would be provided during and after the operation, Hill & Knowlton also interviewed key members of the national news media who had covered the Barney Clark story in Salt Lake City. We were interested in assessing their views of the University of Utah's media relations efforts and in getting their suggestions regarding public relations support for media coverage of subsequent artificial heart patients, but through a third party so the insights could be obtained without making commitments. Their 47-page report, "Communications Implications of the Next Artificial Heart," included excerpts from interviews applying to any media onslaught, not just Barney Clark or Humana. Among the most pertinent of the journalists' observations were:

1. The university failed to live up to its promises to prepare the news media in advance with good background information on the patient, the procedure, and the heart itself.
2. They seemed to think that giving the media some space, some food, and some phones was the extent of their obligation.
3. The media needs access to people who can provide details on both the medical and human interest aspects of the story as well as controlled access to the patient's family.
4. Utah seemed to be playing to the television news, yet they were not well prepared for that medium, especially when they did the video interview with Barney Clark using their own camera crew.
5. Utah underestimated the continuing impact of the story.

They assumed it would be over in a hurry, but it didn't go away.

6. The biggest slipup was that the university consistently issued sugar-coated progress reports on Barney Clark and made it look much more optimistic than it was.

7. The Utah people played favorites with the local media and treated the national news organizations poorly, especially the television networks.

8. Humana would have to be even more forthcoming with data than a university because it is a corporation. It will be vulnerable to criticism simply because of the climate surrounding the artificial heart experiment.

9. Humana people should make sure the family gets accurate information in advance of the press. Disclosures should be straight and unvarnished facts. If the odds are 10 to 1 against the patient, it should be reported as such.

GET THE FACTS FIRSTHAND

You also will need to fully understand the facts regarding the story. That can only come by digesting as much background information as possible, and then getting to know the people you will be working with during the onslaught. Get out of your office and into their surroundings as much as possible so you can get to know them personally. Become one of their team and let them take you to school. Immerse yourself in the details of what will happen but also learn what they do and how they relate to each other. You need to know their personal strengths and weaknesses and who you can go to for an objective second opinion when you can't rely on your primary sources, which unfortunately will happen.

I moved my office from Humana's corporate headquarters to Humana Hospital-Audubon during preparations for the first artificial heart operation, which provided more than an invaluable crash course in open heart surgery. My day began at 6:30 A.M., as I accompanied the Humana Heart Institute medical staff on hospital rounds, and rarely broke before 6:30 that night, but the same was true of the doctors. During those long days, relationships were forged with many of the physicians, nurses, and hospital staff. These relationships would prove immensely helpful later in knowing whom to contact to get things done or to check out details to ensure we had factual information and knew what the disclosure priorities should be.

THE MEDIA RELATIONS PLAN

Call it a protocol, procedure, action plan, or whatever you like, but while you are doing your research, you also should be doing some serious planning for how you're going to deal with the media when the story breaks. No grandiose documents are necessary. The disaster plan that Union Carbide developed for dealing with the Bhopal accident was just six pages long, including the media relations procedures.

You have to distinguish the substance from the noise, so define the objectives and priorities. Then go for outlined ideas and one-liners in three basic areas—information and visuals, administrative details, and logistical considerations. The plan should be as anticipatory and realistic as possible and should reflect the thinking of everyone, including secretaries and even department alumni, who can be recruited to help. Get them involved from the start. Those meetings will charge everyone's batteries and prove immensely helpful in surfacing the details that will make all the difference after the onslaught begins.

To stimulate everyone's thinking in developing a good "what to do" list, include the following in your discussions:

Information and Visuals.

- Background materials—what's available and needed.
- Primary and alternate sources of information.
- Spokespersons—who and how to help them get ready.
- Visuals—production, distribution, and costs.
- Information and visuals for "worst-case" situations.
- Legal/regulatory considerations.

Administrative Details.

- Realistic media relations guidelines, considering the situation.
- Approval of information and visuals to be disclosed.
- The chain of command for resolving disputes.
- Timing of disclosures, briefings, and updates.
- Coordination of press briefings or written updates.

- Media contacts—existing and needed.
- Staffing requirements and schedules.
- Keeping the participants and families informed.
- VIP/management/employee communications.
- Ongoing media coverage.
- Budget considerations.

Logistics.

- Suitable rooms for media briefings and individual interviews.
- Places for the media to wait and the participants to hide.
- Electricity, lights, phones, and parking.
- Hotels, motels, messengers, and meals,
- Security at the site and at the briefing center.

Anticipate your needs in advance by creating the scenario, running your organization through it, and evaluating your performance. In Humana's scenario, we planned for KDU-TV from Dubuque, Iowa, to cover its first artificial heart implant. Their news crew wouldn't know anything about the artificial heart or the patient when they arrived, having flown to Louisville to cover the surgery because the news director's father had died of congestive heart failure. No matter that KDU-TV doesn't exist. Their news crew became the focus of our efforts to anticipate everything journalists would need in covering the story. The question we kept asking at planning meetings was "How can we provide the mythical crew from Dubuque with everything it needs to cover the story, with minimum disruption of our staff?"

We were also fortunate because we had seen what the University of Utah went through during the Barney Clark news coverage. Consequently, we adopted a strategy in preparing for the media that was as simple as it was self-serving: the more background information, visual material, and logistical support we could provide, the easier it would be for the news media to cover the story and the less help the hundreds of them would need from the few of us. We also figured that the more we could facilitate their preparation of solid news stories, the more favorable their attitudes and working relationships would be with us. This was the foundation of our plan, and it worked.

There was some discussion about how Humana could leverage the potential "halo effect" that the artificial heart program could have on its hospitals and health care businesses. In retrospect, that was a mistake. We'd have been better off adopting the approach of the University of Utah and the University of Arizona at Tucson, which gave no thought to how they could use their respective artificial heart programs to enhance the reputations of their medical centers. The business implications and impact, either upside or downside, will depend largely on how well you handle the disclosure and subsequent media coverage. Again, the true value will be in how your important publics perceive the organization through the prism of the media's news reports.

YOUR MOST IMPORTANT AUDIENCE

The effectiveness of your internal communications can have an immense impact on the support from your top management as well as lessen your chances of being blindsided by reporters who have picked up information from someone on the inside. In addition to the grapevine, how do your management and employees find out what is going on? How can you ensure that those people and the families of the participants get the word on any major disclosure from you and not from the news media? Here are the tactics you should adopt:

1. Have a checklist of key people to be contacted, and designate one of your best people to make sure the participants, your management and employees, and especially family members you haven't talked to are not caught by surprise when a disclosure is made. If something newsworthy comes up during a briefing, that person should be responsible for alerting any participants it relates to. In some instances they may have to draft a statement summarizing the question, the response, and any clarification that might be needed. That statement can then be used to update management and employees and for response to subsequent media inquiries.
2. Work closely with whomever is in charge of distributing employee bulletins, so you can get updates posted in a hurry.
3. Provide your management and the participants with a daily compilation of prominent news clips and a summary of phone contacts, so they will know how the media is covering what has been said and done.
4. Establish a system for providing all of your facilities with relevant information on the news event and any important

developments disclosed to the news media. Whenever significant disclosures were being made, each of Humana's 90 hospital administrators were sent bulletins with the text of press releases via Humana's computer system.

Your employees will appreciate your efforts to keep them informed. Those at the facility where the story will break also will appreciate suggestions on how to respond to questions from reporters when an encounter occurs. Most employees are leery of being interviewed, but they also don't want to be discourteous, fearing that the reporter will use their negative response to make them or their organization look bad. So help them out by scheduling orientation sessions regarding the impending news story and giving your employees some guidance in how to handle an impromptu interview.

One good way is to select someone from the audience to be "Mike Wallace" interviewing you. It's fun but also informative for everyone to see how you respond when you are not comfortable with the question and don't want to answer. Then give them a safety valve—a phone number that will be the main line for any media calling in to get an update. That way, if they don't want to talk about the situation with a reporter, they can refer the reporter to that number for the latest information. Also, encourage them to contact you if they are approached by a member of the press and asked specific questions. Those early warnings can be invaluable intelligence should a news organization have its muckraking boots on.

WAR GAMES

The secret of successful media relations during a major news story is found in one word—anticipation. You will have to be prepared for how the various segments of the news media will report the story, the information they will want, the visuals they will need. Your spokespersons need to be ready for what will occur whenever they face the media, the questions reporters are likely to ask, and how to respond. "If you are going to do anything as complicated as dealing with large numbers of media, there's preparations and training that have to be done," Bob Henrie observed. "Nobody can just stand up there based on their natural ability. They will never succeed like they will if they are prepared."[22] For that to happen, you will have to look for ways for everyone to practice how they will work together in dealing with the media.

One of the many ironies of the Challenger accident press coverage is that NASA had planned to stage a mock space shuttle emergency and test the provisions of the STS Public Affairs Contingency Plan, mentioned in Chapter 1. Because of the tight shuttle launch schedule, the simulation had been postponed several times, but had been rescheduled for February—one month after the ill-fated Challenger mission. Humana, on the other hand, was able to conduct a series of dry runs prior to Schroeder's artificial heart operation. Dr. DeVries' "dress rehearsals" were mentioned extensively in the news media, but most reporters were not aware that our press relations also had gone through the rehearsals.

Bill Strode and Art Levy, who would be the photographer and video cameraman for the first operation, practiced during the surgical team's rehearsal in Salt Lake City when an artificial heart was implanted in a calf. A number of logistical problems had to be worked out afterward, but we got a clear sense of the timing for critical phases of the operation and saw where the really important camera shots would be. Strode and Levy practiced again with Dr. DeVries and Dr. Lansing doing an open-heart procedure at Humana Hospital-Audubon in the surgical suite where the artificial heart implants would take place, and things went more smoothly. When Schroeder's artificial heart surgery took place, the photographic or video coverage went smoothly and provided the news media with outstanding visuals, which was an important factor in the extent of the coverage.

Media confrontation training was another part of the preparations. While some journalists have cited it as an example of how Humana "orchestrated" the actions of the physicians in dealing with the press, the training actually was designed to familiarize the spokespersons with the situations and questions we might encounter. If it did anything, the training prepared the participants to respond to the news media in a straightforward manner rather than by clamming up or not giving a good response because of not knowing how to handle difficult questions.[23]

In addition to Dr. DeVries and Dr. Allan Lansing, who was to be the medical spokesman, Patricia Davis, the hospital administrator, and I went through the full day of responding to reporters during simulated press conferences, talk show discussions, telephone interviews, and media stakeouts, all of which were videotaped and critiqued by the other participants. One of the "reporters" was John Dwan, the spokesman for the University of Utah Medical Center, who used his experience during Barney Clark's artificial heart operation to help us get ready. "That training made me aware of how to stand and the important little things in responding to reporters," Dr. Lansing recalled. "It also gave me some good practice in thinking on my feet when you're exposed to tough questions. That was very useful, but I must tell you that there was very little in my own experience with reporters covering the artificial heart patients that was negative or that I'd consider an attack."[24]

Humana also held a media background briefing the week before Bill Schroeder was selected to be the next artificial heart patient to check our readiness while we brought the press up to date on program developments since Barney Clark's implant nearly two years earlier. That one-day session pointed out that we had anticipated most of the media's major information need. Our spokespersons were ready, but the designated media briefing area at the hospital was woefully inadequate for the number of correspondents who would be covering the story. Two months of work and a six-figure budget had gone into adapting the only unused space in the hospital for media briefings, but we knew we had to find much larger facilities. The briefing center turned out to be at the Commonwealth Convention Center, seven miles from the hospital.

ADEQUATE MANPOWER

It's not hard for a spokesperson in the middle of an onslaught to get the idea that he or she is a one-person show and the media's sole source for anything and everything. That's a mistake. "Nobody can do what we have to do 12–14–24 hours a day, seven days a week, for a month or two without losing their edge. You have to get some relief and be able to get away from the fray completely if you are going to be any good over the long haul," said John Dwan, the spokesman during the Barney Clark news story. You can have only one public relations person in charge at a time, but they are going to wear out. You need somebody who can step in and take over."[25] The more qualified people you can pull in to help, the more effective your media relations program is going to be. That may sound simplistic, but now is the time to consider how many people you have who can do the following:

1. Handle Phone Calls from the Media.   Most of the hundreds of calls you'll get each day will be from radio stations asking for a sound bite with basically the same information that has been given out at the last briefing and moved by the wire services. Anyone who has the latest details and uses good judgment can handle a majority of those calls. Having a background in public relations is helpful but not essential, since the best way anyone learns to handle phone interviews is on the job. The people who return those calls need to be articulate but must also know how to defer to the principal spokesperson on questions they are not comfortable in answering.

2. Take Care of the Arrangements for Interviews.   Someone needs to make it as easy as possible for the participants when they are willing to break loose for an interview, even if its over the phone. That often will involve arranging a suitable time and place for the reporter and the participant to get together, briefing the interviewee on what will be covered, and being on hand in case there are details that need to be followed up. Even if everything goes without a hitch, one interview can chew up two or three hours. When it's a major story, like Barbara Walters' interview of Dr. DeVries for "20/20," you're talking nearly two weeks of one public relations manager's time.

3. Coordinate the Shooting and Distribution of Visuals.   This is another job that will be critically important and very time consuming. The person who has this assignment doesn't need to know as much about the subject as about the technical requirements for photography and video, how to get in and out of the location with minimum disruption, and what is needed for good visual elements in a picture. Another important facet of the job will be knowing how to coordinate the photographic development, editing, and distribution so adequate visuals are available quickly to the news organizations.

4. Assist the Media with Their Logistical Problems.   Many of the news organizations descending on you will be looking for someone to help them find a suitable location for a microwave transmitter truck, track down the phone company people, or line up hotel rooms for a weekend relief crew. That often will require more ingenuity than media relations savvy. And true, it's not a regular part of public relations. But when you can help a news organization get its job done with less hassle, two of the results are better reporting and a more favorable attitude toward your organization.

There may be concerns about letting your staff take the brunt of these logistical assignments, but take a hard look at the people you have to help you. How good are they? Why can't they handle a lot of these engine room efforts? The trickiest will be phone duty, but that's also a good way to let them become a part of the news coverage during the unbelievable hours they will be spending after the story breaks. "What most CEOs would find is that they have people in their organization with skills that they never knew they had," Warren Anderson observed. "So, when the fire starts, you've got a lot of firemen. Given the opportunity and the challenge, they will rise to the occasion and do the toughest jobs for you."[26]

If it appears the news media coverage will continue, everyone will need a break after a few 18- to 24-hour days. We frequently used Humana's public relations department alumni at night and on weekends, when the news coverage was lighter. Delta has a procedure for borrowing employees from other departments. NASA uses public affairs personnel who are no longer with the government but are available to help out for short periods of time. In each instance they were immensely helpful. They also had the satisfaction of knowing they helped when they were sorely needed, and were involved in a news event that would become part of history.

KEEP YOUR PEOPLE INFORMED

Delegating assignments can only be done successfully if you make sure your people are kept posted. NASA's Shirley Green made it a point to meet each morning at 7 A.M. with NASA's acting administrator throughout the Challenger crisis and then to brief her headquarters public affairs directors. Delta has specific provisions in its public affairs emergency procedures handbook for keeping its staff briefed on the latest developments after an accident has occurred.

Set aside 30 minutes a day to catch up on what has happened and to go over what to expect in the next 24 hours. Unless there's a crisis, get together at 8:30 A.M. Eastern Standard Time. You'll know how the morning papers and the network TV morning programs covered the latest developments, and there will be a lull before the wire service deadlines for their P.M. cycles approach. The topics will vary and there should be a set agenda to make best use of everyone's time, but make it a point to cover:

1. The number of media phone calls the previous day, and how they broke down by type of news media.
2. What the participants expect will happen during the next 24 hours.
3. Interviews scheduled for today and those to be arranged.
4. Current media interest and focus of questions.
5. What's being heard from the media.
6. Problems, questions, and concerns of the public relations staff.
7. The work schedule for tomorrow.

DOCUMENTATION

One way you can maintain the support of your management team is to keep them informed regarding the news media coverage so they will be aware of what is being reported and can respond authoritatively to influential people with whom they will be talking regarding the situation. Management should know how many journalists are on hand, the news organizations they represent, and how much media coverage the situation is getting at the local and national levels. They also should be aware of news media interest in other parts of the country and overseas. This comes from knowing how many media phone calls are being handled, the news organizations who are calling, and how the information is being used.

Having records of how the news media reported the story could be important later if the situation spawns lawsuits. Getting the clippings and videotapes at the time will be far less expensive than the costs of an attorney's time and the fees charged by video libraries and database services for retrieving various news reports later.

The problem from your position will be time. You'll be lucky if you have a few minutes free during the day to skim the local papers. You rarely will watch TV because you'll be too busy responding to the ongoing deluge of questions and requests for assistance from the media or trying to find out what has happened at the scene. The only time you're likely to concentrate on the details of the news is when something has gone haywire in the coverage and you are trying to figure out how to respond.

Keeping Track of the News Media

Documentation is important; but when you're dealing with a national news story, the expenses, much less the time that would be required to review the print, broadcast, and wire service coverages, could be astronomical. At the same time, with some advance planning and for relatively little money, your organization can keep tabs on the major print and broadcast news coverage. Here's how:

1. Every journalist who shows up should sign up. That doesn't mean he or she has to go through the formal credentialing process that is required by NASA or the White House, unless they will be allowed within the confines of your facilities. In that case they should be handled by your security people as visitors who will be coming and going frequently over the next several days.

If badging is not normally required or if your briefing facilities are away from the scene of the news event, simplify the procedure but maintain it all the same. Rather than having a sign-up sheet, use preprinted five-by-eight cards so you'll have a way of filing each card alphabetically for quick reference. The card should have the following information on each journalist:

```
Name _____    News organization _____
Business address _____    Local address _____
Business phone _____           Home phone _____
Hotel _____ Rm # ____    Local phone _____
```

We used the cards to set up an emergency calling system so Humana could alert both local and out-of-town news media if there was a significant development involving any of the artificial heart patients. The system was first used around 9 P.M. after Schroeder's first stroke, on the 18th day after surgery. The visiting news media who were still in town were called at their hotels. Most had left town by then and were called at home. That gave them the opportunity to alert their newsrooms to the story and discuss how it should be handled. Otherwise, they would have been called from someone in their office who had only the wire service copy and wasn't sure how to play it.

2. Count the house during the first few days to get the number of reporters and TV crews at your briefings. An analysis of how many journalists are still covering the story, and which news organizations they represent, will be very useful in deciding how and when to cut back on news briefings. Later they will help you in analyzing the extent of the national news coverage the story received and the numbers of people you had to deal with personally.

3. Get a skilled photographer to shoot both slides and black-and-white photos of the news coverage during the height of the story as if she were doing a photo essay for a news magazine on your organization's involvement with the media. Have her cover a briefing and then shoot the print and broadcast media at work developing their stories. Get some good shots of the intensity of activity and the interaction of the participants, the PR people, and the press. Those photos are excellent material for your internal publications and for presentations you and the participants will inevitably be asked to make later.

4. Save the hundreds of phone message slips from the media after the calls are returned. I mentioned earlier that rumpling up phone slips will seem like one of the few sources of satisfaction you'll have, but it's also a mistake. Rather than wadding them up, make a note of what transpired on the bottom or the back. "Taped interview for network news—condition"; "Live five-minute interview all-news radio—family plans-Christmas"; "Taped update, radio station, Sydney, Australia—status of stroke recovery." Humana did not do that with the thousands of phone messages we responded to during the artificial heart media coverage. We regretted that later when we wanted to know how many phone calls we had, who called, and how our information was being used by the news media.

Take a few moments at the end of the call to ask how your information will be used, make a note on the slip, and put it in a box marked "Completed." You'll be amazed at how many calls are returned each day. Later, those slips will provide a fascinating, invaluable summary of your involvement with hundreds of news organizations you never saw. They also will tell you a great deal about how their journalists covered the story, even though you never saw or heard it.

5. Have an interview request form, which each journalist can fill out with details about the story angle he or she is pursuing, deadlines, where they can be reached, etc. Initially those forms provide an excellent means of showing the participants the extent of the media interest and the story angles they want to pursue. You and the participants then can decide which requests should be given priority.

When specific interviews occur, make a note on the request form regarding the date, place, length of the discussion, prominent questions, etc. Add those interview sheets to the Completed box so they can become part of your historical record and provide a means to follow up, if the participants or your organization is interested in seeing the results. You'll also have a record of how many one-on-one interviews were conducted, and with whom.

Keeping Track of the News Coverage

If there's time, check with several news monitoring services to determine what types of coverage they could provide for your news story, the costs involved in tracking both the print and broadcast media, and the turnaround time in getting coverage reports to you. Major clipping services like Luce and Burrells can give you reports from the thousands of newspapers across the country as well as from the wire services and television network news programs. For additional cost they will transmit their reports the same day via telephone facsimile machines or computer modems. Regional services can monitor the local newspapers, and in some cases the news coverage of television stations in your area.

In each instance, selectivity will be an important consideration. Thousands of press clippings can be generated by the same news story if it is distributed nationally by one of the wire services. Since the news monitoring services charge for every clipping, you have to decide in advance what level of coverage the service is to provide, the regional and national newspapers that are to be monitored, and the turnaround time for the clippings.

But it doesn't end there. What you will get is a manila envelope stuffed full of press clippings. With all the time pressures and priorities you and your staff will have in dealing with the news media each day, those clippings are likely to remain in their envelopes bundled in rubber bands. One person needs to be designated to review and paste up clippings, to go through videotapes or broadcast transcripts to provide you with a daily summary, and to point out any important statements or problems in the coverage.

In this age of VCRs and boom boxes, the alternative to the commercial monitoring services is to set up your own media monitoring capability. There will be some expense for equipment, supplies, and the time of the people involved, but it's likely to be less than what you'd pay for a commercial service.

1. Find someone who has equipment to monitor radio and television, starting with your audio-visual department, if you have one. If you don't, you will have to rent enough VCRs to record the news coverage on each of the local TV stations, which will include their own newscasts as well as the television network's news programs. Several boom boxes also will be needed to record from AM/FM radio to tape cassette when network and local radio news programs are broadcast.

Line up someone familiar with your organization who has the time to keep track of the news reports on TV and radio and in the newspapers. A retired executive or the spouse of an employee on your staff would be ideal. Another possibility would be a college or graduate student majoring in public relations who could use the project for a thesis or work-study program. You might want more than one person, because their days will usually run from 6 A.M. until after the 11 P.M. news, and include weekends.

Whoever monitors TV and radio newcasts also should clip and paste up any stories in the local newspapers as well as national newspapers and magazines available in your city or town. The optimum would be for that person to have a personal computer equipped with a phone modem that could access data services and scan for stories from the wire services and national publications, which you otherwise might not get for several days or weeks.

Whoever will monitor the news media should go through their own dry run. When you have the VCRs and radios, pick out a current story in the national news and have them track it for two days. The monitoring should get progressively better as they learn to use the equipment and handle several newscasts at the same time on radio and TV as well as on CNN, which will frequently go "live" from the news scene at any time during its round-the-clock newscasts. Editing services can be easily found through local advertising agencies, by calling a nearby TV station, or even in the Yellow Pages. These services have the equipment needed to string the audio and videotape segments onto master tapes. That will allow you and your media monitors to analyze the results and then develop a compilation of news broadcasts for your management.

2. Designate someone to compile the daily summaries of media contacts from the call slips and interview sheets, as well as from the print and broadcast compilations provided by your media monitors. Their job will be to duplicate and distribute the media summaries to top management to keep them informed of the coverage and your actions in handling the media during the past 24 hours.

They should be included in your morning update meetings and should take advantage of the opportunity to "interview" you and your staff for anecdotes, tidbits, and details, which may be interesting to review later when the onslaught has subsided. The "historian's" job can be handled by a secretary, spouse, student, or anyone not involved in the ongoing activities in the briefing center.

THE IMPORTANCE OF TRANSCRIPTS

There will be many uses for a written record of everything said to the news media. Transcripts of briefings are important, but it's also a good idea to get a written record of any one-on-one interviews if you're concerned about legal problems or negative publicity. We didn't provide transcripts during Humana's artificial heart operations, which was an oversight on our part. I recall seeing Larry Altman of the *New York Times*, Christine Russell of the *Washington Post*, and Ed Edelson of the *New York Daily News* huddled over Altman's tape recording of the Schroeder postoperative briefing to get the exact wording from Dr. Lansing on specific details. In retrospect, how useful transcript copies would have been to each of them, and to us later.

The University Medical Center in Tucson, in contrast, provided transcripts of medical briefings on the Creighton artificial heart procedure. Besides helping the media, the transcripts proved useful to medical team members in knowing what questions were being asked by the media and in reviewing the answers so their later responses could reflect those statements. The transcripts also were invaluable in bringing late-arriving journalists up to date on what had already been disclosed.

To create transcripts, all it takes is a tape recorder and good typists. But the trick is in the way the recordings are handled to ensure clarity, accuracy, and speed in making the written record available to the media. Use a good-quality tape recorder with a microphone that can be plugged into the molt box system, if you are using one, or taped beside the speaker's microphone on the podium. To get the transcripts out quickly, switch the tapes every 10 minutes so you can use more than one typist to transcribe the briefing or interview, and then merge them on a word processor.

There were some complaints from journalists in Tucson that the transcript didn't accurately reflect the questions they asked, probably because the typist couldn't clearly pick up voices from the audience. The person operating the tape recorder should have a second microphone so that questions from the audience can be repeated directly onto the tape. Speakers can't be counted on to repeat or accurately paraphrase every question, since they often will be thinking about how to answer it.

With quality transcripts prepared after each briefing or interview, both you and the media will have an "official" record of what was said. From that point, you will be able to document any disclosure in order to point to an inaccuracy in the media coverage or accurately represent your side in the event of litigation. These transcripts will also come in handy months later, when the media requests follow-up information. By having a transcript of what you said the first time and by documenting the coverage to see how it was reported, you will know how to respond to any questions that seem to be asking you for the same information you disclosed earlier. If the facts have changed since the initial onslaught, you'll be able to explain exactly how they've changed by mentioning to the caller the difference between what you said and what was reported earlier.

TIMETABLES

You are looking at a lot of work, and when you begin listing all the details, it can be unnerving. But if you are to be ready, you must establish a realistic timetable based on the priorities, the available personnel, and how much time you actually will have to get ready. One critical mistake Loma Linda made was having an initial discussion in July about Dr. Bailey's plans to perform a xenograph transplant, and then not having a timetable to track and coordinate the preparations of both the public relations staff and the surgical team. Knowing that Dr. Bailey was planning to undertake a highly experimental surgical procedure, Loma Linda's public relations staff had contacted the University of Utah to find out what had occurred during the coverage of Barney Clark but never revealed the specifics of what they were anticipating. They met three months before the Baby Fae procedure and decided to use their conference center near the hospital for media briefings, to serve refreshments, and to begin developing background materials on the procedure, medical institution, and medical team. However, no further planning was done until the week before the procedure, when the public relations staff learned that Dr. Bailey was ready to proceed.

Perhaps you have a systems department or know someone with experience in developing project management timetables using PERT, CPM, or similar techniques. They can be immensely helpful in working through what has to be done to make sure you have considered all the details, defined the related activities, and determined which activities will be the most time consuming—and therefore most critical. An added benefit of this type of scheduling is that it can also define and monitor budget expenditures for press relations materials and activities.

In Humana's case, we relied on Dr. DeVries' estimate that it would take about three months for the hospital's institutional review board to approve the artificial heart protocol and for the FDA to approve Humana Hospital-Audubon as a site for the artificial heart clinical investigation. Our working timetable was based on that estimate; but we also had a contingency timetable, which would begin as soon as FDA approval had been received and Dr. DeVries had begun his search for the next artificial heart recipient. The proverbial "Plan B" allowed us to shift and be ready to make the announcement of the artificial heart patient's selection within 24 hours.

The contingency timetable was activated on November 8, 1984, with our announcement that FDA approval had been received and that Dr. DeVries had begun actively screening patients who might be candidates for the artificial heart. Bill Schroeder became the prime candidate the next week although he had to undergo gall bladder surgery and tooth extraction to clear sources of infection before he would be approved for the implant. Some members of the local media learned about "The Man from Jasper" from their sources within the hospital, but heard he was ruled out because of his gall bladder. Schroeder only had a 1-in-4 chance of getting through the gall bladder operation, considering how severely weakened his heart was; but, in typical Bill Schroeder fashion, he survived and began to recover.

Dr. DeVries had hoped to let Schroeder recuperate for two weeks before performing the artificial heart implant, but on Thanksgiving Day his badly damaged heart began to lose what little strength it had. When I joined DeVries on rounds at 6:30 Friday morning, he had already made the decision to proceed. I drafted the press release and met with Schroeder and his wife to review it and to brief them on what would happen when the media got the word. The announcement was made at 6:10 that night, and the onslaught began minutes later. It would continue for 17 straight days without letup.

We had no way of knowing what it would be like when it began. In looking back, those 11 weeks of intensive planning and preparation that allowed us to handle one of the most complex medical news stories of all time, without hampering the recovery of the patient and without compromising the operations of the hospital and its physicians and staff. This is the type of anticipatory planning you will have to undertake if you expect to survive and succeed in a media onslaught.

CHAPTER FOUR

The Longest Day(s)

The onslaught usually begins with a bulletin over the Associated Press or United Press International wire services. You may trigger it yourself when you first pick up the phone, or it may begin when one of the media learns of a major news story involving your organization. Regardless of how it starts, every telephone in your office will be ringing in less than five minutes. Delta Air Lines had 6,000 media calls during the first week after the Flight 191 crash at Dallas-Fort Worth. NASA's public affairs center at Cape Kennedy handled nearly that many calls in the first 24 hours after the explosion of the Challenger.

Within the first hour, at the most a few hours, microwave and satellite trucks will be pulling into your parking lot while the local newspaper and wire service reporters will be waiting for the next disclosure. TV crews will be stringing cables, trying to make their phone hookups work, and setting up cameras and monitors amidst aluminum shipping cases that shortly before were in the cargo bay of an airliner or on a chartered jet.

No amount of confrontation training will prepare you for the intensity of the first days of a media onslaught. However, a lot can be learned from Schroeder's artificial heart operation and recovery, the search for survivors of the Wilberg Mine fire, the Union Carbide disaster in Bhopal, and the aftermath of the Challenger tragedy. This chapter will show you how you can maintain control of the situation and not be overwhelmed by the sheer pressure and speed of the news media once the story has broken open.

GETTING THE WORD OUT

We've discussed what happens and what you can do when the media finds out about the story without any disclosure being made. But what if you have to make the announcement and the media doesn't know yet? Don't worry about mailing the press release. All you will have time for is two phone calls, one to Associated Press and the other to United Press International. If your community isn't large enough to have a wire service bureau, get the release to any newspapers, radio, or television stations in your local area.

Read the release over the phone or, better yet, have it delivered at a predetermined time so they will get the announcement at the same time—and within five minutes the onslaught will be on. What happens is that the local media or wire service bureaus will have taken your announcement and called the national news desks of the Associated Press and United Press International to dictate a one-paragraph "lead." AP and UPI immediately transmit that brief message at 1,200 words a minute via satellite and computer to the 15,000 news organizations worldwide that are members of the AP and/or subscribe to UPI. Wire service terminals in newspapers and TV and radio stations, which have been churning out the day's news, sports results, and weather, suddenly interrupt in mid-sentence to transmit BULLETIN: followed by that one-paragraph lead.

That's when you hear "We interrupt this program to bring you this special news bulletin" on your radio or have a message begin to scroll across the bottom of your TV screen. That's also when your switchboard begins to go crazy as the media starts calling in for more details or a phone "actuality," which can be used by the network and local radio news in their next broadcasts at the top or bottom of the hour.

The first calls will be from your local media. Moments later you'll have the networks coming in on you as AP and UPI transmit additional details, including the name and phone number for the source for the story. Suddenly you're talking to somebody at NBC, CBS, ABC Radio News who wants to record the conversation for broadcast and asks you to begin with your name so he can get a "level."

Humana's announcement that Bill Schroeder had been selected as the next artificial heart patient was made via a two-page press release at 6:10 P.M. on November 24, 1984, the Friday after Thanksgiving. The release gave general information on Schroeder and indicated a full medical briefing would be held at 9 P.M. Saturday night, with surgery scheduled for 7 A.M. Sunday morning. The phones began ringing less than four minutes later and didn't let up until around 1:30 the next morning. The hundreds of calls we handled in the interim ranged from radio actualities to an in-depth discussion with Dr. Altman of the *New York Times*. There also were numerous calls with questions about what arrangements were being made for briefing the news media. The calls came from every major news organization in the United States and from dozens of newspapers and radio stations, several as far away as Ecuador and Australia.

The radio stations and networks will be looking for the essence of the announcement. You can help them if you have a copy of your release in hand, with the major statements highlighted, when you're on the phone. Start off by reading the lead paragraph slowly and naturally; then, in the course of the conversation, mention the other points you have highlighted, even if they don't directly relate to the question you were asked. Radio networks and stations will build the stories in their hourly newscasts around whatever you say, if it's relevant.

You'll soon begin to hear from network TV news programs and interview shows' producers, who are very persuasive when they want to get somebody on their particular show. A call from a producer for ABC-TV's "Nightline" after the Schroeder announcement provided an indication of what we would be in for during the days and weeks to follow. It is also a good example of how the network news organizations will exert pressure on you and your spokespeople to capitulate to their needs. You have to be straightforward about what you can and cannot give them. And don't be afraid to say no. Here is an excerpt from that conversation:

Producer: Mr. Irvine, Ted Koppel has just canceled the show he had planned for tonight and will interview Bill Schroeder. We're making the arrangements now, and all we need to know is how do we set it up with the hospital? Do we work through you or somebody else?

Response: Thanks, but I'm afraid it's not going to be possible to interview Mr. Schroeder.

Producer: You don't understand. With your timing of this announcement, "Nightline" is the only network news program that can still give Mr. Schroeder the chance to tell the American public why he has decided to have an artificial heart.

Response: I'm very sorry, but that's not going to be possible.

Producer: Why not?

Response: He's dying. I saw Mr. Schroeder about three hours ago, and he was barely able to breathe, much less talk.

Producer: Oh, that's too bad. But, don't you think it's important for him to talk with the American public, in case something happens?

Response: I'm sorry, but that's out.

Producer: OK, we'll just have to build the program around Dr. DeVries. Can you get in touch with him for us?

Response: That's not going to be possible either. Dr. DeVries is at the hospital. He's concentrating on preparations for the operation.

Producer: No problem. We'll do the interview at the hospital. It'll only take a few minutes, and he'll still be near his patient.

Response: Sorry, that's out too.

Producer: You're going to make these decisions arbitrarily, without checking with either Mr. Schroeder or Dr. DeVries?

Response: That's right.

Producer: Mr. Irvine, you're new at this, so I'd like to give you a bit of practical advice. There are a lot of questions about Humana's involvement in the artificial heart program. This would be an excellent chance to tell your company's side of the story, but you're stonewalling us. That's not the way to deal with the news media.

Response: Sorry, but that's the way it's going to have to be.

LESSENING THE PRESSURE ON YOURSELF AND THE MEDIA

You're going to take a psychological pounding from pushy producers and many other members of the media, as they pour in on you over the phone and in person. You will need a realistic game plan for dealing with the media, and you'd better be ready to stick to it no matter what the pressure point is. You can take several steps when the announcement is made to relieve some of the pressure on you, and on the media as well, during the initial hours of the onslaught:

1. Keep the Announcement Simple and Straightforward. The news media will be rushing to get the story out and will be less likely to misconstrue details if they are easily grasped and reported. Keep them as simple, understandable, and accurate as possible. Use clear comparisons and the personal observations of the participants included in quotes. The technical aspects are important but should not override human interest details so the news media and the public can relate personally to the situation and to those who are involved. As far as what will happen next, stay away from speculation about the future, even about when the next important development will occur, unless you are absolutely sure.

2. Give the Announcement to the Wire Services First and at Precisely the Same Time.   AP and UPI will be the primary conduit for the story to the rest of the news media worldwide and should receive your information at virtually the same time so neither will have a competitive advantage in alerting other news organizations. The local news media also is important, but they usually will have more leeway with their deadlines and will use wire service copy if your release is delivered when they are going to press or on the air.

You may be able to take the media's deadlines into consideration in deciding when to send out the announcement, but don't make the mistake of giving anyone a break with an advance copy of the release if you know it will go out close to deadline. This is not the time to be playing favorites with any news organizations, big or little.

If you have local AP and UPI bureaus, two of your people can deliver the releases to each wire service office at the predetermined time. Otherwise, they can begin reading the full text of the announcement to each wire over the phone. If you have a computer terminal and a modem, you can even download the text to AP and UPI in a few seconds. Then follow up by having the release, and any background information and photos, delivered to both wire service bureaus and to any print or broadcast media in your local area.

3. Include Your Background Information and Visuals.   Some people may want you to give out the press release and nothing more. All that does is cause the press to pester your organization for the little details. "The more information we have, the better the story we are going to write. The payoff is to the readers and the participants. The more information we have, the more informed the copy will be," said Al Rossiter, Jr., of UPI. "A lot of PR people will sit on details because they are sure nobody is interested. We are. It may not show up in our copy, but to have that information to draw on gives the writer a much better perspective."[27]

We probably could have reduced follow-up telephone calls from the wire services and local media by 50 or more the night of Schroeder's announcement if we had also included Humana's extensive briefing book on the artificial heart with the press release. Instead we wanted to be fair to everyone, and waited to distribute it the next day when the briefing center opened. By that time the AP bureau in Louisville had moved five separate stories on Schroeder's selection for the artificial heart, the reaction of his family, and his medical history, which it got by interviewing his family physician in Jasper, Indiana.

4. Schedule a Background Briefing. The media pressure will be substantially less if a background briefing is scheduled to review a major disclosure and to answer the questions of reporters. They'll report the basic story but hold off on extensive coverage until they can get an explanation of what has happened from those who are directly involved. The time and place of the briefing should be included in the initial announcement.

5. Find Out about Deadlines. For the first few hours, have your people ask about deadlines while the media calls are pouring in. Radio reporters often will need to talk to you within the next few minutes to be ready for their next newscast at the top of the hour. Newspaper journalists will usually have more time and can develop other parts of their story with wire service copy until you can return their call. A quick sort of the phone message slips marked with deadlines will help you decide which to return first.

THE ONSLAUGHT BEGINS

What you cannot see is how fast the national news organizations are mobilizing. The reaction of ABC News to the Schroeder announcement is typical of how the TV networks will respond, even on a holiday weekend. ABC got the bulletin and then the first wire service story by 6:25 P.M., in time to make the second feed of "ABC Evening News" with Peter Jennings. It also was fed to ABC radio news and became a major part of each network radio news update, four times an hour during the next 24 hours. The network immediately chartered a plane in Chicago and two hours later had a correspondent and camera crew doing a stand-up on the front lawn of Bill Schroeder's house in Jasper, Indiana. The correspondent ran into Schroeder's daughter, Cheryl, who was checking her parents' house, and honored her request not to be interviewed. In the meantime a second ABC crew was being dispatched from Washington with George Strait, the network's medical correspondent. Another camera crew, a free-lance husband-and-wife team from Louisville, was contacted in Illinois, where they had been spending Thanksgiving weekend, and pulled back to Louisville.

Mike King, the Louisville *Courier-Journal*'s medical writer, also was on vacation when I called him in Washington, D.C., about Schroeder, but he was not unprepared. He and the *C-J*'s editorial staff had developed 10 "slugs" for stories on Humana, the family of the patient, and other aspects of the artificial heart program the previous week, after Humana had an orientation briefing for the media. King worked over the phone with Gideon Gil, the paper's other medical writer, on the lead story for Saturday's paper. He then wrote two of the sidebar stories on the flight back to Louisville Saturday morning, while Gil handled three others. King wasn't the only journalist headed for Louisville on Saturday. Within 18 hours of the initial announcement, 325 members of the media had signed in at the briefing center, including 26 TV news organizations. The fact that it was a holiday weekend was irritating but irrelevant.

THE FREE-FOR-ALL

Within hours you will be dealing with hundreds of people, all wanting you to brief them, set up an interview for them, find them a hotel, put them in touch with the phone people, help them out with a live, on-camera update, or tell them where they can park the satellite transmission truck.

There is no more experienced organization than the White House press office in handling the incessant needs of hundreds of journalists who travel with the president. Still Denny Brisley, a former assistant press secretary to the president, described it as like taking your kids on a tour of Europe and having them questioning the validity of your answers while you are simultaneously making sure they are properly clothed, fed, and housed. "The central problem is getting your message across while keeping some kind of dignity. The press, due to the intense competition, are very interested in 'me, me, me.' Help me out. Answer my question right now."[28]

You will be working in an atmosphere of controlled chaos, being torn in several directions at the same time by the myriad of newspeople wanting your assistance. All of them, from the weekly news-paper in a participant's hometown to the *New York Times*, will want the same consideration.

Dozens of newspaper and wire service photographers, TV cam-era crews, and stringers from photo agencies will be after you to tell them how, when, and where they can get the best shots. If they can shoot the participants or the news event itself, lumbering bodies lugging TV cameras with lights and boom microphones and fes-tooned with motor-driven still cameras will surge into the area, jostling each other and going for the best position the minute you open the doors. Your briefing area will quickly be decorated with strips of gaffer's tape on the floor to define the space claimed by various TV crews. They'll spell out their network or station names in crude gray letters made from wide strips of tape.

If you are controlling the distribution of photos, TV cameras will be set up and ready with their lights on waiting to shoot whatever is posted or about to be handed out. Meanwhile, photographers from the newspapers, wire services, and photo agencies will be waiting to pounce on the prints. If there's video as well, you'd better have a means of providing enough dupes or, better yet, a molt box system hooked to one videoplayer so they all can copy the tape at the same time. We'll discuss the hardware needs in Chapter Six, "A Look at the Logistics."

Everyone will want to interview the participants, who probably are too involved to talk to anyone, much less a mob of reporters. After that it will be with members of the participants' families, eyewit-nesses, anyone else who can explain what happened, officials of your organization, and, if all else fails, you. Peg Maloy, director of public affairs for the Federal Emergency Management Agency, pointed out that you always want to get the most authoritative, credible spokes-person you can, but there will be times when that turns out to be you. "As a public affairs person, I always try to have my boss or the experts quoted, not me," she said. "But often the people we really need are tied up with the disaster or whatever we're involved in and it's more critical to have them there. That's when the press will say 'You're our source' and they'll end up quoting you, so you have to be ready for that."[29]

You will hear the most convincing reasons imaginable about why each news organization should have the first interview with the participants or principal figures. After all, it's the hometown paper, or it has umpteen million viewers each night or readers each week, or it services thousands of news organizations worldwide. The dilemma will be agonizing for anyone with a background in public relations. Here is the opportunity of a lifetime to have your organization and key people interviewed by every major news organization you've ever dreamed of. Here is the chance to tell your side of the story, to make the important points that need to be conveyed. The story may well be the lead item on the news for the next few days or on the cover of *Time* or *Newsweek*. Yet you look at the dozens of journalists from major news organizations milling around and realize it's also a finger-in-the-dike situation. Once you take the finger out and the interviews begin, how many can you possibly set up, and who gets priority?

The media also will be pestering you with hundreds of questions that don't concern the latest developments in the news event, with the runaway winner being "when." When will the next update be held? When will you have photos? When will I know if I can do the interview? When will the family be willing to talk to us? The "when" questions are legitimate. In addition to giving a future angle to their stories, the reporters will be trying to plan their stories and figure out what to tell their newsrooms to expect in the next few hours. They also will be trying to decide when to be on hand for whatever you will coordinate while also developing other elements of the story.

You will be inundated with special requests. Reporters, producers, and camera crews will be looking for decent places to stay and eat, places to buy batteries or recording tapes, messenger services, and even medical assistance. A majority of the requests will come from the TV networks and affiliates, which will have the most people. They also will need the most space for editing equipment, setting up for live "feeds," and parking broadcast equipment ranging in size from microwave vans to mobile broadcasting studios in the semi-trucks and trailers usually seen at major sporting events. But there also will be dozens—even hundreds—of individual reporters looking for desks and phones to file stories and receptacles to plug in their portable computer terminals.

Their biggest logistical problem will be having enough phones. The University of Utah put in 10 lines for the reporters covering Barney Clark and wound up with 50. Humana installed 50 and found every one being used during the first week of coverage. NASA has 500 lines installed for the media covering shuttle launches, but they needed 80 more lines the morning after the Challenger explosion. If the news media has special telephone lines, so much the better. It will help to make the situation run more smoothly.

If you are planning for a major news disclosure, include discussions with the local telephone company in your planning. However, if the news disclosure breaks suddenly, you will probably not have the opportunity to provide phone lines for the press. In that instance, make sure that whatever briefing room you set up has facilities for networks to install their own phone lines or at least has telephone booths nearby. Union Carbide, for example, did not have any special phone lines installed at their briefing facility at the Danbury Hilton. The company assumed that the reporters covering the event would have the wherewithal to seek out the pay phones in the hotel lobby or make their own arrangements.

KEEPING CURRENT

Working with the media will be more than a full-time job, but you also will find yourself struggling to get free from reporters so you can stay close to the source of the news itself. You can't be in both places at once, but the more you can balance your time between staying close to your sources and keeping in touch with reporters on the scene, the more effectively the news coverage can be managed. You need to know what's happening firsthand to respond with authority to the media's incessant hammering for updates, but you also have to be in a position to anticipate what the upcoming developments will be to determine how and when they should be disclosed.

You will have to keep reinforcing your rapport with the participants so they will view you as part of their team, not one of the media. That only will come from spending as much time as possible with the key people and getting more than just the information—also a sense of the mood, their concerns about the situation, and their regard for the other people involved. They, in turn, need to know which news organizations are covering the story, how the news coverage is going, why certain stories are taking a particular slant, and what major areas of interest among the news media need to be considered.

Regardless of how strong your relationship has been in the past, the participants will view you with suspicion, because you've been exposed to the media. Some will consider your efforts to get information, or your ideas about what to disclose, to be tainted by the press, and to a certain extent they will be right. They'll be aware of the news coverage if there's a TV set nearby, from reports on their car radios, or from seeing the headlines of a paper. Intellectually they may know better, but in the stress of the situation, you will be blamed for the added burden that's being placed on them by the presence of the news media. If they don't like the news reports they are seeing and hearing, you will be held responsible for letting that happen.

Their families will be even less sophisticated in their attitudes about your role in working with the news media. Initially they will be in a state of shock and will probably accept anything you tell them about relating to the press. But you, as an authority on the news media, also will get the credit or the blame for the ensuing news coverage since they will expect you to control its extent and content. As the story evolves, you may well be viewed by family members as an agent of the media or as the censorship supervisor, depending on how they feel about your organization, the extent of the news coverage, and the accuracy of the stories.

The participants and any families who are involved may expect the public relations people to keep the media under control, and they may even blame you for negative or inaccurate news reports. "A few of the families felt I was responsible for the news coverage, that I determined what went on the air, that I controlled both the quality and quantity of the news," Bob Henrie recalled. "Because there would be a news story where I would be interviewed or quoted, they would get upset with me. I felt badly about that."[30]

Family members who encounter reporters and don't want to be interviewed may indicate you have advised that they not talk to the press. That's an easy way for someone under stress to say no, but it will also give the news media a nice bit of controversy to work on. You should anticipate this and prepare for the worst by briefing all the participants about the direction the news coverage might take. At the same time, encourage them to help you by following the news and relating to you any inaccuracies or blatant mistakes they discover. If they feel that you are going to call the reporters who have distorted the facts, they will feel that they have some control over the situation, even though that control is more perceived than real.

SOURCES OF CONFLICT

Regardless of whether the news story is positive or negative, be ready for conflict. The media will be neutral and generally cooperative when they arrive, but they also will suspect that you are not giving them all the information that's available, which probably will be the case. There always tends to be an adversarial relationship between the news media and public relations, but now the usual roles will be reversed because you control what the media needs. However, those differences will be mild compared to the likely debates and disputes within your organization.

You'll come in with an understanding of the news media's needs and the importance of being forthright. The legal minds, curmudgeons, and conservatives in your organization will take the opposite tack, citing the vulnerability to lawsuits and the impossibility of satisfying the media's appetite for information or of ensuring the accuracy of its reporting. In between will be a diversity of executive viewpoints, based on their limited experience with reporters and on personal reactions to media coverage of other news stories. There will be some angry exchanges as tensions build and fatigue sets in among both the participants and your management team, who may have tolerated the presence of the news media at first but now see the dozens of reporters and TV crews as a disruptive factor.

And then there will be employees who feel they are in the best position to decide what should be disclosed or who want to gratify their egos by being interviewed or quoted as a spokesperson for your organization. "We had the same types of petty politics and power plays that Humana had, but the difference was that ours were controlled by Chase Peterson. He exercised that authority from time to time, and we had some head-bashing sessions," John Dwan recalled. "When those situations arose, he'd get on the phone or into a private meeting, and the rules would be laid out in no uncertain terms."[31] Even with Chase Peterson's leadership and authority as president of the university's Health Sciences Center, Dr. DeVries remembers that it seemed more hours were spent arguing about how much should be disclosed about a specific development in Barney Clark's condition than was needed to decide on the treatment plan for the patient.

The conflict also will come from the outside, sometimes predictably and at other times by complete surprise. While the rescue efforts were still under way at the Wilberg Mine, officials of the United Mine Workers flew to Huntington to stage a press conference and make a number of serious allegations against the mining company. "Anyone who had something against the company, Western coal development, or individuals in the mine, given the immense publicity, had an opportunity to have access to lots of media with whatever they were going to say," Bob Henrie said. "Whatever they said was covered without much discretion. The fire put the company in an extremely vulnerable position for others to exploit the tragedy, and that happened shamelessly."[32]

Union Carbide's Bhopal task force also faced pressure from the outside and from within. On the one hand, congressional committees as well as community leaders in the states where Carbide had chemical plants voiced their concern over plant safety and the company's response to the accident. American attorneys flew to India shortly after the accident, ostensibly to represent the damage claims of the Bhopal victims, and set the stage for the rounds of litigation with the lawsuits seeking billions of dollars.

In the face of these activities, Carbide's lawyers recommended that management remain as closemouthed as possible while the cause of the accident was being investigated. Their point, which is the position most lawyers will take, is that whatever you say publicly can and will be used against you by the other side. The company's Bhopal Team had to balance all of these conflicting points of view while at the same time trying to preserve Union Carbide's integrity with its internal and external publics.

Warren Anderson, who holds degrees in both law and chemistry, shouldered the additional burden of wanting to provide as much "no-strings" assistance as possible to the victims while maintaining good relations with the Indian government and assuring American communities around Carbide's chemical plants that its facilities were safe. "In whatever tort liability issue you can think of, the litigation has never helped any of the pain and suffering going on," Anderson observed. "So legal liability wasn't the right issue. To solve the problem of Bhopal, I felt that we should stay away from that entirely and talk in terms of moral responsibility to make sure we could do whatever was appropriate."[33] You're going to live with dilemmas like Anderson's, which rarely get reported in the headline-oriented news coverage.

The media more likely will focus on the inevitable bystanders awed by the invasion of the news teams. Some will kibbitz in the back of the briefing area or wander through to see the TV equipment and reporters working on stories. Others may take advantage of the gathered newspeople to promote a particular cause, such as missing children or a kidney transplant for a local child. A local radio station wanted to plug a new song, "Plastic Heart," to the news media between medical briefings the week after Schroeder's operation.

Reporters frequently will turn to local people to get a "man on the street" perspective, especially if there are no hard news developments to report. They will be hoping for a few pearls of wisdom among the innocuous comments that most will provide. That will be novelty to some people, but it quickly wears out. After the Challenger shuttle explosion more than 250 journalists and TV crews poured into Concord, New Hampshire, to do interviews with the citizens and especially with faculty and students at Christa McAuliffe's high school. A few days later they overran a memorial service for McAuliffe which was attended by her parents, just as they had a memorial service for the Wilberg miners in the tiny San Rafael Mission near Huntington.

DAYS WITHOUT END

For a spokesperson the first day may not end for several days when you consider their experiences in the following news stories.

News Story	Spokesperson	Typical Workdays
Barney Clark's artificial heart	John Dwan	Worked 44 straight hours during and after surgery, got 4 hours sleep, then went 18 hours. Average day was 12–14 hours during the first month. Handled 10–12 media calls nightly between the time he got home and went to bed, with 3–4 more calls during the night. Only relief during Barney Clark's 112 days came during the month on active reserve duty with the Marines in Korea.
Baby Fae	Dick Schaefer Dick Weismeyer	Schaefer worked 36 hours the first day. Briefing center staffed from 7 A.M. to midnight the first seven days, after which media interest abated somewhat. Public relations staff worked without a day off until Baby Fae died on 20th day.
Bhopal	Jackson Browning Ed Van Den Ameele	First day ran from 2:30 A.M. to 11 P.M. Heavy media coverage of daily press briefings began after Anderson returned from India. Worked seven-day weeks

News Story	Spokesperson	Typical Workdays
		through Christmas. Van Den Ameele forced to get unlisted phone number after *Fortune* article on Bhopal.
Challenger	Shirley Green Hugh Harris Dick Young	Worked 19 hours after Challenger accident. Seven hours off, then 18-hour day. Briefing center staffed 24 hours a day for two weeks, then 18 hours a day for six weeks. Still handling media calls late at night and on weekends six months after the accident.
Wilberg Mine	Bob Henrie	Worked 72 hours without sleep from initial phone call through disclosure of no survivors. Wilberg fire took 100 percent of time during first few months and never less than 50 percent during first year. Weekly media calls regarding the fire numbered as high as 300 and never less than 30. Had to get second phone at home for family use because media called the original number, often beginning at 5 A.M.
Delta 191	Bill Berry Jim Ewing	Initial day went 26 hours, including regular workday before accident occurred. Berry worked several 16-hour shifts from midafternoon through next morning before media pressure let up enough to shift to daytime hours. Press relations staffed 24 hours a day at Atlanta headquarters and Dallas crash site in accordance with Standard Practices.
Bill Schroeder's artificial heart	George Atkins Bob Irvine	Briefing center staffed from 6 A.M. to 11 P.M. for 17 consecutive days. Closed for 4 days, then reopened for 7 straight days following Schroeder's stroke. Used recorded message for overnight updates but still averaged two to three calls a night at home between 11 P.M. and 5 A.M.

As these typical workdays show, you will become as much a slave of the situation as are the participants in the story. Your workday is one of incessant telephone calls, being paged frequently, and having your pocket beeper go off. That's acceptable because it's part of the job, but it never seems to stop. So how do you cope? You'll feel like the beachmaster at Normandy while in the midst of the media onslaught. If you are to stay ahead of the frenzy from both sides, you'd better get and keep the situation under control:

1. Maintain Realistic Disclosure Policies.   The guidelines for what information and visuals your organization will provide should be a clear indication to the media of what to expect so they can plan accordingly. They need to know who will be your spokespersons, where and when disclosures will be made, provisions for photography and video, and how interviews will be handled. The more you tell the media in writing and in advance, the less they will have to ask you.

2. Take Advantage of the News Media's Experience.   The reporters and field producers who pour in on you have been through onslaughts before and will know what is needed for a smooth working relationship between the participants and the press. Let them suggest the best times for briefings and how you can provide information and visuals so nobody gets a jump on the other news organizations. They are competitive and dislike "pool" situations, but when pools are appropriate they can set one up in a few minutes.

3. Choose Your Words Carefully.   You will be under constant pressure to respond, to reply, to react. The worst thing you can do is "wing it" when you are caught by surprise. Peg Maloy of FEMA pointed out that there have been instances where the person to whom the press turned for answers to its questions didn't have the answer. However, because the reporters were pressuring him, he responded and gave them information that turned out to be wrong. The result of the inaccurate news reports was that the person ultimately lost his job. "You need to draw the picture of truth for those people," she said. "And if you come to a point where you don't know or can't say because it's going to hurt somebody, don't be afraid to say, 'I can't answer that question.' The public has the right to know a lot of things but not something that's going to hurt people involved in a disaster."

If there's even the slightest doubt, the only thing you should say is that you will have to find out. That often takes guts, but you will maintain your credibility with the media only as long as they can count on you for accurate information. Even if you do know, take pains to explain details clearly and carefully, especially if you are dealing with newsworthy details. An illustration, even a rough sketch, often can reduce reporting errors by helping the news media explain the story to their audiences.

4. Put the "Lid" on Every Few Hours. When the lid light is on in the White House pressroom, the press knows nothing will be disclosed for a specified time and the wire services will be notified to alert them if there is a sudden development. That gives the news media and the press office staff an all-important break, which you and the press as well will need during the onslaught.

You don't need an actual light, but you can still put the lid on for a few hours. That will give the media time to eat and sleep and you an opportunity to catch up on recent developments with the participants. That also will be your chance to stay in touch with those who really matter. "I called my wife once a day just to maintain our communications. That was my lifeline with the rest of my life," Bob Henrie recalled. "Every time I could do that I came back with renewed strength and a renewed perspective that was so important to maintain, because you get so buried it's very easy to lose sight of everything else."

CHAPTER FIVE

Managing to Maintain Control

How much time do you have before you'll be involved in a major news story? You probably have no way of knowing when, if ever, it will happen, which is the reason organizations have contingency plans. Or the story may break in a few days or weeks, which may be why you're reading this book. Either way, the decisions that you and your management team make now will determine how effectively you can manage the situation and maintain control once the story is out.

NASA and Delta Air Lines both had contingency plans for responding to the news media if a disaster occurred. One worked, the other didn't. Humana and Loma Linda both knew that hospitals that bore their names would be involved in a major news story. In one instance the ensuing worldwide media coverage was favorable, in the other it had a profound negative impact on the reputation of the institution.

Even if there's no way of telling when you and your organization might find yourselves in the midst of a newsworthy situation, the management decisions that are made now will largely determine how well you succeed when it does occur. To be specific:

- Your chain of command needs to be established to hammer out the tough decisions in the midst of a major story and minimize the chances of misstatements and discrepancies that will generate controversy in the news reports.
- Your spokespersons must be designated so there will be no question of who is authorized to speak for the organization.

- Your guidelines, policies, and procedures for responding to the news media must be established and clearly understood throughout the organization so there will be no deviations when the media onslaught begins.
- Careful planning and budgeting will be required to make best use of your manpower and other resources during the initial siege and as the news story drags on in the ensuing months or years.

This chapter discusses the management decisions that have to be made to establish and maintain control of a breaking news story, the first and most important consideration in preparing for a news media onslaught.

SIZING UP THE NEWS POTENTIAL

Too many public relations people "cry wolf" too often with the news media by calling them about a major story that isn't. Just to be sure you really have a newsworthy development on your hands, check its vital signs:

1. *Who's involved and how well known are they?* You may be dealing with a celebrity, not necessarily a show business personality. If he or she is known locally, it's likely to be a local or regional story. The fact that the Humana Heart Institute was adding a surgeon from the University of Utah to its team wasn't newsworthy. What made it a media onslaught was that his name was DeVries.

2. *How unique is the situation?* If you're dealing with a true "first," or even a significant "second," you probably have a major news story on your hands. Artificial hearts had been implanted twice before Barney Clark's surgery, but his was the first that would be permanent. Thus the worldwide news coverage

3. *What's the human interest potential?* How closely can the average person relate to what happened? Is it a life-and-death situation? The "little guy" bucking the odds also can give a news story immense appeal. Bill Schroeder will be remembered by many as the man with an artificial heart; but many more will remember him as the man who wanted a beer

and later asked the president to check into the whereabouts of his social security check.

4. *How much controversy is involved?* Are there any skeletons in the closet? What are the chances that someone will come out against what has happened? If there have been any casualties, you can count on somebody questioning the safety procedures and thus getting media coverage. What kept the Challenger accident such a hot news story over six months were the disclosures of recommendations not to launch because of the cold weather and the memos of frustration regarding the O-ring problem in the solid rocket booster, which exposed the mismanagement that had developed within the space agency.

WHERE ARE YOUR VULNERABILITIES?

If there are a number of casualties and the potential for additional loss of life, you can be sure the media onslaught will be on. But you also can predict to a certain extent how the media will cover the disclosure of a story that may not be a disaster. Their news morgues, electronic and otherwise, will quickly give them what is known about your organization and the participants. Anything controversial will quickly become one of the focus points as different news organizations develop their strategies and news budgets for covering the story.

The disclosure late in 1986 that the Reagan administration secretly had sold arms to Iran was enough of a controversy for the media to finally find a loose plate in the president's image armor. When the diversion of the sale proceeds to the Contras in Nicaragua was revealed, the media had all it needed for a major news story that would sap much of the administration's strength and require the president's attention for months to come.

What criticisms do you have to respond to most often? What doesn't the public know about yet? How are the participants and your organization regarded in their field, in the immediate community where the story is breaking, by state and federal government agencies, or by Wall Street analysts if you're a public company? The answer to each of these questions is a potential source of story ideas for the news media.

Beyond the short-term exposure, there also is the question of long-term impact. It's more important but also more difficult for an organization to maintain its reputation in a crisis situation than in a disclosure of a new development; but, if the disclosure is mishandled, as it was at Loma Linda, the negative media coverage can be just as harmful as if a disaster had occurred. For example, many journalists felt at the time that Humana's real motive was to use the artificial heart news media coverage to generate name recognition for its hospitals and thus increase their patient census. Many still feel that way. To be sure, name recognition was one result of our exposure, and we received millions of dollars in free publicity. But it's impossible to determine if it has had any impact on Humana in terms of increased business. It's even more difficult to know whether there will be any return on the millions of dollars the company has invested in the artificial heart program. (Humana has never disclosed the exact costs for the first two years of the program to its stockholders, the news media, the FDA, or anyone else.)

If the focus of the news story is a development in medical science, another question will be whether talking to the news media will jeopardize the chances of the data being published in a medical journal. Physicians and researchers are particularly apprehensive about violating the "Ingelfinger Rule" of *The New England Journal of Medicine,* which will not publish information on medical experiments that have been discussed in other publications or by the news media.[34]

Researchers need to understand that no newspaper or television station is going to report medical information the same way it will be presented in a peer-review journal. Reporters don't include creatine levels in their story if the patient has a kidney problem or the pro-thrombin time for his blood if there's a concern about clotting and hemorrhaging, as there has been with the artificial heart patients. That's not what the public is interested in. They want to know in understandable terms how the patient is doing.

George Strait, the medical correspondent for ABC News, believes *The New England Journal of Medicine'* s"Ingelfinger Rule" has been abused. "Its sole purpose is protecting the medical research establishment, and it's used to squeeze people out of that establishment," Strait observed. "It's also a wonderful way to sell copies of Dr. Relman's magazine because everytime the media mentions an article in *The Journal* they're talking about something new."[35] Dr.

Lawrence Altman, medical writer for the *New York Times,* observed, "If the scientific journals don't want to publish something because it's already been disclosed, that's their problem. The editors are journalists and are no different from medical journalists who write and edit stories for the *New York Times, Washington Post, Los Angeles Times* or Louisville *Courier-Journal.*"[36]

POWER PLAYS AND POLITICAL CONSIDERATIONS

Step back a moment and take a look at the mentality of your organization, which is basically a reflection of the personalities of its top management team. How comfortable are they in addressing someone who may not be completely supportive? What has been their experience in dealing with the press in the past? How easily do they respond to tough questions and even to attacks by the media? Executive personalities will not change to fit the media coverage. Their strengths and their weaknesses, along with those of the participants, will be accentuated while they are on public display and scrutinized by the news media for days or even weeks.

You will have to make your own private assessment of how your management team will hold up once the shelling starts and of how much you can count on them to follow your directions when confronted by skeptical journalists asking some difficult questions. And you also have to be mindful of how your colleagues will react to you as the company's media quarterback. Will they want to rewrite the game plan themselves or complain to higher management that they don't agree with the decisions you have made? You need to anticipate this and get everyone's agreement, including the CEO, that once the onslaught begins, signals can't be changed arbitrarily at the line of scrimmage. Reporters will seize upon anything that smacks of mismanagement, as they did after the Challenger accident or the disclosure that $30 million in revenues from the Iranian arms sale had been diverted to the Contras. That confusion will become a major subsidiary issue, which can overwhelm any management without a clear sense of leadership.

The chain of command, both from an operational standpoint and for dealing with the media, needs to be clearly and unequivocally defined—in writing. All it takes is a one-paragraph memo from the highest level of management or a specific section from the policy manual that specifies who is in charge, but at some point there will be a power play, which will make that written statement essential. Once the decisions have been made, they should be considered company policy to be followed as closely as possible by all participants.

The key to establishing and maintaining effective media relations in the midst of any onslaught will be the public relations director or whoever is monitoring the evolving news story, staying in touch with the participants, and advising the spokespeople and the rest of the staff. Organizations like Delta Air Lines, which have done an effective job of informing the media, have all had a clear-cut line of command, with the public relations people having direct access to the decision makers. The operational decisions for Delta Air Lines in the aftermath of Flight 191 were made by Hollis Harris, the senior vice president for operations. Delta's public relations staff normally reports to the legal department but was tied in closely with the command center by Delta's Standard Practices and Procedures, which go into effect when an accident occurs.

The same holds true for a news event that is not a disaster. During Barney Clark's 112 days with an artificial heart, Dr. Chase Peterson had the final say on what would be disclosed. Dr. DeVries and John Dwan were among the people who reported directly to him. The relationship worked well in that differences of opinion among those involved in the artificial heart program were resolved by Dr. Peterson, who has since gone on to become the president of the University of Utah.

The optimum management in an onslaught will be enlightened risk takers, because the stakes in how information is disclosed will be high. And if they pinch every penny, you're going to have another problem. It will take a substantial investment of time, personnel, and money to maintain control of the media relations. Realistically, there can be no budget limits for handling a media onslaught, any more than there can be limits to the legal fees in a major lawsuit, simply because there is no way to predict how long the news coverage will continue, how intense it will be, or what steps your organization will have to take in responding.

CRISIS MANAGEMENT PROCEDURES

An important consideration in your planning is whether your organization already has a written policy for handling crisis situations. If it does, the last thing you want to do is fly in the face of that procedure.

A lot of people have invested considerable time in developing and updating it, and many of your top executives may insist on going by the book, especially with something as scary as the propect of having to deal with reporters in addition to the problem itself. A good crisis management policy, like Delta's Standard Procedures, takes into consideration how the media will react to the initial disclosure and the pressure they will exert on the organization to gain more information. It clearly states what the organization's disclosure policy will be, and it provides the same kind of realistic guidance to the spokespersons who will have to face the mob of reporters and TV cameras that is provided to those employees who will be handling the operational side of the crisis.

Consider the differences between Delta Air Lines and NASA, both of which have written policy manuals for major problems that include provisions for dealing with the news media. Everyone at Delta working on the Flight 191 crash knew what the company's disclosure policy was following an accident. Jim Ewing and Bill Berry also knew from the procedure what each was authorized to do as a spokesperson for Delta, the limits of their authority to speak for the company, and the clearance procedure for the information they would provide to the media. Knowing that, Ewing could conduct the first media briefing less than an hour after he arrived at his offices.

If your organization has procedures for handling crisis situations, they probably mention the news media as a responsibility line item and indicate what the approval process will be for any information that will be disseminated to the press. If you have time, get that policy updated as quickly as possible to reflect the likely news media coverage scenario when the onslaught begins so it can become a realistic basis for your media relations plan.

The alternative is to start from scratch. Humana Hospital-Audubon, like all hospitals, has a good disaster plan that includes provisions for dealing with the media. The artificial heart wasn't a disaster and didn't fit into that plan, so we developed a media relations protocol (scientific jargon for procedure) for the first artificial heart operation and patient recovery. The eight-page protocol:

Defined the situation we expected to face.
Outlined the objectives we hoped to achieve.
Assigned responsibilities for the actions to be taken.
Specified medical and nonmedical spokespersons.
Detailed the procedures for disclosure of information.

Established ground rules for individual and pool interviews.

Set up guidelines for shooting, editing, and distribution of photographs and videotape to the news media.

Outlined an optimum communications plan from the time of patient selection through his initial postoperative recovery.

The protocol was not totally based on our vision and foresight. It also was a defensive measure prompted by the growing interference, politics, and power plays within the hospital and Humana Heart Institute during the final month of preparations before Bill Schroeder's selection. I drafted it, and my boss, George Atkins, cleared it with Humana's chairman and president. The protocol was then given to the medical and nonmedical personnel who might be involved with the news media during the artificial heart program so there would be no question about authorized spokespersons and distribution of information and visuals. It worked surprisingly well during Schroeder's operation and throughout the first few weeks of his recovery because it provided a detailed plan that allowed everyone to coordinate their activities. However, as the months dragged on and personality clashes began to develop, the protocol gradually was superseded by political gamesplaying.

Our problem will occur in any organization when inconsistent or contradictory statements are made by different spokespersons. Some will be more concerned about getting publicity than what they are saying, which gives the press all it needs to develop news reports on apparent conflicts within the organization. Bill McAda, a veteran public information officer for the Federal Emergency Management Agency in Washington, noted, "If I were in an industry where I could be facing a major problem at some point, the first thing I would want to know is who my spokesperson is going to be. That needs to be determined long before we have a problem. It should be written into our contingency plans as an admonition to any other members of management that this person is *the* spokesperson. In other words, we're not going to have 10 of our officers or managers telling different stories about what happened or what the situation is."[37]

The news media will want to be briefed by the person in charge of the situation that prompted the news coverage. That's understandable, but it often will not be realistic if the participants or principal figures in the organization are heavily involved in what has happened. Your best bet then is to have an authoritative spokesperson, such as a physician or an appropriate expert, who will work with a public relations person to handle the majority of the media's questions, information needs, and interview requests.

Spokespersons can be most effective if they have a good understanding of the situation but are not directly involved. They can then brief the media without interpreting or second guessing the decisions of the participants. Dr. Chase Peterson, the medical spokesperson at the Utah Medical Center, was an internist who could answer general medical questions without getting into the specifics of the surgical procedure or how Barney Clark's artificial heart was functioning. Dr. Allan Lansing, at the Humana Heart Institute, on the other hand, is a cardiac surgeon trained in artificial heart implants. In some instances he didn't fully agree with Dr. DeVries' medical decisions following Bill Schroeder's first stroke, which occasionally put him in a difficult position when responding to the media's questions.

The authorized spokespersons will need someone designated to fill in for them at media briefings, especially if the news coverage is likely to continue for more than a few days. The principal figure in the news story may want to conduct a briefing from time to time, or you may want to use another of the participants. The alternates should be aware that once they serve as spokespeople, the news media will seek them out whenever they cannot reach their primary information sources or if they want another viewpoint of what has happened.

The news media also needs to know what your policy will be regarding disclosures made by unauthorized spokespersons within the organization who provide information and ask that their names not be used. While there was no way to eliminate the possibilities of reporters using information from an unidentified employee or participant, this was not a significant problem with news coverage of the Humana artificial heart patients. The primary reason was we made every effort to be forthright with the media, but we also had a clearly defined policy in our media briefing book:

> All information will be "on the record" and there will be no "unidentified sources" for information relating to the artificial heart program. Any source of information is to be identified by name to ensure the information can be verified if there is a question about its accuracy. If information is not provided in the briefing area, or is not disclosed during a scheduled interview, it will not be verified, except at a subsequent media briefing when other members of the media can be provided with the same information.[38]

DEFINING RESPONSIBILITIES FOR PUBLIC RELATIONS

In many respects the public relations staff will have the most difficult job of anyone involved in the news story because they will be working in a no-man's-land between the participants and the press. A mistake in either direction can cripple relationships and jeopardize your organization's ability to control the flow of information being provided to the public via the news media. In those critical first hours they will define the focus of the prism or lens through which your organization will be viewed by its publics. This prism will remain intact throughout the disclosure and will either enhance your company's image or taint it.

NASA lost control of the news coverage during the first five hours and would never regain it during the course of the Challenger investigation. The negative media prism has significantly altered public and congressional perceptions of NASA and still influences news coverage of the space agency as it tries to reestablish its manned and unmanned launch programs. "It's hard to imagine how it could have been hurt more. Their whole premise, that this is a can-do agency that can put a man on the moon and explore the heavens, was torn to shreds," said Michael Isikoff of the *Washington Post*. "In fact, as the Rogers Commission said, they were operating an unsafe space vehicle, recklessly endangering the lives of astronauts.[39]

A breaking news story is no place for amateurs, engineers, or astronauts to be making decisions about what will or will not be disclosed to the news media. If top management has any sense, the most experienced public relations people will be put in charge of dealing with the media and allowed to use their best judgment in deciding what to disclose.

Whoever is in this position will, of necessity, play the role of devil's advocate in a news story and have the difficult job of keeping both participants and institution honest in what they say. They have to. They will represent both the media and the public. That's one reason for having the public relations spokesperson report directly to whomever is in charge. "They cannot be subject to the whims and whimsies of every physician or administrator in the place," John Dwan noted. "They have to answer directly to the boss, so when the tough fights occur, they have a way of getting a final decision without having to work it through different layers or political channels."[40]

There will even be basic facts that the participants may not want to disclose, and the public relations people will have the tough job of pointing out why that approach isn't realistic. They still may get shot down. That's another reason why it's essential that you have only one link in the chain of command between public relations and top management during an onslaught. The person in charge of public relations also needs the authority to make decisions regarding disclosures to the press if the CEO is not available.

The media relations chaos at the Kennedy Space Center after the Challenger explosion might well have been avoided if Shirley Green, NASA's director of public affairs, had been authorized to provide any verified information to reporters until Jesse Moore was available to brief the media. She could not reach the administrator to get that authorization.[41] By the time Moore finally held the briefing, NASA's working relationship with the news media had virtually disintegrated.

It's important to be aware that a "kill the messenger" mentality develops quickly as pressure builds up within an organization involved in an onslaught, and the public relations person's comments, much less his or her presence, will not necessarily be welcomed. The natural tendency for any organization, as it was at NASA, is to avoid saying anything if there's a problem or to defer an announcement as long as possible, preferably until it's over. Many corporate lawyers will urge this approach, citing the potential for legal action and the advantages of fighting on their terms in court rather than having the media serve as judge and jury.

Ironically, just the opposite tactics will be employed by many plaintiffs' attorneys who are highly astute at press relations. They are skilled at generating adverse publicity, which can be devastating to an organization's sales, its business and professional relationships, and ultimately its future. Embarrassing disclosures in the press, thanks to the information provided by plaintiffs' attorneys, have resulted in many out-of-court settlements, with an agreement that nothing further will be disclosed, including the amount of the settlement.

THE TOUGH POLICY DECISIONS

"When disaster strikes it is only human to look for someone to blame, but in the Challenger tragedy the real culprit might have been the decision-making system rather than any individual decision makers."[42] The time to be hammering out the tough policy decisions is not when the pressure is on. If you wait until the onslaught is imminent, your top management team will be concentrating on the situation itself, and disclosures to the news media are likely to be secondary, or near the bottom, in their list of priorities. You have to get to them ahead of time, before they freeze up in their decision making, to get the closure your organization needs on these tough policy questions regarding press relations:

1. Disclosure of Information

What information will be provided to the media during the course of the news story so they can report the news with your organization as their primary source. When will disclosures be made at briefings or with written updates? What specific facts and figures will and will not be provided? How much detail do the participants want disclosed? What areas are particularly sensitive from a business, legal, or personal standpoint? If you don't provide the information, what are the chances of the media obtaining it through other sources and forcing you into a position of responding rather than disclosing?

Deciding what details will be disclosed to the media won't be easy, but those philosophical issues need to be resolved *before* the onslaught begins. Dr. Chase Peterson and Dr. Allan Lansing had similar briefing styles in that both medical spokespersons provided as much detail as they had on the condition of the artificial heart patients. Dr. DeVries, in contrast, preferred to give out little more than vital signs and a general statement of condition before responding to questions. That put him at a disadvantage and was one of the factors that caused him to announce after two months of medical briefings on Humana's artificial heart patients that future information on the patient's condition was going to be disclosed in medical journals.

2. Review and Approvals

There also needs to be a decision on who has to approve information before it is disclosed to the news media. Every organization has its politicians and bureaucrats, and with something as important as a major news story, some would like to get involved in the approval process. You may have a technical review committee going over every update and advisory, but they obviously will not be able to screen the answers your spokespersons provide to the questions raised by the news media.

The straighter and cleaner the lines of communication between the spokespersons and whoever is in charge, the better. At Union Carbide, for example, because of the highly technical nature of the Bhopal accident and the impending threat of litigation, all disclosures to the press were fully discussed by the Bhopal Team before Jackson Browning, Carbide's chief spokesperson, briefed the media. While this was time consuming and sometimes frustrating to the media, who wanted quick answers to the complex questions, it protected Carbide's credibility and helped guarantee a level of accuracy for which the company was later applauded by other members of the chemical industry.

3. Photography and Video

Decisions also need to be made about the shooting and distribution of photos and video. The visual element of the story can be an expensive proposition if your organization is to maintain control of what is released. But once again, the rules of the game cannot be changed after the news story has begun. After the Challenger accident, NASA arbitrarily impounded all of the still and movie film shot by the media's cameras, which were run by remote control in isolated locations surrounding the launch site. The results were another bitter fight between the press and the space agency and a lawsuit filed by the *New York Times* for violation of its basic rights under the First Amendment.

MAKING THE POLICIES KNOWN

Resolving the disclosure questions and issues may seem to go quite smoothly at first, especially if the discussions occur several weeks or even months before the actual news event. The problem is, "The road to hell is paved with good intentions," and attitudes are likely to change when the onslaught is imminent. If they don't then, it's even more likely when there is a negative development or when everyone's patience wears thin as the story drags on for more than a few days. Those media disclosure policies should therefore be in writing. You may have time to work them into an overall procedure for handling the situation, or it may just be in minutes of your meetings summarizing what was agreed to, but get it down on paper and distribute it to everyone who will be involved, including the CEO.

SETTING THE LIMITS OF DISCLOSURE

The biggest dilemma you'll face during an onslaught is how to accommodate the media's voracious news-gathering appetite while still maintaining control of the situation and preserving some semblance of privacy for the participants and their families. If you were ever looking for a minefield situation, this is it. You and your public relations people will serve as the gatekeepers, which naturally is a source of frustration for the news media.

For example, when NASA decided not to provide any details on recovery operations involving the Challenger crew compartment, the wire services, TV networks, and several major newspapers responded by acquiring sophisticated ship-to-shore radios to monitor messages from the recovery ships. As a result they often had information on what had been found before NASA's public affairs staff and, in some cases, before the astronauts' family members were officially notified. Some members of astronauts' families were asked to comment on the recovery of crew cabin debris before they had been informed that the debris had been found. This situation further damaged NASA's credibility and caused increasing tension between the families and the organization.

The last thing journalists want is a filter between themselves and the sources of the story, and they will exert continual pressure to hear from those who are directly involved or affected by what has happened. Their most frequently cited reason for deserving that access is that "the public has a right to know." In fact, as far as your organization is concerned, the public does *not* have an automatic right to know.

Some journalists may tell you they are the eyes and ears of the taxpayer. That's stretching it. They are representing their individual news organizations, which are competing with each other and making money in the process. With the artificial heart disclosures, reporters who felt stymied in their quest for information frequently pointed out to us that $200 million in government funding had gone into artificial heart research efforts over the years, and the American public was therefore entitled to know how their tax money had been spent. We rejected that argument. There never has been a government program or research grant stipulating that the news media would be entitled to have direct access to those who were involved in the experiment. And as for *the public's right to know,* that term doesn't come from the

Constitution; it was coined by an Associated Press editor and has since become a battle cry of the news media. They would like you to think otherwise, but the public's right to know is strictly a matter of individual choice.

However, you must consider the realities. First, everyone involved in the news event, including public relations spokespersons, needs to understand that they will become public figures the minute the disclosure is made. It will be especially difficult for the families of those involved, because the stress of the situation will be multiplied by the media pressure to know how they feel about what has happened.

The participants themselves will have very little privacy as long as the media continues to cover the story, and for a certain period afterward they will find it difficult to be alone without a well-wisher asking how things are going or wanting an autograph from someone they have seen on national television. "The experience of becoming a public figure has changed every single aspect of my life," Dr. DeVries observed. "Whether it involves a concept that's political, religious, economic, professional, or personal, one way or another the artificial heart is totally a part of everything I do now. Everything you do, your entire life, is recorded and audited by other people."[43] The bigger the story, the more difficult it becomes to maintain that personal privacy. In dealing with hundreds of news organizations, a few unreasonable journalists' questionable tactics can require as much attention as the rest of the media combined. Again, it's the pack journalism situation, and the bigger the pack, the more pressure on privacy.

You will naturally be on the lookout for the *National Enquirer* and its supermarket tabloid competitors, which will be looking for anything that can be turned into a sensational article, but the difficulties may come from other quarters. The University of Utah had its problems with *Life*, and we at Humana had our hands full with *People*, which wound up doing a derogatory story on Humana's chairman and president after it found that it really would not be given an exclusive interview with the Schroeders.

The most blatant privacy invasions seem to occur among the TV networks, perhaps because they are the most intrusive news medium. While most of the TV newspeople are reputable, there are some whose journalistic standards are perplexing. CBS interviewed the grief-stricken wife of a Wilberg miner before it was known whether he was dead or alive. Her speculation about the cause of the fire was a major part of the story, even though she was distraught and had never been in a coal mine.[44] The television coverage of Christa McAuliffe's parents watching the explosion of Challenger evoked strong feelings and differences of opinion, even within the news media.

> There has been a lot of criticism of the networks in showing the pictures of Christa McAuliffe's parents sitting there watching the accident. I don't think that criticism was valid because there was no intrusion upon their reaction," said David Cohen of ABC News. "The camera was there, and they knew it was there. It wasn't like anybody came up and yelled at them, "How does it feel to see your daughter blown up in a spaceship?" The effect and the purpose were the same in that we got the reaction that we needed to flesh out the story. It was a nonintrusive reaction. There was no screaming or yelling that we were there. We were observers. It was the kind of thing that I've always felt. Just let the camera be an observer. That's what it is.[45]

> I thought the pictures of the family members at the VIP site who watched the explosion in the video were terrible. I felt the camera was an intrusion into their privacy," said Mark Mayfield of *USA Today*. "That puts me at odds with other reporters and my editors, I suppose, but I believe that was one case where a family had a right to privacy.[46]

There is no way the media can assure the personal privacy of those who are enmeshed in the news event. As individuals, they will sympathize with their plight. As professionals, they cannot and will not allow another news organization to get a significant edge, at least not consistently, if they want to keep their jobs. If there is going to be any respect for individual privacy, some standards will have to be established by someone other than the journalists, although they can certainly be involved in drawing them up. But the final say will have to remain with the public relations people, not the press.

WORKING WITH THE NEWS MEDIA

If your organization is to maintain control, it has to be willing to work with the journalists who are covering the story. The first step is to realize that you're probably a novice in coordinating a major news story, so seek the advice of veteran newspeople about how to lessen the pressure on both the participants and the press in getting their respective jobs done. They can provide you with useful insights and invaluable assistance in making life easier for the people who have more important things to worry about than how the press is going to report what is happening.

We at Humana had learned a great deal from the University of Utah, but it was the field producers and reporters from national news organizations who gave us the important insights and assistance enabling us to accommodate over 300 news organizations covering Bill Schroeder's artificial heart implant. A week before we announced Schroeder's selection, they confirmed our suspicions that the briefing center at Humana Hospital-Audubon would be too small, and suggested a place away from the hospital with enough room for briefings and working space for the print and broadcast media. When we selected the Commonwealth Convention Center, seven miles from the hospital, the major news organizations met to set a pool interview system and arranged for microwave transmission facilities from the hospital to the convention center, at no cost to Humana.

There also has to be an understanding about what information, visuals, and interviews the organization will provide and what it expects in return from the press covering the story. The media is not unreasonable, and they understand the organization's primary priorities. They also know you have the high cards in that you have access to the sources of the news. That puts you in a position to indicate what you will provide and what you expect in return.

Humana's understanding with the news media was that we would provide as much information and visual material as possible at the briefing center, and in return we expected the media to stay out of the hospital. The television crews could do stand-ups outside but would not enter the building unless accompanied by one of our public relations people. That agreement was reasonable, and they honored it because we provided the media at the convention center with twice-a-day medical briefings, as well as updates and photos, so they would have plenty of material to work with. Emery Mining, in contrast, had difficulty keeping the media away from the Wilberg Mine, primarily because all they were getting were the telephone reports from the mine site to the mining office in Huntington.

And then there are the practical considerations. The more you can do to accommodate the logistical needs of the news media in covering the story, the more they will continue to rely on you. They need space to work, phones, power, hotel rooms, and myriad other things that are secondary to reporting the story but important all the same. The same holds true for the participants, who may need the privacy, protection, and the practical advice that you can provide to help them in dealing with the media. You will be the conduit between the two. Give them what they need, but also give them some distance between each other to maintain control.

THE IMPORTANCE OF ANTICIPATION

Anticipation, more than anything else, is the key to maintaining control. You and other members of management have to be thinking ahead and working out how the organization will handle the details for something that has yet to happen. You need to anticipate how the news media will cover likely developments, to figure out the best way to handle their visual needs, or to just think about the questions that may come up at the next briefing. NASA, for example, knew that the news media would focus on the recovery of Challenger's crew compartment and the solid rocket booster section suspected of causing the explosion. They had the option of establishing realistic guidelines for disclosing information and visuals during the recovery of wreckage, including the crew compartment and the SRB casing. Those guidelines could have stipulated that general information would be provided on the types of wreckage being recovered so that the media would have something to work with, but nothing would be disclosed regarding the remains of the astronauts. That would have eliminated the media's need for ship-to-shore radio equipment and would have allowed NASA to manage the disclosure of information more effectively.

There has to be parallel planning whenever you are involved in a newsworthy situation. Operational decisions are going to be made by your management team to resolve the situation, but somebody also needs to be thinking about how those actions can be explained most effectively to the important internal and external publics whose support you need, and who will be influenced by what they read, see, and hear in the news media.

Nobody on President Reagan's staff who was involved in the Iranian arms sale discussions evidently bothered to consider how the news media would react when they found out, which they undoubtedly would. Nobody had the job of trying to develop a rationale that would be acceptable to Congress, foreign governments, the news media, and the American people, and which would be used to test the recommendation before the decision was made to send that first planeload of arms to Iran. That kind of parallel planning would have allowed the president to avoid the most disastrous situation his administration has faced. It's the kind of anticipatory thinking that has to be a major element in top management's decision making whenever their organization is being scrutinized by the news media.

CHAPTER SIX

A Look at the Logistics

"They who control the terrain control the battle," military historians have written, and the same holds true for media onslaughts. T. H. White reported that in the 1960 presidential campaign, John F. Kennedy won the hearts and minds of the news media because he provided for their every need when they accompanied him. He made sure that his press releases took their deadlines into account and that they had access to phones and briefing areas. Richard Nixon, on the other hand, was less accommodating to the needs of the reporters who followed him, and the results translated into more favorable press coverage for the senator from Massachusetts than for the then vice president of the United States.

The same will hold true for your organization. You will have a much better chance of getting favorable coverage from the news media if you consider their logistical needs in working on a major news story and provide facilities that will accommodate those needs so they can get their jobs done more easily and effectively. Your arena will be the briefing area that you set up to meet the press's needs.

This chapter explains what to consider in setting up a briefing area for news organizations. It also will take you through the other facilities you and the news media will need to work effectively together—and stay out of each other's way. The little things that make a big difference will be discussed, as will some of the logistical blunders that can lose the day for you with the participants or the press.

THE ULTIMATE BRIEFING CENTER

The news media are often faced with covering a major story and having nothing to work with in the way of facilities. The other extreme is the most elaborate media briefing facilities in the world— those at the Kennedy Space Center in Florida. NASA's facilities were handling an average of 500 journalists for each launch of the space shuttle at the time of the Challenger accident, but then had to deal with an additional 1,100 newspeople who poured into the Kennedy Space Center during the next 12 hours to cover the story.

NASA has a covered grandstand for the news media at the Kennedy Space Center four miles from the shuttle launch pads. Even though it is outdoors, the grandstand is equipped with writing tables for journalists, as well as TV monitors and capabilities to have simultaneous press briefings via satellite with other NASA facilities. The space agency also holds media briefings in the adjacent television production building, where its large studio can be set up with risers in the back to accommodate TV crews and folding chairs for approximately 250 reporters. Other journalists can watch media briefings from the grandstand or the TV studio via closed-circuit television at the "Dome," a geodetic domed building that serves as NASA's press facility at the Kennedy Space Center.

The media grandstand had to be pressed back into service after the explosion when the hoard of journalists and camera operators descending on the Cape could not be accommodated anywhere else. You may remember seeing coverage of that first briefing, with both the participants and the press huddling in their overcoats and winter jackets. The temperature at the time was in the 40s.

NASA also used the 500-seat Galaxy Theatre at the Kennedy Space Center's "Spaceport, U.S.A.," facilities whenever hearings of the presidential commission investigating the Challenger accident were held at the Cape. The theatre normally is part of the space agency's complex of displays, tours, and facilities for more than two million tourists who visit the Kennedy Space Center annually. During hearings of the Rogers Commission, reporters, photographers, and TV crews occupied the front sections of the theatre, and the public was allowed to sit in the back. Again, the journalists covering the proceedings also could watch from the "Dome" several miles away. There they could file stories more readily as their deadlines approached, while they watched the hearings on NASA's closed-circuit television system.

NASA's domed press center has been designed, staffed, and equipped to assist working journalists doing stories on spaceflight or specific launches at the Cape. In addition to containing the office area for NASA's media relations staff, desk space is provided for approximately 70 journalists in the large circular room and is allocated on a first-come, first-served basis. Each desk has its own electrical outlet and telephone jack, so a reporter can write stories on a portable computer terminal and then file them immediately by plugging into the telephone outlet. The rear wall behind the journalists' desks is lined with compartments filled with fact sheets and other types of background information on a myriad of topics relating to spaceflight and launches undertaken by NASA or the Department of Defense.

Across from the journalists' work area is a curved counter that sets off the public affairs staff offices but also provides a convenient place for stacks of the latest press information released by NASA. Off to one side is another curved counter with signs indicating Tours and Interviews for reporters, photographers, and TV crews who want to see NASA's facilities or interview specific people. A photo/video library is located in the same large room, which permits the news media to order any NASA photo or video footage they need to support their stories. Visuals are provided without charge to accredited members of the press.

A veritable trailer park of portable buildings is clustered to one side of the Public Affairs Center, providing working space and darkrooms for the wire services and other news organizations. The three major TV networks have gone one step beyond, erecting studio buildings on stilts in the same area to provide a clear view of launch pads during their coverage. Space is also provided for parking television trucks equipped for microwave transmission or satellite uplink, but away from the other buildings so their microwave and radio signals can be transmitted without interference.

As far back as the 1960s, NASA realized that its facilities would be the focus of an assemblage of the worldwide media and planned accordingly. As a result, reporters are made to feel welcome and accommodated by the organization, which has resulted in over 25 years of favorable press coverage. And as far as creature comforts are concerned, NASA's cafeteria is open 24 hours a day for employees as well as reporters during launches. It's a pleasant, two-block walk from the Public Affairs Center, past the Saturn rocket display, and across from the Vehicle Assembly Building. The only problem is hotels and motels, the nearest of which are 20 miles away.

NASA's media briefing facilities are impressive, but they didn't happen overnight. The $1.5 million complex at the Kennedy Space Center evolved during the years of spaceflight and has handled as many as 2,700 journalists (for the first flight of the space shuttle in 1981). The size and extent of these facilities admittedly is far beyond anything you will need in relating to the news media, but a lot can be learned from what the space agency has done, which can then be scaled down to fit your specific requirements.

MEDIA BRIEFINGS CAN BE HELD ANYWHERE YOU WANT

You may have several options for a place to hold news media briefings, depending on how much time you have, the location of the news event, and the nearest available facilities. The most important consideration, by far, will be in finding enough space. You need to be able to meet with the news media but in a place that also provides you and the participants with space for work and for privacy. Rather than having the media set up camp in the wrong place, you're better off using the largest available area you can find, even if it's in the lobby, until you are sure of where you will hold briefings on a regular basis.

If your facilities are too confined, it will start you off on the wrong foot with the press, which the University of Arizona at Tucson quickly found out when the media rushed in to cover the first emergency use of an artificial heart. "We did that first briefing in the wrong place, the dean's conference room," Dr. Allan Biegel recalled. "I had reporters and cameras literally in front of my nose. It was very uncomfortable for me, trying to answer all those questions when I had 25 people breathing down my neck."[47] Bob Henrie also felt that using the library and conference room in the Emery Mining Company office as the briefing center created rather than solved problems during the Wilberg Mine fire coverage. "In looking back we should never have let the media set up in our office building because once they were there, it was virtually impossible to get them out," Henrie recalls. "They ate there, they slept there, they used the typewriters, the telephones, and the restrooms. When the plumbing clogged, they were upset, and there were even reports that some of them were rummaging through our files."[48]

It will take considerable room for dozens of TV camera crews, in addition to reporters and other media people. And those people will need space nearby to edit videotape, write and transmit copy, talk to their newsrooms, and wait for the next update. That means an unusual demand for telephones, electrical service, food, coffee, couches, and restrooms, to name just a few of their needs. The media preference is for briefings held at or near the scene of the news so they will have access to the participants in the surroundings where the story has occurred. That's nice but often may not be practical. President Reagan has never held a press briefing at Camp David or at his Santa Barbara ranch. NASA has never held one at the launch pad.

The news media will gather wherever you indicate disclosures will be made. There may be room at the site of the story for news media briefings, as was the case at Tucson when the University Medical Center's auditorium finally became available. The University of Utah Medical Center used the back half of its cafeteria for press briefings on Barney Clark. Loma Linda used its Randall Conference Center, a block from the hospital, during the media coverage of Baby Fae. The White House has a small but permanent briefing area in the West Wing with adjacent workspace for the press corps which is about 50 yards away from the Oval Office.

The benefit of proximity for the participants is in having quick access to the news media when it is desired. They can provide an update, be interviewed, or hold a briefing and still be within walking distance or a few floors away from where they're working. For the press, beyond having more convenient access to the participants, additional information and insights will be gleaned from conversations in elevators, hallways, and the cafeteria.

On the other hand, if you don't have facilities to host a gathering of several hundred journalists for who knows how long, don't force it. Bob Henrie meant well, but it was a mistake to use the library in the Emery Mining Company building for press briefings and to let the media stay in the building because of the snow and the fact that the town's only motel quickly ran out of rooms. He and the miners' families would have been much better off if briefings and updates had been held in the American Legion hall across the street or at the nearby elementary school, which was out for Christmas vacation.

The important thing is to hold the updates in a place that has enough room to accommodate all of the media but also provides you and the participants with some distance and breathing room. You are going to need to meet, make phone calls, and do whatever has to be done without having to be concerned about whether your comments are being overheard.

It's always a good idea to know who's around you, especially when you're on the phone, because eavesdropping is one of the media's irritating but effective newsgathering techniques. "One of the most annoying things was that we would call to get a condition update on Baby Fae and the news media would be hovering around to listen to our end of the conversation. We just couldn't talk comfortably," said Anita Rockwell, assistant director of community relations at Loma Linda Medical Center.[49]

Dr. Jack Copeland, the Tucson surgeon who implanted an artificial heart in Tom Creighton on an emergency basis, recalled how his transplant coordinator took a phone call from a hospital in Oklahoma City that had a possible donor heart. The coordinator didn't realize that as she wrote down the details, a reporter was right beside her doing the same thing. Within minutes the Oklahoma hospital was getting press calls and one of the networks indicated it was coming to the hospital. "The organ donation was being made by the family under the condition that the patient's name would not be given out," Dr. Copeland said. "There was to be no publicity so we were at great risk of losing a possible donor heart, and of not being able to communicate with that hospital again in the future."[50]

WHAT TO LOOK FOR IN A BRIEFING CENTER

You will need enough space to conduct the briefings, which may be attended by as many as 200 members of the media, including two or three dozen TV crews, depending on the nature and location of the story. You're also going to need adjacent rooms for individual meetings and interviews, as well as a large area that can be used by the print, wire services, and radio reporters for developing and filing stories immediately after briefings. Your own telephones and working area should be nearby to facilitate talking with the hundreds of media covering the story in person and on the phone.

You're obviously not going to get all that ready in 90 minutes. The key decision right now is to pick a location for media briefings that can be used throughout the duration of the news event. The media wants to be as close to the action as it possibly can get. The only thing they want more is to be able to report the news with the least possible disruption, which means not having to move their phones and workspaces. So pick the place that best meets your needs and theirs, and stick there.

Start first with your own meeting facilities. If you don't have sufficient space for the media, or it won't be practical to use it for a period of several days or even weeks, begin checking the nearest hotels with conference facilities. Long before the Bhopal crisis, Union Carbide established the Danbury Hilton for its briefing center; first, because it had sufficient space, and second, because Carbide wanted to keep the media away from its corporate headquarters. Any hotel which is used for media briefings will have a bonanza on its hands. You should get an excellent rate on your briefing facilities, considering how much they will make on room charges and other expenses that will be paid by the media.

Have someone personally check out the proposed briefing area, and have the banquet manager show them the location of the telephone room, power sources, and access to the parking lot. Ask about hotel security, doors in and out of the briefing area from which you and your spokespeople can make quick exits, and the ability of the hotel staff to service the needs of reporters on a 24-hour basis.

The quality of the room's audio system needs to be checked out. Some meeting facilities have modern systems for amplifying and equalizing the sound, but in many instances you'll find that the public address system is used primarily for luncheon speakers. For the first briefing you can get away with the electronic spaghetti of microphones hanging over the podium, but for the long haul you need to talk to someone who understands audiovisual needs and can rig the room with adequate lighting and a molt box or DA system for the media to use in getting their audio signals from one microphone. It's nothing more than a box connected to the sound system with receptacles that allow a number of TV and radio jounalists to plug in and record any remarks directly from the speaker's microphone.

It's a good idea to listen to the technical people from the TV stations—and especially to those from the networks—as they begin to arrive. They make their living by knowing how to adapt quickly to a breaking news story and can be invaluable in giving you advice and tips on what will be needed by all the media.

Finally, make sure you have a small room adjacent to the briefing area, which can be used for meetings, pre-briefing discussions, or just plain hiding out to collect your thoughts when things get hectic. Get a layout of the facilities, and if they look satisfactory, do some serious horse trading to get the space you need at the best price.

HUMANA'S BRIEFING CENTER FOR THE ARTIFICIAL HEART

As mentioned earlier, Humana had planned to use the largest classroom at Humana Hospital-Audubon as a media briefing center. We had the room equipped with risers at one end for the speakers and at the other for TV cameras. Theatre lights were installed in the ceiling for video coverage, and molt boxes were provided in the walls and risers to eliminate the need for every electronic journalist to string microphones over the podium. An adjacent room was set up as a media work area with phones and a coffee machine, and a door was cut into the exterior wall to provide the media with direct access to the parking lot.

The design was optimum. The only problem was that the briefing room turned out to be too small, even though it would accommodate 19 TV camera tripods and seat 85 journalists. That one-day artificial heart media orientation revealed how cramped the briefing room would be and prompted a quick search for other facilities that would provide more space for briefing, working, and sleeping, if necessary. The choice was the Commonwealth Convention Center in downtown Louisville.

"The Bomb Shelter," as it was lovingly known because of the basement location, provided ample space for media briefings and had a stage of low risers facing 275 chairs. Low, terraced risers for TV cameras were set up behind the chairs and to both sides for cutaway shots. The large room adjoining the briefing area was lined with double rows of eight-foot tables, which served as the media's work area. Fifty telephone lines were strung to the tables, and heavy-duty extension cords were provided to supply power for the correspondents' computer terminals. Rented couches and soft chairs were arranged in an alcove at the far end of the room, which could be darkened if we went through the night and anyone wanted to sleep between updates.

Meeting rooms across the hall from the briefing area were rented from the convention center by NBC, CBS, and CNN, and were equipped with editing equipment as well as "sets" for live feeds to the network news programs. ABC's facilities were on the loading dock in a portable building that was to be set up in Humana Hospital-Audubon's parking lot before our plans were changed at the last minute.

Humana's workspace was in the same large room with the media's work area and lounge, which turned out to be beneficial to both the press and our public relations staff. Any journalist with a question had only to walk a few feet to ask us if we knew or could get the answer. At the same time, if we were ready to hold a briefing, had photos to release, or needed to clarify something, all that was necessary was to walk over to the media's tables and tell everyone. As the days passed, the working relationships became very solid, and we were able to discuss details as if we all were from the same newsroom.

THE LITTLE THINGS THAT WILL MAKE A BIG DIFFERENCE

Staffing Requirements

Have at least one person from your staff on hand to assist the media whenever the briefing center is officially open. That will mean setting up work schedules for 16 to 24 hours a day, seven days a week, depending on the situation. The NASA and Delta Air Lines briefing centers were staffed 24 hours a day. If that seems like overkill, consider the time differences from where you are to Europe and the Far East. In this era of global news coverage and satellite broadcasts, you're going to have news organizations somewhere in the world ready to talk about your story at any hour of the day or night, and in many instances they will want to talk directly with a spokesperson. The options will be to have them call someone at your briefing center or to rouse you in the middle of the night to answer a few routine questions over the phone.

Access and Security

Give the media access to the briefing area 24 hours a day. The TV networks keep odd hours in preparing for live feeds to the morning shows, especially if your news event is not in the Eastern time zone, and may be preparing for an update at 4 A.M. If your staff is not always present in the briefing area, you will need to have a security guard on hand because curious people will be coming through at strange hours, and the journalists will want to leave some of their equipment and phones in place once they are set up.

Media Alert System

Set up an emergency calling procedure for the media. Have both the local and out-of-town journalists fill out a card with their names, news organizations, and the phone numbers for their business, home or hotel where they will be staying while they are covering the story. Use cards like the one shown on page 46 so they can be divided among several people if phone calls have to be made when there is a sudden development while they are in town or after the story has subsided.

Home phone numbers may seem like an invasion of the media's privacy on your part, but journalists greatly appreciate being called at home if there has been a major development. They would much rather get the call from the source of the news than from someone in their newsroom who reads them wire service copy before they can call their editors to discuss how the story should be handled. In some instances, especially with network TV, those calls at home give the field producers valuable information and a little additional time to make logistical decisions on whether to send in camera crews and on what will be the fastest way for them to get the story on the air.

Connect with the Phone Company

Get to know the person at your phone company who handles large orders for special events, because he or she will be deluged by media for overnight phone installation as soon as the disclosure is made. We arranged to have 50 phone lines installed in the media workroom for journalists who needed to talk to their editors or transmit copy from their portable computer terminals (which have replaced the traditional typewriters) directly to their newsrooms. Humana paid for the installation and monthly line rental, but the calls were charged to the journalists' credit cards, just as they would be if made from a pay phone or a hotel room.

You may want to disconnect the phone sets that are not being used when the number of media covering the story begins to drop off, but keep the lines in place if there's a chance you might have a sudden crisis that will bring everyone back. It took us less than 30 minutes to reconnect the 25 sets we had disconnected when we reopened the briefing center after Schroeder's first stroke, and we were very glad the lines were still there.

Many of the national news organizations, particularly the broadcast media, will want the phone company to install lines for their own use. ABC News, for example, had 16 phone lines in their trailer, 7 in the briefing room, and 4 at the main entrance of the hospital (for live feeds). The "Today" show had 30 phone lines involved in a live feed from the Kennedy Space Center the morning after the Challenger accident.

Messengers

You're also going to need couriers to get information or film from the scene to a darkroom or the briefing center. They also can be used to get copies of updates to participants and other key people and for dozens of other assignments. We used interns in Humana's management training program and had them work in pairs when the pressure was heaviest, so one could double-park or drive around the block while the other went in to pick up or deliver whatever was needed.

The media also are going to need couriers for picking up and delivering videotape and photos to the airport at all hours of the day and night but will make their own arrangements.

Provisions for TV Cameras

Make room for the TV cameras *behind* the reporters, not in front. During the medical briefings in Tucson, the cameras were set up in the open space between the auditorium seats and the stage. When they had their lights on during briefings, the participants couldn't see which journalists wanted to ask a question. A far better arrangement is to place risers or sturdy platforms for the TV cameras 25–35 feet from the stage so they are on the same level as the podium but far enough back so the speakers can see and respond to the journalists sitting in front.

You'll also need provisions for the TV crews wanting to get cutaway shots of the spokesperson from the side as well as shots of the audience. Keep the aisles wide enough for the crews to move back and forth, and have someone on hand at the briefings to work with the TV crews. The White House briefing room has designated areas for cutaways. TV crews can even go up on stage if it's OKed by a member of the press office staff, who ensures that they don't get too close to the speaker.

Logos or Signs

Remember that most photos and TV pictures of the speakers will be tight head-and-shoulders shots, so any logos or signs on the front of the podium will get cropped out. If you want your organization identified during briefings, keep the sign or logo around 36 inches in size, and position it behind and slightly above the speaker. The White House identification in the media briefing room is an excellent example. It's solid, tasteful, and mounted on the wall above and behind the podium.

Ample Amperage

Make sure you have enough electrical power. A minimum of 100 amps should be available to provide sufficient lighting for the TV crews, regardless of whether you provide the lights or allow the crews to plug in their own. There is nothing more disconcerting than to have a TV crew switch on an additional light during a briefing and have everything go dark, which has happened all too often.

Parking for the Media

Allow considerable parking space for the diversity of media vehicles that will descend on you. You'll see everything from newspaper reporters in their own cars to the network TV crews, which will rent anything with a large trunk for their cameras and tripods. There will be vans and trucks with telescoping microwave transmitters and others with satellite dishes aimed skyward. And if it isn't football season, you may even have one or more of the TV network broadcast control rooms in a semitruck and trailer.

The TV networks and stations will want to park as close to the briefing area as possible so there will be less distance to string the miles of cable that will have to be run from their cameras to the transmission equipment in the vehicles outside. If there is any duct work, windows or doors to the outside that can be used to shorten the cable route, so much the better. And while they will want to be close to the building, the television engineers will be looking for places where their microwave trucks will have an unimpeded line of sight in the direction of their station's microwave receivers. Satellite trucks will need a clear view in a southwesterly direction to aim their dishes at communications satellites in orbit.

Sustenance for the Press and Public Relations

Provide coffee and donuts for yourself and the media early in the morning, and maybe even sandwiches and soft drinks later in the day and into the evening. With the ungodly hours, everyone will be groggy. Having something to eat and drink when they don't have time to get it themselves can do a lot to improve the attitudes of journalists when they are fighting a deadline. It also will help your own alertness and attitude in responding to the hundreds of phone calls and inquiries from the media.

Show and Tell

Have a blackboard, flipchart, or large bulletin board to post briefing schedules, recent photos, copies of the latest updates, or anything else the media should be aware of. We used three bulletin boards, one for that day's schedule and written updates, one for the latest photos, and one for old information and photos.

Useful Hardware

You are going to need two business-quality phone recording machines, which usually can be rented by the month from a local retailer. Make sure you order extra outgoing message tapes of one-, two-, and three-minute lengths since the tapes wear out rapidly and you will have messages of different lengths, depending on what has happened. The White House press office keeps its phone recording machines on 24 hours a day with the daily schedule of events involving the president so the news media can plan its coverage.

The recording machines will become indispensable in providing the media with updates, especially when a bulletin has been released or when they call in late at night. You'll need two machines because the calls will often back up and roll over to the next line when deadlines are approaching or when a new development has been announced.

You're also going to need a good-quality cassette recorder with a tape meter that can be plugged into your sound system and used to record the remarks at each of the briefings so your organization will have the means of transcribing what is said.

And finally, you will need several pocket radio page beepers for those on your staff whom you may have to contact in a hurry. Get the kind that will display the phone numbers visually rather then blaring out the caller's message. It's bad enough whenever a beeper goes off, but the media and everyone else doesn't need to know who's calling or what has happened.

The Importance of Backup Communications

The problem you'll be dealing with will be difficult enough, but if your lines of communication break down for any reason, it's going to multiply. Your organization must have the ability to stay in touch with the site of the news story as well as with the briefing center, and the last thing it needs is the kind of two-phone-line dilemma that Union Carbide had to deal with in Bhopal.

Phones are the communications lifeblood of any organization in a crisis, and especially news organizations. Even if the phones are working, will you have enough? The 500 lines at the Kennedy Space Center weren't sufficient to handle the news media's needs the morning after the Challenger accident—NASA could have used another 100 lines. Bill McAda of FEMA believes that having the ability to communicate is the most important consideration in any crisis, especially one that will attract the news media, and that the best thing any organization can do is plan for the worst situation imaginable.

The question you need to be asking is how would you manage the situation if the phones were knocked out? What about microwave, satellite communications from a nearby hotel, or having the ability to patch into radio communications systems? Start with the phone company, which has its own disaster plans, but find out what you and the news media can use if the normal lines of communications are down and out.

Have a Hideout

Set aside a place to hide for a few minutes. You and your staff will use it frequently during the long days to go over recent developments and likely questions with the participants before a briefing, to conduct one-on-one interviews, to wolf a sandwich without a phone ringing, or to call home and let your family know you're OK. We'll discuss the importance of the hideout in more detail in Chapter 13, Battle Fatigue.

SETTING UP A SAFE HAVEN

The participants also will need a place where they can gather without having to worry about running into the news media. This should be where the families will find out first what has happened and where they can question the participants or grieve in private, if that's the case, before going out to face the glare of TV camera lights and a mob of people bombarding them with questions. The families of Humana's artificial heart patients stayed in empty patient rooms on the 5th floor of Humana Hospital-Audubon and later used the transition apartment across the street.

After the Challenger accident the public never saw the next of kin of the astronauts. They were in a VIP section atop the building housing the launch control facilities and thus could be escorted downstairs and out of sight. Because next of kin was limited to the spouse and children of married astronauts, Christa McAuliffe's parents were in the bleachers reserved for relatives and close friends of the astronauts where TV cameras could show their reactions to millions.

During the Wilberg fire the only place the miners' families could get any information was at the Emery Mining Company office in Huntington. The problem was that also was the place where the media was being briefed. The families thus had to run a gauntlet of reporters and camera crews to get in and out of the basement of the building, which had been set up as a place where Bob Henrie could brief them on the latest developments.

In retrospect, the families would have been much better off if a neutral place had been set up where they could come without being concerned about having to talk to reporters. That would have avoided the kind of angry confrontation that occurred outside the mining office when a grief-stricken relative of a miner lost his temper and beat up a TV cameraman. The San Rafael Mission church building, just outside of Huntington, and on the road to the mine would have been a good haven. The dirt road to the church could have been blocked by a mine security person or local law enforcement officer to be sure the family members could come and go without being disturbed. It's tough asking someone a question when they are in their car and driving away.

These are good examples of the nuts and bolts details that all too often get short shrift when you're preparing for an onslaught. Yet they also show how anticipatory thinking ultimately will determine how effectively your organization, the participants and the press can work together in the midst of the news story.

CHAPTER SEVEN

Backgrounding the Media

It's one thing to announce that someone named Bill Schroeder will be the next recipient of an artificial heart; it's something else to provide the background information and visuals that will enable reporters to develop the comprehensive news reports, commentaries, editorials, human interest stories, and sidebars to set themselves apart from their competition. But that's what they need if they are to understand the story and report it accurately. The background information you provide will be a critical factor in determining how informed and objective the news reporting will be, because a large majority of the journalists, photographers, and field producers will know little or nothing about the subject or the organization involved when they arrive on the scene.

Journalists will be looking for any background material they can get, and if you don't provide it they will start to dig into your organization, feeding on whatever facts they can gather to create their own context for the story. After the Challenger accident reporters at the Press Center were scanning the telephone directory for the Kennedy Space Center and arbitrarily phoning NASA employees whose job title or area of responsibility sounded as if it might provide some insights into what had happened.

Any journalist will tell you that being adept at the "quick study" is a routine part of the news business. That's why it's imperative that they have whatever background information you can pull together if you expect the details in the story to be reported accurately. The question is, what background materials, visuals, and briefings can you offer that will enable them to understand the subject and the people involved so they can file accurate, authoritative reports on the story within hours?

This chapter will show how the quality and quantity of background information you provide will help establish a good working relationship with the news media covering a major story so they will rely more on your organization than their own scavenging for details and facts. Although it will be time consuming and it can be expensive, providing appropriate background to the media will be well worth the investment at the time and over the long term as well.

BASIC BACKGROUND INFORMATION

> One of the biggest problems for a general assignment reporter is getting up to speed in a hurry. I'm a fast study, but I need information on what's happened as well as the background on the situation. It just isn't enough to wait for the first briefing. Schroeder was the lead story for us, and I had my first story on the air within three hours after getting off the plane in Louisville.[51]

The needs of Mark Knoller, an AP network radio correspondent, are no different than those of hundreds of his colleagues when they arrive to cover a major story. Reporters don't go shopping for sources, not with the time and competitive pressures they are under. Their first stop will be at whatever facilities have been set up to inform the press, and they'll seek out the public relations people to get the background information and visuals they need to understand the situation and cover the story to the satisfaction of their newsrooms. The same will hold true during the ensuing days and weeks, as a seemingly endless stream of newcomers appear to relieve their colleagues or to develop a specific story angle. They will take any biographies, fact sheets, background information, or other relevant material you can provide. The shorter and less technical, the better, and don't worry about the appearance. A reporter would much rather pick up important facts from a double-spaced backgrounder on Xeroxed paper than to get the same information by wading through a technical manual or slick brochure from the marketing department.

A good approach in deciding what to cover in your background information is to list the who, what, where, why, when and how topics mentioned in Chapter 2. That will help define the useful information for someone who knows little or nothing about what has happened, the organization, or the people involved. In the "who" area you are going to need biographies or personnel press releases on the key participants. If a physician is involved, he's likely to have a six-page curriculum vitae, which lists everything, including his grade school. Have someone combine the essentials into a one-page summary. The important thing is to have as much consistency as possible in the types of information provided on the participants.

In the other areas of news interest, you should consider a one- or two-page fact sheet on the equipment, the process, or whatever is involved in the news story. The news media also will be interested in background on the facilities, your organization, a chronology of the important dates in the situation, and a list of authorities on the subject. Newspaper clippings or magazine articles that pertain to what has happened make excellent background material, as do computerized data retrieval services. On-line services, such as NEXIS or Dow Jones News Retrieval, will list what has already been written on the subject, by whom, and what their specific angle of interest was. That kind of bibliography can be very helpful in defining what is being reported about the subject and your organization by newspapers, wire services, magazines, journals, and newsletters, as well as on television. Some of the articles and information these database services provide may be relevant background material in itself. You may even pinpoint a controversial aspect of the situation, which should be addressed in a backgrounder or fact sheet so you will have a prepared response if the question is raised, as it undoubtedly will be.

In addition, there may well be books or internal documents with relevant information that would be useful to the media but can't be copied. In these instances someone can probably transcribe or photocopy relevant sections and paste them together. You can also have one of your people transcribe paragraphs of general background information from a company-confidential publication. Under favorable circumstances you'll have enough time to do all of this before any of the information is put to use.

QUESTIONS AND ANSWERS

You and the other spokespersons are going to be faced with myriad questions from the media, most of which will deal with the same areas of interest. If you subscribe to the theory that the best defense is a good offense, you are much better off if you can anticipate and answer every conceivable question in advance, from the most obvious to the most obnoxious.

Again, start with the who, what, how, why, where, and when approach, this time to come up with the most likely questions. Then get into specific questions that may be triggered by what is already known about the organization, the participants, or the situation itself. While you are at it, think about the costs, social considerations, ethics, profit potential, availability for the masses, alternatives to what is being done, environmental concerns, potential impact on minorities, government intervention, legal liability, long-term implications, and other issue-oriented questions that may be raised initially or in the ensuing days and weeks.

You also should get into the nastier questions regarding safety, informed consent, adequacy of training, and anything else that you'd normally be too embarrassed to ask. "Has there been any indication of negligence among those who are directly involved in this situation?" "What alternatives were investigated before the decision was made to proceed?" "Who was consulted, and what was their reaction?"

If there is anything confidential regarding the situation, include questions that address these areas both directly and obliquely. Local reporters have an amazing network of sources that may tip them off. They also may hear rumors or innuendos regarding the situation that arouse their curiosity. Either way, you and the other spokespersons should be prepared to respond to questions regarding something that nobody is supposed to know anything about.

Organize the questions by general category and begin typing them up, leaving about one or two inches of space between each question for answers to be inserted. If you can, use a word processor because you may well add to the list of questions as more becomes known about the situation, as new developments occur, or as the media raises important questions that you hadn't considered.

While the chances of all these questions being asked is small, especially at the first briefing, they will help you and the other spokespersons prepare mentally for any tough questions that come up. You also will find them very helpful in developing your other backgrounders and fact sheets as well as position papers or written responses to inquiries from reporters, government officials, customers, students, and who knows who else.

PHOTOGRAPHS

The newspapers, wire services, and TV news crews will be anxious to get any appropriate photographs you can provide. They will want working portraits or head-and-shoulder shots of the participants, which can be used in the initial coverage. Beyond that if you have any good photos of the facilities, the procedures, or the equipment involved in the story, set those aside as well.

Your best photos for the news media are 8 × 10 black-and-white or color prints with a sharp image. The size is important because the wire services transmit 8 × 10 prints, and the TV cameras can pan around the picture more easily. Snapshots and Polaroid shots should not be included unless you are absolutely sure no other photos can be obtained. Steer clear of the shots used in your marketing brochures—the ones that are carefully lit, with models dressed appropriately, and the organization's name prominently displayed. The media needs photographs relating to the story. They are not going to give some company a free endorsement just because nothing else was provided.

Make sure each photo has a typed caption pasted on the back that identifies any persons in the picture by name and title and what is happening, if it depicts action. It's also a good idea to have a statement in indelible ink across the lower edge on the back that indicates the photo is being distributed free of charge and cannot be resold without written permission of your organization. That may seem unnecessary, but we'll talk about the aftermarket for photography in Chapter 9.

You should provide at least three prints to the press: one each should go to AP and UPI, with an additional photo to post on a bulletin board so the TV cameras can pan across it for their news coverage. If you have additional prints, the next priority should be the photo editors of any daily newspapers in your city. (If you are short on prints, they can order the photo through the wire services.)

OTHER VISUALS

If you have any videotapes showing the facilities, the principals, the participants, the process, or anything else related to the news coverage, include it as possible file footage for the media. The TV news crews routinely shoot ¾-inch video, but they can convert what you have. Considering their desire to get anything visual that can be used right away, the different TV crews can work out an arrangement to dub your footage for use by all the media at no charge to you.

Diagrams and maps showing locations of important aspects of the story are another visual that can be extremely useful in helping the news media understand and report the details accurately. They should be included with any background materials, and you may also want to enlarge some of them to provide the participants with a reference visual during their media briefings. They also will provide a much more interesting background for photographers and TV camera crews than just a talking head. Similarly, if there are scale models that can be used to explain how something works or where the development occurred, they may prove to be very helpful to the spokesperson. We kept a demonstration model of the JARVIK-7 artificial heart handy, and it was used on several occasions by Dr. Lansing and Dr. DeVries to clarify a detail or in answering a question during medical briefings.

SIDEBAR INFORMATION

Make it a point to include background materials on indirectly related facets of the story, as long as they are relevant to what has happened. This can be especially helpful to those members of the news media who want to broaden the scope of their coverage. It also will benefit you and the other spokespersons by diverting some of the direct media pressure away from you.

Having background information and spokespersons available from other organizations is also especially helpful if the media onslaught has been caused by a crisis. Morton Thiokol, the manufacturer of the solid rocket boosters for the Challenger space shuttle, absorbed a lot of the media pressure that had previously been directed at NASA after the first disclosures about "black puffs of smoke." Utah Power and Light, the owners of the Wilberg Mine, made their engineers available at the company's headquarters in Salt Lake City with schematic diagrams to explain how the mine was laid out and where the fire had started. After the crash of Delta Flight 191, representatives of Lockheed Aircraft Company provided the news media with background information and responded to questions regarding L-1011 jumbo jets.

There may be a temptation to provide unrelated background information on your organization or its products and services in the hope it will stimulate a story when there aren't any new developments to report. Be careful. You won't be dealing with newspeople looking to write something about other than what they have been assigned to cover. Rather than including chaff in the background materials, you'd be better off summarizing the interesting things you'd like the media to cover as one-paragraph items in a backgrounder with a title like "Interesting Facts About . . . ". Some of those items may get plugged into the stories that develop, and if a reporter wants to get more detail, he or she will ask you. That's much better than having the news media wading through and throwing out irrelevant background materials.

What you wind up providing in background information and visuals for the news media obviously is going to depend on several variables, the most significant of which is the amount of time and personnel available before the onslaught breaks loose. Then it's a question of how much material you have to work with and how much your management is willing to say and spend. If you have a disaster on your hands, photocopy whatever information you can pull together and slip it into folders, which can be stacked and handed out easily as the media arrives. On the other hand, if you have a few days or even weeks, you can do a more effective job of developing and presenting the background information the press will need.

BACKGROUND ON THE HUMANA ARTIFICIAL HEART PROGRAM

Humana was fortunate to have 11 weeks between the announcement that Dr. DeVries would be joining the Humana Heart Institute and the disclosure that Bill Schroeder would receive an artificial heart, but we needed every minute. After the hospital received FDA approval and we switched to the contingency timetable, two solid weeks went into finishing the briefing books, photos, and video newsclips that would be the backbone of the artificial heart background materials, even though we didn't know who the patient would be.

The Humana Briefing Book

The centerpiece of Humana's background materials for the artificial heart programs was a 62-page briefing book in a three-hole binder, divided into the following sections:

Biographies.   One-page fact sheets on the principal physicians.
William C. DeVries, M.D.
Allan M. Lansing, M.D., Ph.D.
Robert K. Jarvik, M.D.
Ronald N. Barbie, M.D.

One-paragraph biographical summaries also were provided for physicians, technical personnel, and administrative staff at the hospital, as well as for executives at Humana who were likely to be interviewed by the news media.

Background Information.   Fact sheets were provided on:
Humana, Inc.
Humana Hospital-Audubon.
The Humana Heart Institute International.
Heart disease.
Artificial heart patient selection protocol.
Artificial heart patient consent form (copy of the document).
JARVIK-7 artificial heart (illustrated).
UTAHDRIVE system controller (illustrated).
HEIMES portable heart driver (illustrated).
Chronology of artificial heart development.
Glossary of medical terms.

Media Policies and Guidelines.
Overview.
General policies.
Television and radio coverage.
Interviews.
Photographs and videotape.
Authorized spokespersons.
Media relations representatives.
Media briefing area.

Questions and Answers.
Humana's previous experience in medical research.
Humana's involvement with teaching hospitals.
Humana's prices in comparison to other hospitals.
The ethics of making money from sick people.
Humana's policy regarding treatment of indigent patients.

Medicare and medicaid patient care at Humana hospitals.

What Humana expects to gain from participation in the artificial heart research.

Humana's ownership rights to artificial heart technology.

The employment status of Dr. DeVries.

Ownership of Symbion, Inc., stock by Humana or Dr. DeVries. (Symbion developed and manufactured the JARVIK-7 artificial heart.)

Patient Progress Reports.

(Space was provided for journalists to insert copies of updates and advisories.)

The briefing book was developed by the Humana public relations staff and provided to all members of the media when they signed in at the briefing center to cover Bill Schroeder's artificial heart implant. Copies also were distributed to the administrators of Humana's 90 hospitals and to other company executives who would undoubtedly be asked questions about the artificial heart program.

Background Photos

Humana also supplied 100 sets of color slides and black-and-white pictures to the media as background photography on the artificial heart program. The series of 12 slides and 25 photographs included pictures of the Humana surgical team implanting an artificial heart on a calf to illustrate what occurs at various points during the surgical procedure. Portrait photos of Dr. DeVries in surgical greens and white clinic coat also were provided, along with "working portraits" of the surgical team standing around the operating table, with masks down and the JARVIK-7 artificial heart positioned in the foreground. Other pictures included studio shots of the JARVIK-7, UTAH-DRIVE, and HEIMES portable heart driver and both aerial and ground-level exteriors of Humana Hospital-Audubon.

The background photos were used extensively by the print media. The color slides of the working portraits were especially popular with such newspapers as *USA Today*, which have increased emphasis on color, especially on the front page. *Newsweek* used one of the background slides from the surgical procedure on the calf as part of its three-page photo coverage of Schroeder's artificial heart operation to show a close-up of the Jarvik-7 being inserted into the chest cavity. We knew it was one of the background photos because a thin white band was visible across the base of the mechanical heart. What wasn't legible was the lettering on the band, "Not for Clinical Use."

Video Backgrounders

My initial fact-finding trip to Salt Lake City revealed that the public was fascinated with the mechanical heart but had a difficult time understanding how the Jarvik-7 worked when it replaced Barney Clark's natural heart. Most people also were not aware of the 50-year evolution of the artificial heart from the time the first model was developed by a French scientist, with financial support from Charles Lindbergh. The design of a mechanical pump that would work 40 million times a year inside the human body was another fascinating story. That led to the decision to develop a series of video backgrounders, which would allow television news to explain and illustrate the interesting history and inside story of the artificial heart.

The seven video vignettes that we produced dealt with:

1. Trends in cardiovascular surgery.
2. History and future of the artificial heart.
3. How the artificial heart works.
4. Manufacturing the artificial heart.
5. Power systems for the artificial heart.
6. Clinical training for artificial heart implantation.
7. Profile of the Humana Heart Institute's surgical team.

Production was handled by Medstar Communications of Allentown, Pennsylvania, the firm we had selected to provide video coverage of Humana's first artificial heart operation. Each vignette was produced as a 90-second newsclip similar in format to the TV news segments frequently distributed to television stations by corporations and nonprofit organizations. Initially the video vignettes were intended for the hundreds of independent TV stations in the United States that could not afford to send crews to cover the artificial heart surgery but might want to expand on the coverage provided by the networks. We also had planned to offer the vignettes to many of the European television networks and in a number of countries, including Japan and Australia, that would have the same basic interest.

Distribution in the United States was to be via satellite, and a

30-minute segment of time was reserved for Monday, November 26, before Schroeder's condition started to deteriorate and the operation was moved up. Mailgrams had been sent out to TV station news directors across the United States, alerting them to the availability of the video backgrounders on the artificial heart and indicating the satellite broadcast time and frequency.

The sudden deterioration of Schroeder's condition and the subsequent artificial heart operation on Sunday, November 25, meant that the satellite feed of the video backgrounders occurred after the operation. The transmission was made anyway, but with 18 minutes of videotape from the actual operation added to the 10 minutes needed for the backgrounders. A number of news directors who called in during the ensuing weeks indicated they had used the backgrounders in their local news broadcasts. The TV networks also picked up parts of the backgrounders, especially the animation showing a cross section of the artificial heart pumping blood.

Position Papers

One area where Humana initially came up short was in not having sufficient background information on controversial issues raised by the news media on its own or through the comments of Humana's critics. Answers to the controversial questions in the background information section of the Humana briefing book were not enough. We needed a position paper to state Humana's views on these topics, and so will you if your organization is immersed in a news story that has both proponents and opponents.

Humana's position paper was written by Tom Noland, a former journalist who joined the company's public relations staff the Monday after Schroeder's operation and found himself working an 18-hour day in the Bomb Shelter. He began work on the paper several weeks later and had the typewritten draft completed and approved in time for distribution to the press when they arrived to cover Murray Haydon's artificial heart operation in mid-February. The paper, which subsequently was published as a 17-page pamphlet entitled *Humana and the Artificial Heart*, addresses:

- The history of funding for the development of the artificial heart and the clinical investigation of the JARVIK-7.

- The potential costs to society of the artificial heart if it proves to be beneficial for many of the 600,000 Americans who die each year from cardiovascular disease.
- The priorities that must be weighed by society, the medical profession, and the families of patients considering the implant of an artificial heart.
- Whether patients can expect to have a satisfactory quality of life when they are sustained by the artificial heart.
- Humana's previous experience in clinical research and its commitment to underwrite the hospital costs for up to 100 artificial heart patients.
- Humana's response to critics regarding the motives for its involvement in the artificial heart program, and its forthright approach in providing information to the public via the news media.

The problem you will find is that a good position paper isn't easy to write, much less get approved by your management, especially if everyone is focusing on the news event. In reflecting on his experiences in writing the paper, Noland believes the ideal scenario is to have someone do the work who knows the organization and is paid to spend a majority of his or her time pounding a typewriter or word processor. "He or she can't shoehorn this kind of assignment in between press calls and other projects. It should be a full-time project, which is tough when you're being pulled in six different directions."[52]

Noland, now a senior public affairs manager at Humana, feels the writer should start out with a day or two at the site to interview and understand the participants so the text will convey their professional views and personal feelings as if they had written it themselves. Then there needs to be time spent researching the subject and reviewing documents and reports in the files, perhaps even using a database terminal or any other sources of background information on the company and the issue. Finally the writer should have ample time with top management to discuss the organization's position on the pertinent issues so the text will be influenced by their views, even if they are not quoted directly. "Then he should be locked up in his cell with a deadline for delivering the final draft," Noland added. "Any journalist has been faced with that many times. You don't necessarily like it, but that's the only way this kind of thing gets done when you're working in 'Emergency City.'"

Background Briefings

Personal backgrounding can be another important information source, especially if it can be done before the news event occurs. The White House press office sets up background briefings for the news media prior to and sometimes after the president's involvement in any significant development that will get worldwide news coverage. Briefings often are conducted by a senior administration or White House official, who is not named. The rationale of the White House for the use of unnamed sources is that the means justify the end. "You don't want anyone to go on record as speaking directly for the president, or even for the White House, but you have to give reporters guidance," said Denny Brisley, who was an assistant White House press secretary. "It's better to let them know the situation, which includes pointing out when they are a little bit off, than to let them go off on a tangent that's completely wrong. If you don't background properly, you might spend all day doing damage control."[53]

The use of background briefings also is a routine part of the work done by other government press offices, especially those with heavy media coverage like the Department of State and NASA. Each NASA facility has its spokespersons on hand at the Kennedy Space Center for shuttle launches to provide background information and handle any questions relating to their area of the space program. Spokespersons for the organizations whose payloads or personnel are on each shuttle mission also are there to provide background information to the news media.

You also can do a lot to help the cause if background briefings are held for your top management, employees, and any VIPs who might be in a position to influence the future of your organization. These kinds of briefings are best done by personal presentations, if you have the time and the participants are available. They also can be done electronically. NASA has its spokespersons in Houston, Cape Kennedy, and Huntsville participate in background briefings prior to shuttle launches, using the space agency's satellite communications system to provide closed-circuit television coverage between the facilities. The media often are not present but can still cover them by picking up what's being carried by the NASA satellite.

Background briefings become an essential response mechanism if the media coverage has been caused by a crisis, especially if the crisis involves some form of complicated technology. Shirley Green at

NASA recalls that in the first few hours after the Challenger explosion, the press center at Kennedy Space Center was flooded with many reporters who had little, if any, background information about the space program in general or the space shuttle in particular. One problem in providing technical briefings for general assignment reporters was pointed out by Jackson Browning at Union Carbide who believes that the complex nature of what happened at the Bhopal plant made quick, one-sentence explanations a virtual impossibility. He is among the many onslaught veterans who are quick to point out the virtues of having background information and handouts that are understandable by reporters who do not normally cover technical stories.

THE RETURN ON THE INVESTMENT

If all this seems expensive, it is. Humana spent $125,000 in preparing background information and visuals for the artificial heart program before Bill Schroeder's operation. It can be an excellent investment, however, if you consider how much it enhances the media coverage of the news event. Another benefit is that the materials often can be used for other audiences besides the media. Humana still gets hundreds of requests each month for information on the artificial heart program. Much of what they send out was developed originally for the news media and now has a second, even longer, life span.

CHAPTER EIGHT

Feeding the Bears

The old saying "Feed the bears or they'll eat you" was used in identical ways by three of the spokespersons interviewed for this book. What John Dwan of the University of Utah, Ira Furman of the NTSB, and Hugh Harris of NASA were saying is that if you do nothing else, you'd better update the news media with useful, accurate information. Otherwise, they will eat you alive just as they did the Loma Linda Medical Center when they covered Baby Fae and NASA after the Challenger accident.

You don't have to give them everything. It's your call to decide what will be provided. Just keep in mind that there are dozens of skilled journalists out there competing with each other and looking for the facts, the details, and the latest information they can shape into solid news stories that will satisfy the demands of their editors or news directors. Your organization will be their primary source as long as the quality and quantity of raw material you provide is sufficient, consistent, and credible. If it's not, they will come up with any number of other sources in a few hours.

THE DISCLOSURE GAMUT

If you do any developing of a game plan for an onslaught, know how the media updates are going to be handled. The options for keeping the media informed run the gamut from the Soviet approach after the Chernobyl nuclear power plant accident, which was almost complete silence, to giving the news media anything it asks for. Neither is realistic; but, as we discussed in Chapter 5, your organization and the participants have the right to set the limits on what will be disclosed, which should be somewhere in between. The participants and top management probably would prefer to take the Soviet approach—play it safe and say as little as possible. They will be under enough stress already and will view the prospects of divulging information to the news media and the world as an immense imponderable that they don't want to deal with.

The problem is that somebody has to be thinking about what effects negative news media coverage will have on your organization, and you may be the only one with that perspective. That means you're probably going to have to take a minority viewpoint and argue persuasively for being forthright with the news media if your organization is to avoid the kinds of problems that have been experienced by NASA, Loma Linda, the Soviet government, and the Reagan administration after the Iranian arms sale.

Management needs to understand that they are not opening the disclosure floodgates by providing the news media with basic facts that can be confirmed. Just the opposite. Every bit of relevant information you provide will reduce the pressure that's going to be exerted by the news media on everyone involved. Hugh Harris, the director of public information at the Kennedy Space Center, said that after the Challenger explosion, the tremendous frustration that he and his press relations staff had was in not being able to give the news media some of the basic facts. "That was creating a greater problem of more pressure and distrust on the part of the press," Harris recalled. "We tried to be very straight with the press at all times, but we had as hard a time getting information out of people as they did. We should have had a greater role in deciding what could and could not be released. This is typical, though, of this type of exercise."[54]

Part of the problem may be that you'll encounter some vivid examples of siege mentality, especially if a crisis has occurred. After the Challenger accident, the Air Force meteorologists refused to provide the NASA public affairs staff with information on the weather at Cape Kennedy, which obviously was of interest to the news media, considering the cold temperatures. Because they couldn't get it through NASA, the news media called the National Weather Service and the FAA to find out the weather conditions at the Cape at the time of launch. That further damaged the strained relations between NASA and the press, who have cited the weather as an example of being stonewalled by the space agency.

HOW MUCH DETAIL DO YOU PROVIDE?

One issue debated constantly during Barney Clark's 112 days and the recovery of Humana's three artificial heart patients was how much in the way of specifics should be provided. What a patient has for breakfast, who came to visit, what he said in response to a question, or the color of his pajamas is one type of detail that the media will be interested in having. But what if the patient is hemorrhaging? Do you give the amount of blood lost? Is that something the public is entitled to know? Will the disclosure of this type of information affect the decisions made by the participants in deciding what actions to take?

The answer is *yes*, which means that you and the participants will have to decide in advance how much detail will be provided when there are significant developments. Dr. Lansing disclosed the extent of artificial heart patient Jack Burcham's hemorrhaging in cc's. The news media promptly converted the metric number and reported that Burcham had lost nine gallons of blood, which was more than all the blood in his body. Lansing would have been better off using "severe" or "serious" to describe the hemorrhaging and declining to give the specific amount.

NBC medical correspondent Robert Bazell described the information that was provided to reporters covering the Baby Fae experiment and the Schroeder artificial heart implant as ranging from "significant medical data to idiotic trivia, which gave the public the chance to root for the underdog."[55] Although many journalists disagree with me, Humana probably provided too much information and too many visuals to the news media during their coverage of the first three artificial heart patients, especially in the case of Bill Schroeder.

Humana's approach was dictated by the knowledge that the company's involvement with the artificial heart would automatically be viewed with suspicion by the media. Our plan also was based on avoiding the press relations problems during coverage of Barney Clark and Baby Fae. Humana's George Atkins recalls, "They came in skeptical, anticipating that it would be like the previous medical news events and they would have difficulty getting information. When that did not materialize after the first two or three days, and the material they got was adequate and accurate, then there was the trust and the confidence that really made it a nice working relationship."[56]

The news media highlighted Humana's openness in a number of

stories at the time, and many journalists still recall the abundance of information, photographs, video, and interview possibilities Humana provided. Others have had second thoughts. "Humana overreacted in the beginning," recalls Steve Lyons, who was the *Louisville Times* medical writer. "They made available more information than the press really needed or wanted. The press took advantage of it, especially TV. That created unrealistically high expectations in the beginning that were strengthened by Schroeder's miraculous recovery. That approach has boomeranged because people now have a more negative attitude about the artificial heart than they would have had if their expectations had not been built up so high in the beginning."[57]

REALISTIC DISCLOSURE GUIDELINES

You are not going to satisfy everyone in the news media, but your organization will have the best chance of coming out of the onslaught intact if you and the other members of management put yourselves in the place of a general assignment reporter in deciding how much information you're going to provide. As mentioned in Chapter 5, those decisions need to be made *before* the first encounter with the press so guidelines can be established and understood within your organization. They also need to be conveyed to the news media from the outset of the story so they will know what to expect and can plan accordingly. The important thing is to stick to them once they are established, because they will be one basis of your credibility.

The danger you always face is that everyone will agree in advance on the disclosure guidelines or procedures and then ignore them when the siege is on, which is what happened after the Challenger explosion. "It was a madhouse with all the phones completely jammed, wanting information and not really having anything to give them," Hugh Harris of NASA recalls. "Dick [Young, Harris' deputy press officer] was primarily concerned about when we would be able to get someone over for a briefing. I kept saying I think we'll be able to do it very fast, but that just went on and on and on. The four or five hours went very, very fast."

Take a lesson from what NASA didn't do. If your operations people are tied up and unwilling or unable to brief the news media, the senior public relations person had better step into the void before whatever rapport your organization has with the press is lost. This is what Shirley Green wanted to do. Had she been at NASA longer, she realizes now she would have met with the news media and made an initial statement. "I regret that we didn't do it ourselves," Green observed later. "If I hadn't been so new, I probably would have . . . . If it ever happened again and I couldn't get a program person, I'd go to the microphone and tell the press what they were doing."[58]

A move like that takes courage, but it can be handled intelligently and will maintain your working relationship with the news media for a few hours until the appropriate people are available to talk to the press. Explain that the participants are tied up with the situation and here are the facts that can be confirmed at the present time. Also indicate what information you don't have or are in the process of verifying, and ask what other details the press is seeking so those questions can be added to the list. That may be all that is needed to maintain control of the situation until one of your principal spokespersons is available.

The members of management need to understand that there is a broad middle ground between clamming up and opening the kimono. No matter how sensitive the situation, there will be some basic facts that can be provided on a timely basis. "An adage I learned years ago as a journalist is 'Nothing improves a story like a few facts,' and that's very important to help the press, to give them the sense that we appreciate what their needs are," said Ira Furman of the NTSB. "Because some of our investigators don't understand that, I often wound up in a little conflict when I went after them for some nonperishable miscellaneous information, like the length of the runway."[59] After the Challenger exploded, NASA could have disclosed that helicopters and ships could not enter the recovery area for nearly an hour because wreckage was continuing to fall into the sea. It also could have provided information on the number of ships and aircraft involved or what was being done to embargo the launch data to ensure that all of the details would be available for later analysis. A great deal could have been said in the 4 hours and 50 minutes from the launch to the initial briefing.

GATHERING AND CHECKING THE FACTS

There is no system or set routine for finding out what can be disclosed. If you use a fill-in-the-blank sheet to get your information from the participants, they are going to respond with a fill-in-the-blank attitude, which means that you will have little, if any, newsworthy details to disclose. The only way you can provide useful information to keep the news media at bay is to stay close to the participants and stay abreast of what they are thinking and doing. That only can come from spending time where the news is and being able to say that this is what I saw and heard from those who are involved. For Ira Furman at the NTSB, that perspective could only come from going out to the burned-out remains of Delta 191 and talking with members of the NTSB Go Team as they worked through the debris in the sweltering heat and smells of kerosene and charred materials and remains. For Denny Brisley at the White House, that perspective came from the three meetings of the press office staff each day and their constant involvement with the president and members of his staff, whose offices were down the hall.

During the Wilberg fire, Bob Henrie was the only spokesperson, and he stayed with the media at the mining office command center in Huntington. Henrie had to rely on information phoned down from the mine, twelve miles away, and thus was providing secondhand information to the media. Had he put the lid on disclosing anything new for a couple of hours in the early morning, and taken the time to visit the mine to get his own perspective, his first-person observations might well have lessened the media's efforts to penetrate the mine's security provisions with helicopters and on foot to get whatever information and visuals they could.

COMING UP WITH RELEVANT DETAILS

You can learn a great deal from casual conversations with the people who have been involved in the news story. They may not tell you anything directly, but you'll be able to sense how things are going. I always tried to get to Schroeder's room a few minutes before my 6:30 A.M. meeting with Dr. DeVries for the overnight update. Chatting with the guard outside the room and with the night shift nurses and technical staff usually allowed me to glean enough to know what questions to ask DeVries when he came down the hall. Another good source was the guard's log book, which noted who had been in to see Schroeder as well as who was expected that day.

During the fact finding you will feel as if you are the reporter rather than the other way around, but it's going to take that kind of digging on your part to come up with relevant details that would otherwise be overlooked by the participants. It takes a lot of piecing together of bits of information and "by the way" comments from dozens of people for you to fully understand what the situation is and to know what should or should not be discussed in public and the reasons why. It may be premature, it may be an opinion, or it may turn out to be dead wrong when you check it out with the people who really know what's going on. The important thing is to find out so you can check it out.

In the process you often will uncover things the participants don't think you know or may not want you to be aware of. There may have been a basic disagreement regarding what should be done, or the most recent reports may indicate the situation has taken a turn for the worse, or the latest information may contradict statements made to the press earlier. The University of Utah's John Dwan has observed, "You can't trust the principals to give you all the information because they are going to be looking out for their own personal interests, regardless of whether they are physicians, presidents, or politicians. You also can't trust the principals to be the final arbitrators of what information is to be given out because they are going to be most interested in covering their butts. You can't defer completely to the patient, because if they are smart they are not going to want any information out. Who wants to become a public person like Barney Clark or Bill Schroeder? Knowing what we know about how it will affect their lives, who wants to do that?"[60]

As the pressure and stress of the situation build, some of your sources may want you to disclose what they want the press to hear—and not necessarily the full story. It's good to have a network of reliable sources to check with when you have a funny feeling that you're not being told everything, or that what is being emphasized may not be the most important development. You will need those second and third opinions in sorting things out and in deciding how an objective assessment of the situation can be provided to the press.

It's also important to stay in touch with the families of those involved. The media is going to want to know as much as they can get about the individual family members so they can fill out the human interest angles of their stories, and the more information you can provide, the less the pressure on the reporters to contact the families directly. The families obviously will be aware of the news coverage from what they are seeing and hearing and also from what their friends will be telling them about the extent of the publicity. That can be overwhelming to people whose only previous coverage may have been having their names mentioned in their hometown paper when they applied for a marriage license or bought their home.

Make it a point to talk with some of the principal family members each day in person or by phone to let them know what's going on and to tell them about the news stories they are likely to see and hear in the next few hours. Even if the news will be negative, family members are better off hearing from you than being shocked and dismayed when they pick up the paper or turn on the television. You'll find they often will have questions about the publicity and will want your guidance in how to respond to reporters who have contacted them directly. At the same time they often will give you one or two personal insights or quotes and allow you to pass them along to the news media. That helps the press, as well as you and the families, by ensuring they will have a little more privacy.

TIMING OF DISCLOSURES

You will become aware of many newsworthy details and will constantly have to determine if and when that information should be disclosed. The dilemma will be compounded by the incessant hounding of the news media for any new information, details, or tidbits you can provide. Most won't care whether it's preliminary or premature; they want something to disclose, and after days or weeks of incessant pounding by the press, there's a danger a spokesperson will give in to their demands. The problem is if you make a premature disclosure that turns out to be wrong, the press won't be there to accept the blame for urging you on. Just the opposite. They'll blast you for disclosing information that turned out to be incorrect.

NASA announced that the preliminary analysis of the tape recordings of the Challenger crew's internal conversations indicated they were not aware of the impending disaster. That was on July 17, 1986. The space agency then had to reverse itself 11 days later when it disclosed that the last comment of the pilot, Michael J. Smith, was "Uh oh" and that three of the emergency breathing packs had been activated, indicating there had been attempts to survive, at least briefly.

NASA's Shirley Green feels that the premature disclosure was in part due to the heavy media criticism leveled at the space agency.

"That was one time when we decided to go ahead and disclose what we thought we knew. We were wrong, and we really got beat up on it," Green recalls. "When we had waited until we were sure of something, we were beat up because we weren't forthcoming. So it's been a Catch-22 throughout all of this, but I think it's similar to other crises. Do you go with what you think you know or do you wait until you know it?"

The Union Carbide Bhopal Team took the opposite approach and refused to disclose or even discuss "preliminary" information until it was confirmed—but they also "got beat up." "We deliberately refrained from telling newspeople even though we took a lot of heat because we were supposed to know," Jackson Browning said. "They assumed you're too smart not to know, therefore you must be hiding something."[61] The company's policy frustrated the press, and indeed Carbide was criticized by the news media for not providing certain technical information or commenting on the in-depth series of articles in the *New York Times* on the Bhopal accident until the company's analysis of the accident had been completed. Browning's view is that the first and most obvious answer is seldom the one that stands up under complete analysis.

Some members of the media understand the timing dilemmas you face. "As a journalist I favor full cooperation and letting it all hang out," said Morton Kondracke, a senior editor for *The New Republic*. "But there are times you can tell the press is just going to get it wrong and the more information you give them, the more they will have to clobber you. If you can tell that the pack is in a feeding frenzy and you are about to be the meat, you might be better off letting them chew on their own shoes for a while. The rule ought to be full disclosure, but there will be exceptions."[62]

You and the participants will have to grapple with the question of when a specific disclosure should be made many times during the course of the news story. The basic answer should be not until the information can be confirmed. Then, when you're sure, don't sit on it. If it's good news, the natural inclination will be to disclose it as soon as possible; but the same needs to hold true if it's bad news. The longer you hold onto bad news, the more rotten it gets and the more likely the media is to pick up the scent and start asking some of their other sources.

If the data is preliminary, as with the Challenger crew tapes, how long will it be until the final analysis will be available? If it will take a few more days or even weeks, why not wait? If the final data will be confirmed only after months of research and analysis, it may be appropriate to disclose the preliminary findings, but put "preliminary" in all capital letters so there will be no misunderstanding that the final results are not in. Then indicate when they are likely to be available, and make a note on your calendar two weeks before that date to begin checking on the status of the findings, so you can prepare to make the disclosure at the appropriate time. And until you are ready to release the final data, refuse to speculate any further on the results of the findings.

People in your organization may want to delay disclosing significant developments until the afternoon or even the next day for a variety of reasons, which may include waiting for the stock market to close or needing to contact specific people before the announcement is made. That's usually the logic of top management or staff officers, but they and you had better be careful. The longer you hold onto the news, the greater the jeopardy to the organization and the participants, including yourself.

When you have a problem to disclose, it's imperative to come as clean as you can as quickly as you can. Your organization may absorb a beating from the news media and your other important publics who are affected by the news, but if you disclose everything quickly, you will pre-empt the investigative reporting possibilities for the news media and lessen the chances of the situation being turned into a scandal.

The alternative is to disclose as little as possible, which is like lighting a long string of firecrackers. There will be a series of loud explosions, but you have no way of telling when or where the next one will occur or how long they will continue. Each new bang will be startling and seem as loud as the first, with the overall damage to your organization and the integrity of its management far more serious than if they all had gone off at once.

President Reagan could have avoided the damage to his administration from the thousands of media firecrackers that have gone off in the months after the disclosure of the Iranian arms deal and diversion of funds to the Contras. There would have been very little left for the news media to dig up and report if the president had obtained a full disclosure from Admiral Poindexter and Colonel North, preferably before they were dismissed, and then released the information promptly to the American public. *Time* summed it up, "The messages kept coming at Ronald Reagan, from friends, senior leaders in both parties, veteran public officials belatedly summoned to provide outside counsel, even his wife. Their essence can be put in one word: *act.*"[63]

The other major problem in delaying bad news is that journalists often will learn of the development through one of their many other sources and then break the news on their own. Then you have two problems. You will have lost control of the announcement and will have to respond to questions rather than being in a position to disclose what's happened. You also are going to be accused of covering up and being secretive, and will lay yourself wide open to a frenzy of investigative journalism by every reporter assigned to the story. Consider the damage done to the image of the Gorbachev regime in the West because of its delay in disclosing that the Chernobyl accident had occurred several days earlier.

You'll often have to be hard-nosed in fighting for the type of prompt disclosure that should have followed the Challenger accident but didn't. And always make sure the participants and the families of those involved know before the press, preferably right before. That will take some planning and coordination, but it's vital if you are to maintain your rapport with them.

DEADLINES

If the disclosure involves a routine update or status report, consider the deadlines of the news media and the optimum time to provide the facts. Denny Brisley knows from her White House days that you can't hold a press briefing at 4 P.M. and expect very much coverage, especially from television, because there are deadlines and they have to get their stories in. "If you do hold a briefing late in the afternoon, your information might not make it in the papers or on the air that evening due to various deadlines. In addition there are likely to be more errors because reporters won't have as much time to do the story right," Brisley said. "If you hold a briefing at 9 A.M. on the other hand, they have all day to question as many people as they need and to gather other information."[64]

The best time for disclosures is in the morning, preferably before 10 A.M. Eastern Standard Time. That will allow both wire services to include your news in their P.M. cycle, and also give the television networks maximum time to develop and refine their stories before they are broadcast on the evening news programs. President Reagan's press secretary, Larry Speakes, briefed the White House press corps at 9:15 A.M. and then responded to questions at 11 A.M. The second session was on the record but not recorded for live broadcast.

It doesn't end when you update the news media, however. You need to be available to respond to the hundreds of questions and phone calls that will follow any disclosure that's made, especially as the deadlines for the different news organizations approach. UPI's Al Rossiter, Jr. observed, "Most people don't understand or appreciate the deadlines of the wire services or other news organizations. That's true of doctors but also of PR people. To support a breaking story we can't wait three hours for a call to be returned."

A far more intelligent approach is to respond to every press call, but develop your priorities based on the specific news organization and how close it is to deadline. "The White House absolutely gave different consideration to different news media," added Denny Brisley. "We knew the news magazines close on Friday night, so if you wanted them to carry the story you had to figure out how they can get it before then. The news wires can always be accommodated, but you can't let something go on for two hours and not expect them to go running out of the room to break the story. They've got to file, so give them a filing break on a major story. We did that for TV as well."

Barbara Dolan of *Time* made basically the same point from the journalistic side, "So many public relations people try to treat each journalist as if they are equal and we are *not* at all equal! Each reporter is representing a different kind of news organization. It really shows when they deal with the news magazines because there are very few public relations people, press aides, or whatever who really understand what we really need. What happens is that they don't know what our rules are or, worse yet, our deadlines. They have no conception of what goes into a *Time* article versus a newspaper story or the TV report on the same news."[66]

BRIEFING THE NEWS MEDIA

Many people don't realize there's a big difference between press conferences and media briefings. Press conferences are called to make an announcement like the introduction of a new product or the decision of a political candidate to run for office. That's a different ball game than the media briefings, which will be the most important source of information for the news media during their coverage of a major story. The briefings elaborate on what has already been disclosed, with new details often added by the spokesperson during the initial remarks or in response to questions from reporters. Dr. DeVries recalls that the general interest of the media surprised him when he first began to brief the news media. "I was surprised they were interested in anything about the patient that was unusual, including what he had for lunch or dinner, where his family spent the night, that sort of thing. I also didn't think there would be as many newspeople involved in it for as long a time."[67]

It's a good idea to start off each briefing by summarizing what has occurred since your last meeting with the news media, even if it was only an hour ago. You also should use the opening to clarify information from previous briefings that may not have been stated correctly or was misinterpreted in the news reports and to respond to questions that were raised earlier but could not be answered at the time. Then give the details that you want to disclose.

Everyone has their own style for making presentations, but the quickest, easiest, and most natural approach for a media briefing is to have the important facts listed as one-liners rather than in a prepared statement. Each point can then be disclosed and elaborated on, if the spokesperson has additional details to provide. Leave some space between those one-liners when they are being drawn up because you'll find points will be added to clarify or explain many of them during your pre-briefing discussions. Denny Brisley suggests that you "Practice sentences. Short, concise sentences with a little color get quoted or make the videotape. You can use that to your advantage in getting your point across. For example, you could describe someone's health as, 'He's doing just fine,' or you can say, 'He is as fine as frog's hair—very fine indeed.' Which one would you use if you're the journalist?"

Try to include direct quotes from the participants and the family members whenever possible, because the media will be looking for the personal views and observations of those involved. That also will present an opportunity to give recognition to some of the people who are heavily involved but would not otherwise be mentioned. If there's an opportunity to record some of their observations on a cassette tape while you're gathering information for the briefing, that will be very interesting and useful to the news media. The radio and television reporters can plug parts of those actualities directly into their coverage, but they also will be of use to the wire service and print reporters who will have direct quotes from the participants themselves.

If complex points can be illustrated, sketch out the diagrams in advance and arrange to have a flip chart or clean chalkboard near the podium so the spokesperson has something to use in explaining the points to the news media. Dr. Chase Peterson, a former medical school professor, explained anatomical details to reporters covering the Barney Clark story with diagrams on a chalkboard. Besides helping the press to understand what he was saying, Dr. Peterson's drawings added visual opportunities for the television and still photographers, which they greatly appreciated.

RESPONDING TO QUESTIONS

The most important part of any briefing for the press, and the most difficult for the participants, will be the questions and answers that follow the initial disclosures. Don't let what you've seen on television give you the wrong impression. You're not going to have to put up with what the president's press secretary goes through every day with the White House press corps, and there won't be a Sam Donaldson shouting questions at you.

A large number of the questions will be general, almost naive in nature because the reporters will have little background on the story and will be looking for you to give them a solid lead or human interest angle. If the story is medical or highly technical, reporters who know the field will ask more-detailed questions to build depth into their coverage, and the general assignment media will defer to them for most of the questions. The only time the questioning may get hostile is if information has been provided to the news media that turns out to be incorrect or if they have uncovered an inconsistency or controversy. We'll discuss that in Chapter 11, When the News Coverage Turns Negative.

Spokespersons usually get themselves in trouble without the help of the media. However, they can avoid most of the problems that occur in responding to reporters' questions if they use good common sense. Specifically:

1. Be Sure of What You Are Saying

That's already been mentioned, but it deserves repeating because some spokespersons tend to get puffed up by all the national media exposure and let their egos override the extent of their information. "I was amazed at how much influence the news media has on the project. The media will influence the making of everyday decisions and change the personalities of the people involved," Dr. DeVries observed.

Dr. Lansing was not prepared to discuss Bill Schroeder's condition at the medical briefing the morning after an artificial heart had been implanted in Murray Haydon. As a matter of fact, he had not seen Schroeder or reviewed his charts. When a reporter asked how Schroeder was doing, Lansing should have indicated he had not had a chance to see the patient that morning but would make it a point to check on him before the afternoon briefing. Instead he responded with information from the previous week, when Schroeder had been depressed, which caused some concern about suicide. The hospital was in an uproar before he got back from the briefing center, and Lansing's credibility with many members of the news media was seriously damaged when he had to disclose later that day that Schroeder was, in fact, feeling much better.

We all make mistakes, and the media will accept that as long as we point out the error as soon as we're aware of it. But that doesn't include guessing to answer a question. Watch out when "possibility, suppose, expect, chances" or similar uncertainties are the primary part of the question. The press isn't necessarily trying to trap you, but they would sure love you to forecast so their stories can look ahead to what is likely to happen.

2. Be Very Careful with Good News

Reporters will be looking for answers that can be easily explained in lay terms, and they may overreact if there is any implication of good news in a disastrous situation. Bob Henrie was asked during a briefing on the Wilberg Mine fire whether there was any place where the miners might be able to escape from the fire and toxic smoke. Henrie indicated that the only possibility was a dead-end tunnel and that the miners would have had to seal it off with a waterproof fabric used in the mine. The answer was correct but should have been more carefully hedged, or described as a remote possibility, because within minutes the idea that the Wilberg Mine had a "safe chamber" was hatched in news reports, which fed on each other and grew more distorted as the day progressed.

3. Don't Respond Too Quickly

This is no time to be acting like a contestant on a game show, especially if you know the answer. Take your time in responding. Repeat the question slowly for the benefit of the other correspondents and also to allow whoever is documenting the briefing to get down exactly what was asked. By repeating the question you will have those few moments to be sure you understood the question and to have the answer framed in your mind. Then keep your response short, concise, and directly to the point. It should be no more than two or three sentences.

Part of the "wing it" tendency is to think that you can answer any question if you keep talking long enough. Just the opposite usually will be true. You will only be digging yourself into a hole that will get deeper with each word you utter. The more you talk and the more you elaborate, the more you're likely to say things that you'll later regret. Keep your answers short and directly on the question being asked. And once you've answered the question, stop talking.

4. Move the Questions around the Room

Some reporters are very good at dominating a question-and-answer session if you give them a chance. In fairness to the rest of the media, and to yourself, make it a point not to respond to shouted questions. Instead ask for reporters with questions to raise their hands, and then take each question from a different part of the room so you don't get cornered. You'll quickly get to know who asks hostile questions, who asks you to speculate, and who lobs the easy ones right over the plate. If you can balance the types of questions you take, you can move the briefing along quickly and give it a greater sense of impartiality and fair play. You can also get yourself out of a jam if there are too many follow-ups by moving to someone who has a tendency to ask friendlier questions.

OTHER OPTIONS FOR KEEPING THE MEDIA INFORMED

Briefings are important but time consuming for spokespersons. In some instances other people who are involved can be on hand for some of the briefings. One of the participants may fill in at a media briefing on behalf of the chief spokesperson, or the CEO could provide an overview or general update before introducing experts to discuss the specific aspects of the situation that may be of interest to the news media at the time. That allows the press to broaden the scope of its coverage and also relieves some of the pressure on your organization to provide more information.

Be sure the alternate spokesperson is really interested in presenting what he knows to the press and has not been coerced to fill in for the regular spokesperson. When that happens, the tension will be evident and the interaction between the spokesperson and the news media may turn unfriendly. You also need to be sure the alternate spokesperson is fully briefed on what has been said previously. Part of Loma Linda's problem was that they used several different spokespersons, who often contradicted each other. A good way to avoid that is to make sure the alternate spokespersons look over the transcripts of previous briefings as well as any written updates that have been distributed so they feel comfortable and informed. Then discuss the media's principal areas of interest and most likely questions.

Written advisories are also an effective way of keeping the press informed without the participants having to be present. They are especially helpful when the news media's deadlines come at an inconvenient time for the spokesperson to be on hand but the news organizations need an update on the situation before they lock up their stories. These status reports can be provided to the wire services for distribution to other news organizations. They also can be put on a telephone answering machine and used to update anyone who calls in for the latest information.

MAINTAINING A CONSISTENT DISCLOSURE PACE

Take a look at the expected duration of the news story. The brunt of the coverage is likely to be over in a week with disasters like the Wilberg Mine fire or the Delta 191 crash, although the residual coverage will continue for months. On the other hand, you could wind up in a media marathon with something like Bhopal, the Challenger, or the artificial heart. Humana made a tactical error by not factoring into our planning for the artificial heart program the possibility that this story would run for months or years and that we'd better pace ourselves from the start with a consistent disclosure routine that we could maintain for months. Instead we established a twice-daily schedule of media briefings on Schroeder's recovery, with two additional written updates per day, but then we had no graceful way of shutting it off. After two weeks, the medical spokespeople and our public relations staff were wearing out, while the local and national media had sent in their reserves to continue covering the story at the initial level we had established.

Our decision to close the briefing center and replace the two-a-day briefings with daily written updates was met by angry comments from the press, who implied we were trying to control their reporting of the story. That sentiment would be even more strongly voiced after Schroeder's stroke, when it was impossible to describe his progress on a daily basis. CNN's medical correspondent, Gary Schwitzer, observed the evolution from the time of Schroeder's implant through Dr. DeVries' decision not to disclose details to the news media. "A standard was set on November 24 that was hard for Humana to live up to on December 13 and in February," Schwitzer said. "That's what the PR people probably need to think about, because it is not written up. So many people learned from preparing for the onslaught, but they didn't think that a good offensive always has a second wave. Are you going to be ready for that?"[68]

CONSISTENCY AND CONTINUITY

The strength of your working relationship with the news media will be determined over the course of the news story by the degree of consistency and continuity you can maintain in what is disclosed. That's often very difficult during the height of an onslaught because of the extreme pressure on both the participants and the press. It will be even more difficult later, because most of the participants will get tired of thinking about how the media is going to report what they will say, much less having to go out there again to brief the press and face questions that will range from the inane to the icepick variety.

Journalists are trained to be skeptical and question the information they get, which quickly becomes evident if they sense a discrepancy. Steve Lyons of the *Times* observed that "It's not very satisfactory to tell your boss, 'It doesn't add up. Lansing says one thing and DeVries says another, and they just want us to take the difference on faith.' " Spokespersons often will have differing views, especially physicians. The best way to avoid inconsistencies that the press can report as controversies is to have one chief spokesperson who speaks for the organization, who can clarify any differences of opinion, and who serves as the media's primary source of information.

Part of NASA's problem after the Challenger accident was that revelations were coming from Cape Kennedy, Huntsville, Houston, and Washington, with any number of NASA officials and public affairs people being quoted in the disclosures. Granted, each facility had different responsibilities in the investigation, and NASA permits any employee to speak openly to the media, but this was a major news story that called for one central informed source of information for the press. What the space agency needed was a single spokesperson, and a designated backup, who would be the official source for any NASA disclosures about the Challenger, and who would communicate its position or response to all news media questions regarding the accident. That source would have had to be in different locations during the hearings of the presidential commission, but the media can adjust to that.

The president of the United States may be in Boston or Bali, but the press knows who is authorized to speak for the administration and where information will be provided. "It's best to have one designated spokesperson, maybe two," Denny Brisley observed. "Don't have everyone who is involved speaking. Instruct everyone to defer to the designated spokesperson. If you don't, you'll have 15 different people using 15 different terms to describe one event, and it will lead to confusion as well as controversy."

George Strait of ABC News is a former White House correspondent who also has covered the artificial heart in Utah and at Humana. "We're never going to get all the information we want and need to do a story, but you sure can have a much better relationship when there's consistency in what we're told about the good and bad developments," Strait observed. "After Schroeder's first stroke we all got briefed. After his second stroke we didn't hear anything for a week. You can't do that. It's basically unfair. It's like a cute woman who keeps leading you on."[69] That can be avoided if management and the public relations staff work closely in maintaining a consistent flow of information to the news media. They will be the glue, the heat, the whatever it takes to ensure that the consistency remains in the disclosure policy your organization set forth initially—or risk having the press turn against you.

CHAPTER NINE

Calling the Shots

The ancient Chinese proverb about a picture being worth a thousand words takes on a completely new significance when it's applied to a major news event. While the details of the story will determine the initial news potential, the photos and television coverage from the scene will determine the positioning, the extent, and the duration of the coverage in the print and broadcast media. The converse also is true—the less the visual impact, the less coverage the story is likely to get.

The problem is that you may not be able to control the photography and video as much as the distribution of information. The burglary of Barney Clark's house in which his photo albums were taken, the helicopters flying into the canyon to film the Wilberg Mine fire, and the network television camera that magnified light 55,000 times to shoot the nighttime arrival of the NASA recovery ships are examples of the extremes the news media will go to in obtaining visuals for their stories. These are the realities. The ethics of these efforts are another issue, which we'll address when we discuss the media in Chapter 10.

If your news event is in the national and international headlines, some news organizations in the United States and abroad may be willing to pay substantial amounts to get good photographs and video footage of the story, knowing that the visual element really is what will attract and hold the attention of their readers and viewers. There also is a profitable aftermarket for the photos from some major stories, even those that originally were provided free of charge to the news media. The point is that money will be spent and made getting good photos and video in a major news event, and mistakes by public relations people who think they know the complexities of the picture business can cause their organization to lose control of the visuals. In some instances, they may deprive participants of thousands of dollars in potential income.

This chapter will discuss the complexities of providing the news media with photography and video, which can be a primary factor in controlling the extent of the press coverage. It will discuss the options available to any organization in deciding how visuals will be supplied and distributed in the United States and abroad, and it will point out some of the important considerations involving copyrights and compensation. Whichever way you decide to go, you're going to need expert advice if you are to get the best visual results and establish the most equitable distribution arrangement. We'll discuss who you can turn to for objective advice and also what can be done to ensure you'll still have access to those visuals years from now.

THE DETERMINING FACTOR

Let's face it, you can only go so far with a word story for a general news audience before it has to be supplemented by visuals. Regardless of whether it's a newspaper, news magazine, or television news program, the fastest way to inform or catch someone's attention is with good pictures. Even *The Wall Street Journal* uses line drawings. The more extensive the photography and video coverage, the more likely the story is to be the lead item on local and network television news programs, a major front-page story in your daily newspaper or included in the weekly coverage of *Time* and *Newsweek*, perhaps even as a cover story.

The opposite doesn't necessarily apply, however, especially if you're involved in a news story that will be covered by the national and international news media. Anyone who thinks that they can minimize the news coverage by limiting the visuals should consider what happened at Chernobyl. The Soviets released only one black-and-white photo of the nuclear power plant after the accident. That one shot and several pictures of Chernobyl in *Soviet Life Magazine* were all the news media had to work with during the first few weeks, but it did nothing to slow the intensity of the coverage.

The lack of visuals, combined with the dearth of information from the scene of the accident in the Ukraine, caused some news organizations to report rumors, including one indicating that as many as 2,000 people were dead. The Soviet government reacted angrily to the exaggerated news reports, but they could have dispelled the misconceptions by providing visual evidence to the contrary, which they chose not to do.

What the Soviets failed to consider was that pictures during a major news event, as much if not more than words, will inform, communicate, present the realities, tell you what "is." They really can establish the parameters of many stories. Chernobyl also shows how disparate the Soviet approach to informing the public via the news media is from the news reporting system that we take for granted. Imagine what would happen—and what the news coverage would be like—if the United States had another nuclear accident like Three Mile Island and the utility company chose only to confirm that it had occurred and provide one black-and-white photograph of the damaged facility.

The more photography and video you can provide or help the news media to obtain, the greater your chances of having some control over the coverage of the story. "Once the photos and video went out on Baby Fae, we saw a whole new sense of reality in the news reports," recalled Joyce McClintock of Loma Linda. "Here was an adorable baby yawning and drinking her bottle—people could relate to that in a second. They saw that she wasn't some kind of strange infant but a beautiful baby girl and they began pulling for her. The photo of Baby Fae listening to her mother's voice on the phone was in papers all over the world."[70]

News organizations obviously would prefer to shoot their own pictures using photographers and TV camera crews paid to understand their specific journalistic needs and formats. They also don't like to give credit to another organization for using their photos and video. However, if they can't shoot their own, you'll find any news organization very glad to accept whatever you can supply. NASA and the White House are major suppliers of photos and video to the news media, but the same holds for private organizations as well. Humana distributed more than 360 black-and-white and color prints of Bill Schroeder's artificial heart operation and recovery, and the media wanted every one.

You quickly find that the news media has an enormous, insatiable appetite for visuals. That can be a problem because they will adjust their expectations to whatever you can provide and then constantly hound you for more. As with the updates and briefings on the artificial heart, Humana would have been much better off if we had selected and distributed an assortment of the best photos rather than giving out virtually all of the newsworthy pictures. Besides reducing the photo processing costs, the remaining photographs could then have been distributed later by Humana or the Schroeder family in response to the continuing interest in the artificial heart program.

One of the most surprising uses of still photos will be in television news coverage. Whenever color or black-and-white photographs are to be distributed, television cameras with their lights on will be sitting in front of a bulletin board or wall and waiting for the pictures. As soon as the prints are pinned up, the camera operators will pan around the important elements in each photograph, providing visual background for the voice-over commentary in their news reports.

Your story will be part of a daily crapshoot with other worldwide news developments. During the initial coverage and on days where the story ranks high in the news items of the day, heavy pressure will be exerted on reporters, camera crews, and photographers to come up with solid visuals to illustrate their coverage. They in turn will be after you for new photographs or video, knowing that whatever you provide can make the difference between their coverage being a major news item and buried somewhere.

The photography and video will provide some benefits and a few potential drawbacks for any organization in the ongoing coverage of the story. The more you can provide on any given day, the less the pressure for new disclosures, particularly from the television news-people. Even the print and wire service journalists will have more to work with because they can build or enhance their news reports with details from the photographs or video material. The flip side is that those details also may trigger questions, which are likely to be raised at the next briefing, if not before. Dr. Lawrence Altman, of the *New York Times*, was able to define the type of stroke suffered by Bill Schroeder from the news photos we released. When he asked me about the condition, I checked with the physicians and learned Altman was correct in his assumption.

THE VISUAL GAME PLAN

If your organization is involved in a disaster in which the general public has been affected, you won't have to worry about how the visuals will be handled. Law enforcement agencies will take control of the area and determine who is allowed in to shoot photographs or television news footage. On the other hand, with a positive news development or a crisis within the boundaries of your facilities, you need to know what your game plan will be for supplying the news media with photos and video, just as you have to decide what background information and updates will be provided. If it's your call, here's what needs to be considered:

1. What will be the most visual aspects of the news story? To what extent will news photographs or television coverage of these situations benefit or penalize the organization?
2. Who and what would good news photographers or television camera crews want to shoot if they had free rein? To what extent would their presence actually disrupt the activities that are the focus of the news media's interest?
3. Will there be any danger in having photographers and television camera crews in the area? Who's liable if something happens?
4. What assistance would they need from your organization to get the best news photographs or broadcast quality video footage?
5. How many still photographers and television camera persons with sound technicians can you accommodate in the areas with the greatest news media interest?
6. What wouldn't you want to have photographed because it is sensitive, confidential, or personal? Can that be controlled?
7. To what extent is personal privacy an important consideration for the participants? Who has the authority to make that decision, and how much photography and video are they willing to allow?
8. How much interest will there be in the photos or video beyond the local news media? Nationwide? Worldwide?
9. If any of the photography or video is purchased by news organizations, who should get the income? The participants? The organization? Distributors?

10. How much money is the organization willing to spend on shooting, processing, and distributing photographs and/or video? To what extent does it want to get involved in these activities during the news event and for an indefinite period afterward?

11. How important is it to have control over photography or video footage distributed to the news media? What kind of control? Will that be acceptable to the print and broadcast media?

12. Who should have the copyright to any photos or video that the organization allows to be taken during the news event? What steps will the organization take to protect that copyright?

13. Will there be any uses for photography and video other than supplying the news media? What about documenting what happened? Presentations and publication of papers, articles, or books? Material for employee publications or in-house television?

The pivotal question is number 7—personal privacy. If the participants are not willing to permit any photography or video to be taken or distributed to the news media, that's as far as it goes. The participants, however, need to realize that if they are not going to allow visual materials to be distributed to the news media and if the press wants visuals, they are going to get them someway or from someone.

NASA, which normally is very forthcoming about providing visuals, had several skirmishes with the media after the Challenger accident over the question of photography and video. First they impounded the news media's cameras and film in remote locations, which prompted the *New York Times* to file a lawsuit. NASA compounded the problem by not allowing any of the news media's film to be processed in the media's darkrooms at the Kennedy Space Center. As a result, they were delayed in releasing still photos because NASA's darkrooms were backed up in processing both its own and the news film for use in the accident analysis. Later, the edict restricting photography and television cameras from getting within one mile of the crew cabin salvage operations resulted in the television networks bringing in the gyroscopically controlled television cameras at sea and spy cameras in the harbor.

NASA had good intentions in deciding not to provide any visuals of the recovery of the crew compartment, but those intentions weren't realistic considering the public interest in the fate of the Challenger crew. All it would have taken to eliminate the need for the extreme measures taken by the TV networks would have been to provide one or two still photos shot by NASA of the wreckage being recovered, and pictures of the honor guard bringing the flag-draped caskets off the recovery ships. In the latter instance, a camera pool would have helped to relieve the pressure and also would have allowed the public to know for sure that the astronauts were not lost at sea but had been found and were being honored as they returned to the Cape for the final time.

There are a number of options between allowing no visuals at all and providing the media with everything it wants. You and the participants need to give some careful consideration to what's appropriate. Then it's a question of whether that will be acceptable to the organization, while also satisfying the needs of the news media. The guidelines for photos and video can run the gamut from the Russian government's one photograph of Chernobyl to NASA's extraordinary photographic and video coverage of space shuttle launches.

Even though it was the 25th shuttle mission, NASA had 123 still and motion picture cameras and nearly 70 TV cameras covering the lift-off and ascent of the Challenger. That persistence in providing the same visual support for the 25th flight as was provided for the first made all the difference in isolating the possible cause of the accident so quickly. Myopic mistakes were made by NASA, but it's important to remember that it was the visual images from those NASA cameras that allowed the space agency to pinpoint the black puffs of smoke within three days.

Before the Challenger accident, NASA and the media had a close working relationship with regard to the sharing of photographs and tapes, primarily because the agency was capable of shooting good film and was willing to make it available to the press. A number of the NASA cameras were remote controlled and equipped with high resolution lenses that recorded the explosion and breakup at 79,000 feet. Many shot four to seven frames a second, yielding massive quantities of negative film that had to be developed and analyzed in a matter of hours. In addition, 60 black-and-white television cameras were used to analyze mechanical movements at the time of launch, and nine color television cameras recorded the ignition, lift-off and ascent.

The television networks had cut back on their coverage since the early shuttle missions, when they picked up the pictures from all nine NASA color television cameras. For the Challenger mission, they let the space agency choose among the different television pictures and recorded the NASA select feed. After the explosion the media were left with a single videotape, which would be played and replayed thousands of times. The space agency impounded the rest of the videotape in order to analyze the cause of the accident.

WEIGHING THE OPTIONS

If you decide that you will need the capability to provide photographs and video of the news event, you'll have several options, depending on your budget and the amount of control you want to have over the shooting and distribution of pictures. The three basic approaches you can take are to use in-house capabilities if you have them, work out a pool arrangement with news media, or hire free-lancers. Each has benefits and drawbacks.

In-house photography and video is by far the easiest road to take if you already have photographers, camera personnel, and production capabilities within your organization. The advantages are obvious. They are likely to know the people who are involved in the news story. They also will be familiar with the technical aspects of what is happening as well as the facilities where it all is taking place. Because they are employees, you won't have to worry about copyrights, work-for-hire agreements, daily rates, or distribution charges. Most important, they will be working for your organization, so you'll call the shots and make the decisions about what will be released.

The epitome of in-house photography and video staffs will be found at the White House, where a staff of photographers and cameramen document any presidential activities that may be of historical significance. On many occasions they also provide the news media with visuals when the president is at Camp David or involved in activities not open to the press. Members of the White House photographic staff have been selected primarily for their skill in catching the personal and human interest activities of the president with his staff, government leaders, important visitors, and members of his family.

Some organizations, particularly corporations, have spent hundreds of thousands of dollars on audiovisual equipment and facilities, and with that capability their photographers and cameramen are likely to tell management they are well qualified to handle any news assignment. If nothing else, it's a matter of their own professional pride; but just because someone is in-house and being paid a salary doesn't mean they're right to do a specific job. "If you have an in-house attorney and you suddenly find yourself with a big merger or acquisition, you are likely to go to outside legal talent," observed Ben Chapnick of Black Star, a photographic agency. "You have to judge your photographic capability just as you would judge your business capability, your accounting capability, or your legal capability. It's no different."[71]

The biggest drawback to using your in-house photographic and video capabilities to supply the news media is likely to be in the quality of the results. The videotaped interview of Barney Clark three months after his artificial heart implant was handled by the University of Utah Medical Center and was of such poor quality that it made Clark appear and sound even worse than he was.

There's a world of difference between news photographers and cameramen who are constantly fighting deadlines and trying to get shots that will satisfy a demanding photo editor or news director, and the photographers who work in an institutional environment, whether it's corporate, nonprofit, academic, or governmental. They may have started out in the news business, but it doesn't take many weeks of shooting for the employee newspaper, setting up technical photographs, or videotaping sales training sessions before any good photographer or camera person begins to lose his or her deadline mentality and photojournalism skills.

That doesn't mean you shouldn't use them during an onslaught. On the contrary, take advantage of that resource where they are best suited. Your photographers and camera people can be very important in documenting the situation and providing the technical photography and video that will be of no interest to the news media. They also can shoot for your internal communications programs and photograph special situations for the participants when you wouldn't want to use a free-lancer or news photographer.[72]

Using the media for photography and video is an effective way of supplying suitable visuals that has the distinct advantage of ensuring good-quality photojournalism and not costing you anything to provide. You have two options to consider: arranging photo opportunities or using a pool.

Even if it's only for a few minutes, news organizations prefer to shoot their own still and video pictures and then get out. It takes advance planning and clear-cut understandings with the participants and the news media, but in many instances that kind of photo opportunity can be the best way to handle the situation, if it can be done quickly without disrupting the activities that are the focus of the news. "In an Oval Office photo opportunity, you had to get five or six reporters and about 70 still and TV cameras in and out fast," Denny Brisley recalled. "We didn't want to waste the time of the president and the people with him, considering what they were waiting to discuss, but the media had to get those pictures out. We had a number of ways to herd the press in and out of there in a few minutes. The general public only sees the end result of the photo opportunity, but people wouldn't believe what it's like behind the scenes during those few minutes when everything is happening."[73] Brisley also suggested that you build in some distance between the photographers and the participants and keep stray aides out of the picture. The press may miss something that's said, but there often will be jostling for position which in one instance resulted in a high government official being poked in the face with a microphone boom.

If your organization doesn't want to have a media mob scene for a few minutes at the news site, and if you want to reduce the chances of having helicopters flying into your canyon, then the best approach may be to use a pool. The way a pool works is that a designated still photographer and video camera crew are permitted to shoot and distribute the visuals to all news organizations, including their own. You have the option of deciding who will be in the pool, but you're better off letting the news media work that out among themselves, in case there is a foul-up in the handling of the photography or video. Pool arrangements are supposed to be gentlemen's agreements between the news organizations covering the story, but if the photographer or camera crew that has the assignment can get any advantage on its competition, they will. That's when you don't want to be in the middle.

Even if you are using in-house or free-lance photographers, it's a good idea to have a media pool arrangement set up in advance in case your primary photographers are not available or there's a good opportunity for the news organizations to shoot their own pictures. Although they are fiercely competitive, the news organizations can get together and set up a pool in a matter of minutes. Tell them how many people can be included and what the general parameters should be, and within an hour the media can set up a pool according to your specifications and be ready to go.

The optimum photo pool is two still photographers and one television crew consisting of a camera person and sound technician. Tell them you want a wire service photographer to shoot black-and-white photos for wire service distribution to daily newspapers and a news magazine or photo agency photographer to shoot in color for magazines, newspapers that print color photos, and television. If there's only room for one photographer, he can shoot in color negative film, which can be converted to color or black and white. The television crew should be from one of the networks, because they are more accustomed than the local stations to pool arrangements and the network television news formats.

If the pool can be expanded, plan to include four reporters so you will have written as well as visual coverage at the scene. One wire service correspondent should be from the other major wire service. The same is true of the television correspondent, who should be from a different network than the camera crew. Include a radio correspondent from a third network and one newspaper reporter from the nearby area so your local media is represented along with the national news organizations.

The only question you should be asking is how the news organizations in the pool can handle all of the requests for photos, video, and information from other members of the media in time for everyone's deadline. The networks and wire services do that routinely. The potential problem would be with a photographer or camera crew from a news organization that has never been in a pool situation before and doesn't have the capability for producing large numbers of photos or video copies to meet the demand. To avoid an uproar later on, ask the members of the media who set up the pool to resolve that distribution problem before you will accept the pool and arrange to get them into the site of the news story.

For a pool situation to be handled quickly and effectively, there has to be some advance preparations so no surprises will occur when you show up with the news media. Visit the site an hour or two before the pool is scheduled to be there to see how things are going and to decide where the media can go to get their shots and ask questions, if reporters are to be included. The best bet is to take along one of the pool photographers to scout the scene. He can take light meter readings and suggest the best locations to get good visuals and ask questions in the shortest possible time. When you get back from the site, he'll brief the other members of the pool on what to plan for and what equipment will be needed.

It's also a good idea to take some notes that will help the media. You may even want to make a rough sketch of where the subjects will be and the areas that are being set aside for the pool. Estimate the distances and note that on the diagram. Also do a sensory check. What's the temperature? How much light will there be and from what direction? Is there any wind? What's the noise level?

While you're there, make sure the participants at the scene know what will happen, and also brief any security or law enforcement personnel on duty so they will be expecting you. You may even want them to help you in setting up the areas where the media will be allowed to go, but request that they stay clear of the cameras. With the right kind of planning and preparations, you'll find that pool situations go far more easily and quickly than you or the participants expect. The media is used to getting things done in a hurry when they have to, and with a little assistance from you they can get good to excellent results in a few minutes at the site.

Hiring free-lancers to shoot your photographs and video pictures can give you skill in providing news-quality photography and video and allow you to maintain control of the picture selection and distribution. The free-lance option can run from hiring someone to shoot photos or video to selecting photographers affiliated with major agencies, which can serve as the pool by distributing photos and video to the news media in the United States and abroad. The trade-offs are that good free-lance photographers and video crews are expensive, with rates running from $1,000 to $2,500 a day plus expenses, although there will be plenty of room for horse trading if more than just the shooting is involved.

You also will be adding an additional area of supervision, one that can chew up to 25 to 33 percent of your time unless you have someone working for you with a background in photojournalism. "When you hire your own free-lancer, you hire on another level of problems, worries, and responsibilities," observed Tom Hardin of the *Courier-Journal*. "The person who manages that free-lancer has to decide who will edit the pictures and sign off on their distribution. Does the free-lancer have the experience to work quickly in order to meet the media's deadlines? Is the free-lancer's lab set up to turn out a lot of pictures in a big hurry?" When you hire a free-lancer you suddenly have a jillion more questions. If that person screws up, everybody's going to know it because it's your area of responsibility."[74]

Good free-lance photographers and, to a lesser extent, video camera crews often will be tied into agencies and syndicates, which contact them to handle specific assignments, and in other instances will find a publication or television outlet that is interested in their material. The benefit of this arrangement to the organization is that most agencies represent an array of photographers or video crews and can provide one with the specific skills and experience required for your assignment. They also service the major news magazines and other news organizations in the United States and abroad on a regular basis and thus are accustomed to handling rapid processing and distribution.

Selecting free-lancers is not as difficult as it may seem. The optimum situation is to use photographers and camera crews from the locality where the news event will be occurring so they can be readily available when you need them and you will not be saddled with their living expenses while they have the assignment. Start off by checking with members of the media to find out who the best free-lancers are in your area. Ben Chapnick of Black Star suggests that you can call any newspaper photo editors in the United States with a question like that on a news story, and they will give you legitimate recommendations. "Suddenly you'll have friends everywhere, and you'll get good information because they know they will be a part of it," Chapnick said.

If you've been impressed with the photography in a local daily newspaper, ask the photo editor for several recommendations. Don't be surprised if you are given the names of photographers on the paper's staff. Many have employment agreements that permit free-lancing. In other instances the name may be a photographer who used to be with the paper but now shoots free-lance and has done assignments like yours. Other good sources are the photo editors for *Time*, *Newsweek*, or other major news magazines. Who would they call if they had an assignment in your locality like the one you've outlined?

The same relationship is true of television news camera crews. Many free-lance news camera people started with local television stations and then went on to the networks. The good ones have maintained their ties with newsrooms while also shooting for video production houses, advertising agencies, and companies. News directors will call them because they know using free-lance video crews will be more efficient or less expensive in many instances than flying in one of their regular crews for the assignment.

Whether you use photographers from a local newspaper or TV station, free-lancers, or in-house people, they all should be asked the same basic questions before you decide which visual approach to take:

1. What's their professional background, and how many years of experience have they had?
2. What networks, news services, or photo agencies are they affiliated with, and what are their contractual obligations?
3. What have been their most noteworthy news assignments?
4. What assignments have they had that are similar to yours, and what examples do they have that show the results?
5. What types of shooting do they prefer and are they most comfortable with? What don't they like?
6. What would they recommend you do in planning to shoot this assignment? (That may seem like free advice, but it's also an indication of their creativity and pragmatism.)
7. What sets them apart from the other photographers and camera crews you are considering?
8. After the pictures have been shot, what capabilities can they provide for processing, duplication, and distribution to any member of the news media? What will be the turnaround time?
9. How will photo editing and distribution be handled?
10. Who owns the pictures?
11. What would be the costs of their services?

Each photographer or camera person should provide you with a portfolio or videotapes of their work, which should be reviewed carefully after they leave. Consider which candidates provided samples of the kind of shooting you are going to need, and which ones gave you overly artistic and unrelated examples? Then check their references to see how they get along with other people when the pressure is on, and whether they listen and grasp what is being explained to them. More than anything else you will need someone you can work with easily, who is sensitive to your needs and to the politics of the situation, and who will be aware of more than just what's coming through the camera lens.

THE COMPLEXITIES OF DISTRIBUTION

Shooting your own photographs and video is one thing; providing them to the worldwide news media is something else. Distribution of news photos and video in the United States and abroad can get very complicated and is a process where mistakes can be costly if the participants are to share in the revenues those visuals will generate. You should decide at the outset of the event what your distribution policy will be, because it can affect your entire relationship with the media and with the participants in many instances.

The White House, NASA, and any government agency have a very simple distribution process for photos and video—they give it away. The shooting and processing costs were paid for by the American taxpayer, so visuals are considered public domain and are given out free of charge. Accredited members of the news media, as well as photo agencies and other distribution sources, can then sell them for whatever price they can get. "We really don't care. It's public domain anyway," NASA's Ed Harrison observed. "It's in NASA's best interests to get it on the counter so you as the American public see it. If you're a commercial user, all you have to do is pay the charge for the print or transparency and sell it any way you can."[75] Photos issued by NASA have the following caption on the back defining the provisions for its use:

> Photo credit: NASA or National Aeronautics and Space Administration. No copyright protection is asserted for this photography. If a recognizable person appears in this photograph, use may infringe a right of privacy or publicity. It may not be used to state or imply the endorsement by NASA or any NASA employee of any commercial product, process, or service, or used in any other manner that may mislead. Accordingly it is requested that if this photograph is used in advertising, and other commercial promotion, layout and copy be submitted to NASA prior to release.[76]

The initial interest in photographs and video can seem overwhelming, but it may be the tip of the iceberg compared to the potential aftermarket. The Associated Press and United Press International operate the most extensive photographic distribution systems for the news media. They usually try to shoot their own pictures or obtain photos from one of their member news organizations. If outside news media are not allowed to take pictures, they will pick up whatever photos are being distributed and transmit them by photographic facsimile machines via phone lines and satellites from the nearest AP or UPI bureau. Nonsubscribers also can obtain the pictures from AP or UPI but at prices ranging upward from $75. The photos are then archived by Wide World Photos and Bettmann Photos, subsidiaries of AP or UPI, respectively, which offer them for sale to anyone requesting specific pictures or photos of a general situation or scene.

Photo agencies like Black Star, Gamma Liaison, and Sygma also want black-and-white prints and color transparencies, as well as the video. Rather than servicing a vast network of newspapers on a daily basis, their primary market will be magazines in the United States and abroad as well as foreign television networks, which pay for exclusive pictures from any source in developing color photo spreads or video to broaden their coverage of the story.

The important point is that the wire services and photo agencies are anything but nonprofit entities. They are providing an important service to the news media, and they are going to make considerable money in the process, with pictures from the news event as their source of revenue. The participants may be employees or public figures who cannot participate in the revenues generated by the worldwide photo and video distribution process. However, if they are private citizens, there had better be a clear understanding beforehand with the participants regarding who owns any photography and video and whether they will be allowed to receive any revenues from the distribution of these visuals.

Bill Schroeder, Murray Haydon, and Jack Burcham each signed a patient consent form authorizing the artificial heart operation, which, among other things, stated in Paragraph 13.0:

> I am fully aware of the considerable public interest anticipated in my story as a recipient of a Total Artificial Heart. I am also aware that the Humana Hospital-Audubon has an obligation to disseminate medical information concerning my hospital course as deemed appropriate in the judgment of my physician. In addition to those materials identified in Paragraph 12 [information and visuals for medical education] the Humana Hospital-Audubon, as approved by my physician, is authorized to make, or permit to be made, photographs, slides, films, videotapes, recordings, or other material(s) that may be used in newspapers, magazine articles, television, radio broadcasts, movies, or any other media or means of dissemination. I consent to the use of my name, likeness, or voice for such purposes and I release the Humana Heart

Institute, Humana Hospital-Audubon, their officers, agents, and employees from all claims of liability with respect to the showing, use, or dissemination of such materials(s). I understand that the materials which are public, as described in this paragraph, will protect my modesty and be within generally accepted bounds of good taste.[77]

The primary concern of Schroeder and his family at the time was staying alive and helping science, but the Schroeders had no idea that they were giving up the rights to share in at least $300,000 in revenues. Lacking its own capabilities to provide the media with visuals of the artificial heart procedure and patient recovery, Humana hired a free-lance photographer and video crew. We felt some control over editing and distribution of pictures should be maintained, rather than letting the media shoot and distribute whatever they chose. MedStar Communications, which had produced the video backgrounders on the artificial heart, handled the video, and William Strode, a former Louisville *Courier-Journal* photographer who was a co-recipient of two Pulitzer Prizes while he was with the paper, shot both color and black-and-white photographs.

Strode, who lives near Louisville, was to be the primary source of visuals for the news media during the operation and throughout Bill Schroeder's long recovery. He is affiliated with Black Star, and to lessen Humana's involvement in photographic and video distribution, Black Star was to have been used for distribution of photographs to magazines in the United States and abroad and for overseas distribution of television materials. The arrangement, however, was vetoed at the last minute by Humana's George Atkins, after the Associated Press urged that all photos and video be given to everyone free of charge.

Chapnick of Black Star believes the exclusive first-usage rights to the still photographs and videotape of the Schroeder surgery would have been worth prices ranging from $5,000 in less-developed countries to $50,000 in Western Europe. There also would have been residual sales from monthly magazines, smaller publications, and books. According to Chapnick, "That story, in Germany alone, conservatively would have brought $50,000, maybe more, if one of the major magazines knew they would be the only ones getting it. And a situation existed like that."[78]

What Atkins failed to grasp was that visuals that are given away will be resold by photo and video distribution services, including the Associated Press. Pictures of Bill Schroeder's artificial heart operation, shot by Bill Strode and distributed by Black Star for Humana free of charge to the news media, could have been purchased for use in this book even though they are copyrighted by Strode and Humana. The prices quoted by Wide World Photos (a subsidiary of AP), Bettmann Photos (the UPI counterpart), and Black Star or Gamma Liaison (two photographic agencies) provide an interesting perspective on the aftermarket for news pictures. For one-time usage of a full-page photo in a book distributed only in North America, the prices quoted were as follows:

	Color	*Black-and-White*
Wide World (AP)	$175	$ 90
Bettmann Photos (UPI)*	200	65
Gamma Liaison	300	200
Black Star†	312	218

*Bettmann would not sell pictures of the artificial heart, stating they were distributed free by Humana on a one-time basis and there would be legal problems if they were resold. Bettmann's prices are for photos in their library, which are available for resale.

†Black Star provides one third of revenues from resale of the Schroeder photos to the Schroeder family under an agreement with Humana and the Schroeders signed approximately a year after the operation. However, sales have been nil because the photos originally were given away by all sources.

Substantial revenues were lost from potential sales to news organizations that were willing to purchase the videotape of the operation. "Italian television wanted to buy the video of the operation and the coverage for $50,000, which was a lot of money," Chapnick said. "The sale was canceled because all of the video was out free over the satellite. Television in Britain was interested and prepared under a negotiating setup to consider a very large sum that might have been close to $30,000. Again it was canceled."

The complexities of worldwide news photo and video distribution make this a business where amateurs can easily make costly mistakes. Yet you need to protect your organization's rights, and those of the participants, if the visuals prove to be valuable from a historical as well as financial perspective. Here's what you can do in advance to eliminate the confusion and consternation that will occur when people suddenly realize they don't have rights to the photos or the money they thought was theirs.

1. Decide Who Owns the Copyright

Any photographic or video material produced is copyrighted, and the provisions of the U.S. copyright law regarding its ownership are very clearly defined. Whenever your organization hires a still or video photographer on a free-lance basis, you are purchasing the one-time use of the visuals they produce for that specific assignment. Ownership of the copyright remains with the photographer or camera person, and the materials cannot be used again without their permission.

The copyright for any visuals will only be owned by the organization if (1) the photographer/camera person is an employee and has signed an agreement assigning the rights to the employer or (2) the organization has signed a work-for-hire agreement with the free-lancer, which specifies that the copyright and ownership of the materials to be produced will remain with the organization. Work-for-hire agreements obviously are beneficial if there is any chance you may want the visuals for more than one purpose. You are likely to find that the photographer or camera person will ask for a higher daily rate if they are to sign an agreement in return for giving up the residual rights to the materials they produce.

2. Define the Copyright and Distribution Provisions

Any photograph, video material, or written information distributed to the news media should carry a © followed by the year it was produced and the name of the copyright owner. The copyright caption should be clearly legible on the border of photos or in the leader on videotapes. It also should specify any conditions tied to the distribution and use.

The options run from NASA's approach of giving up its copyright and allowing anyone to sell the visuals to stipulating that the photo or video is not to be sold without the written permission of the copyright owner. The latter approach will severely restrict your initial distribution because resellers won't have time to get that kind of written authorization and still meet the media's news deadlines. It also will raise the ire of the wire services and photo agencies, which will lose out on substantial revenues; but it's up to the copyright owner, not the media, to decide how the material will be distributed and paid for.

If you want video distribution limited to the U.S. media so its use can be sold overseas, the videotape leader should have a legend that shows who owns the copyright and gives the name and phone number of the person the overseas media must contact for rights to use the pictures.

If your organization retains the copyright, you had better have access to attorneys who are in a position to take legal action when infringements occur. A picture of Bill Schroeder given by Humana to the Louisville representative of Gamma Liaison, a photographic agency, subsequently appeared in the *New York Times*—crediting the agency as the source and its representative as the photographer. The agency had altered Bill Strode's copyright and photo credit on the back of the picture before it was sold to the *Times*. On other occasions pictures that ran in local newspapers across the country gave credit to the Associated Press when the photos were actually provided by Humana and carried Strode's copyright on the back. Both are clear violations of the copyright law, but these kinds of infractions will slip by unless you have an attorney who will go after the offenders. When that happens, the word will get out and copyright violations will fall off in a hurry because no news organization wants to be accused of copyright infringement.

3. Decide about Compensation

You can take the NASA approach and distribute the visuals free of charge or for a slight charge to cover the processing costs. However, retain the copyright ownership. As far as whether the participants will share in any revenues, that should be clearly understood in advance and outlined in writing so there will be no misunderstandings later on, as there have been with the Schroeders. The family thought Humana owned the pictures. That was our plan, and an agreement was being worked out with Black Star to sell the photos and video overseas, which would have provided the Schroeders with revenues from the sale. However, after Atkins's decision to give the pictures away, we didn't have time before Schroeder's surgery to draw up a new agreement. That meant Strode owned the copyright. Worse yet, because pictures were to be given out without restriction, we had no way of knowing who sold the pictures to other news organizations.

If the participants want to sell the pictures and your organization is willing to give them the rights, you'll be smart to let someone else be their broker with the news media. There should be a written agreement specifying who owns the copyright to any photos or video and what the rights of the organization and participants will be in the use of the pictures. They should have their own agent negotiate with potential photo and video distributors, just as they will if they get involved in checkbook journalism situations.

It's also a good idea to get a photo/video release for any participant who will be actively involved in the news story. This can be done in advance so you don't have to worry about it when the story breaks, but it's one of those "Murphy's Law" situations that needs to be considered. Dale Minor, the MedStar producer for the videotaping of Schroeder's operation and the videotape backgrounders, noted, "Whenever possible we get people who are in our pictures to sign a release, not just the people we interview. We sign everybody. When we do a job with Humana you'd think we wouldn't have to worry about that, but we do. Lawsuits will hit the deepest pockets. We sign people with the understanding that they are not being paid for this."[79]

4. Let Someone Else Handle Picture Distribution and Retention

The only businesses equipped to handle the processing and distribution of news photos and video are those already in the news business. Even if your organization has an extensive audiovisual capability, it doesn't have the equipment, the people, or the experience to process the large numbers of photographic prints or videotapes the media needs daily, often in a matter of minutes.

You may have a good working relationship with a local newspaper and TV station and, therefore, can use them to handle distribution to other members of the print and broadcast media. Another alternative is to use one of the major photo agencies since it is not affiliated with any news organizations. The agency can be paid a straight distribution charge if the photos or video are to be given free of charge, or it can collect a commission from news organizations which will pay for the visuals.

The other sevice they can provide is cataloging and safe-keeping of photos and videotapes. If you leave that to novices, the originals will quickly disappear into someone's slide carousel or pile of videotapes in a file cabinet somewhere after they were used once for a presentation. Then when someone needs them, the head scratching and rummaging around will begin.

Your local newspaper and TV stations know the importance of storing the originals and having a system for making duplicates so the masters are never lost. Leave it in their hands, have a photo agency to do it for you, or pay them to help you in setting up an in-house system. The important point is not to leave those visuals in the hands of someone who doesn't understand their value and know how to protect them so you always will have access to the pictures you need.

5. Put Someone in Charge of Coordinating Photography and Video

Unless your professional background is in news photography or TV, you need someone who understands the technicalities and speaks the language of the media to help them get the pictures they need or order copies of still photos or video in the correct format. They also should know how to get the visuals to specific locations by the fastest possible means, which often involves the use of intercity or overseas messenger services and even satellite uplinks.

The smartest move you can make is to get someone who understands the photographic and video needs of the news media and to give them that responsibility, so you can concentrate on the media's information needs. Let them arrange photography and video, handle editing and distribution, and supervise anything else that involves visuals. Let them use their professional judgment in deciding what will work and what's the best way to get the job done with minimum disruption to the participants.

"To me the White House people are the best at planning and attending to the many details of their news events. They just plain get their ducks in a row in working with the media for an appearance of the president," Hardin of the *Courier-Journal* observed. "They also have tremendous autonomy to make decisions about pictures. Does your news organization need something special? An unusual angle or vantage point? They'll work with you on getting it as long as you've planned ahead. You can't ask for the unusual just 10 minutes before the president arrives, everyone is too busy at that time. They won't talk to you and they shouldn't be expected to under the circumstances."

HAVING A VISUALS DISTRIBUTION POLICY IS CRITICAL

The photo distribution component of your onslaught planning is critical to its success because much of your relationship with the media will depend on how you provide visuals as well as information. Your best intentions to be forthright with reporters, timely with regard to briefings and updates, accessible at all times, concerned about the media's needs, and honest about any mistakes you might have made will founder badly if you have not set forth a realistic distribution policy for photographs and video.

Your decision may be to allow the media to handle the shooting and distribution or to give the photos and video away free and wash your hands of all subsidiary rights. That's OK as long as your organization and the participants understand that news organizations and photo agencies will broker the pictures and compromise the rights of participants in the news disclosure to any compensation.

If you will be making the photo/video decisions, be prepared to spend a considerable amount of time working with news organizations trying to get photos and video, having to supervise your own camera crews or the media pool people, and dealing with photo agencies and other potential buyers, who will corner you with their requests. Finally, if you are dealing exclusively with a photographic agency, be prepared for hurt feelings, gripes from media people who feel they are being shortchanged, and complaints from the participants who believe that the photo business is getting in the way of the organization's business.

Whatever policy you adopt, make sure that it's clearly understood and that your organization can live with it. Top management may feel that picture distribution is no more than icing on the cake, but in reality it's an important element in the overall plan that can make relations with the media flow very smoothly. That's especially true when the pressure is intense and hard facts are slow in coming out of your office.

CHAPTER TEN

The News Media Is an Enigma

Reporters and journalists are, in my estimation, as interesting a crowd of rascals and misfits as will ever darken the gates of hell. Despite their tendency to run in packs and fly off like blackbirds at the sound of the first loud noise, they are a great breed of individuals because they are like most of us.[80]

There's been a lot of very good reporting of the Challenger story in my view. Some terrific work has been done, both investigative and straight coverage, but we've had a few who really came at it from the approach that they wanted to make a name for themselves. I don't think there's much a public affairs person can do to turn around that mindset.[81]

WHO ARE THESE GUYS?

The news media is an enigma that few outside the journalistic community really understand. The press often seems to have a narcissistic desire to make itself look bad, especially on television. Why else would we be shown so much footage of camera crews and dozens of reporters mobbing the innocent and the indicted night after night after night? At the same time, the reporters, producers, camera crews, and photographers who will be covering a breaking story will be realists. They know they are an added burden and will be distrusted by many of those involved in the news event. They will be looking for the path of least resistance that will allow them to provide the most information to their newsrooms with the least amount of hassle.

Regardless of whether they are local or national, the journalists will have certain similarities. You'll be dealing with a professional group that tends to be intelligent, well educated, and underpaid, especially in smaller markets. By nature they will be inquisitive, suspicious, and skeptical. Their professional training emphasizes independent thinking and consideration of all facets of a situation, both good and bad. They didn't go into the news business to make a fortune but rather because they like the action, the diversity of their assignments, and the challenge of ferreting out information that can be developed into an interesting news story.

There's also the satisfaction of seeing the results of their work in public. But during a major story they pay a price in the long hours that are required and the lack of understanding that occurs all too often with editors or news directors who make the assignments and then the final decisions about how the story will be published or broadcast. You will find that the bureaucracy, politics, and breakdowns in communications are no different in news organizations than in any other type of institution.

You will be dealing with a diversity of professional skills among the journalists. Often the local wire service bureaus will be supplemented by correspondents and radio reporters from other offices or their New York or Washington headquarters. The major newspapers, such as *The Wall Street Journal*, the *New York Times*, the *Washington Post*, the *Los Angeles Times*, and *USA Today*, are likely to have correspondents from the nearest bureau on hand, but they also may send in specialized reporters as well.

The major broadcast networks will be represented by correspondents who will feed their television news programs but often will handle network radio news broadcasts as well. They will work closely with a small army of producers, camera crews, and technical people who will descend on the scene with tons of equipment in aluminum shipping cases stuffed in vans or the largest sedans they can rent at the airport.

While your attention may be dominated by the presence of the national news organizations, they will be outnumbered by their local counterparts as well as media from other cities in the region. Some of them will show up with their new satellite transmission trucks to give the folks back home live updates from the scene. The local reporters will suddenly find themselves having the chance to cover a story that for some could be an important step toward the big leagues of journalism. They will be dealing with a wide range of stories on the news event itself, as well as a diversity of stories of local interest, all the time going head to head with correspondents from the networks, the wire services, and the national newspapers and magazines. Many of them are no more competent or qualified to cover the story than the local journalists.

The nearest AP and UPI bureaus, often a one-person operation jammed into a small room in the back of the local newspaper, suddenly will be transformed into major distribution points for news and photos that will be transmitted worldwide. The local affiliates of the major TV and radio networks will be trying to satisfy the heightened community interest in the story as well as dealing with requests from their networks for specific types of coverage to be carried nationally. Reporters and photographers who are "stringers" for national publications, and may receive one or two calls a year if they are lucky, will find themselves facing the same editorial demands and deadline pressures as the publication's regular staffers.

For the national news media, the assignment will be another in an endless odyssey that carries them hundreds of thousands of miles a year to big cities and remote places across the country and, in many instances, abroad. The reporters will be seasoned newspeople who frequently know nothing about the situation at the time they are handed the assignment. The trip to your location will be consumed in boning up on whatever details are available and planning for the first coverage. The producers for the TV crews will be working out their logistical needs considering the crews and equipment they will have to work with and the news deadlines they will be facing. Most will begin dispatching their first stories within four hours after arriving.

The national media will arrive on the scene with much the same attitude as the Marines had when landing on yet another beachhead toward the end of World War II. They know intrusion is a part of their job, and they intrude better than anybody. There is little novelty in what they do; that wore off the veteran journalists long ago. The correspondents, camera crews, and producers have learned from innumerable stories that they will have to overcome obstacles imposed by developments in the news event, the people involved, and the location. They'll be looking for all the help they can get, as long as those who help don't try to interfere with the assignment they have been given. Your job is to make sure that they get the correct information, that they report it accurately, and that they interfere as little as possible with the actual news event as it unfolds.

A REVERSED ROLE FOR THE PUBLIC RELATIONS PROFESSIONALS

Public relations people who have dealt with journalists in the past will find themselves in a totally new supply-and-demand situation. The pressure from the news media for information and interviews will far exceed anything you can provide. You probably are accustomed to accommodating any journalist who was doing a favorable story and trying to dissuade reporters pursuing a negative angle. You won't have as much latitude now. With hundreds of journalists wanting information at the very moment you receive it, you will have all you can do to keep pace with their demands for information, visuals, and interviews and also maintain control of the situation.

Why the difference between pure public relations material and the sudden ravenous appetite for hard facts? You're no longer talking about feature material which can be run any time there's time or space. This is hard news, where deadlines will be minutes away and the competition for interviews and an exclusive angle will be immense. It's a new ball game that will be covered very differently by the people you've dealt with in the past and by a whole new breed of journalists you've never dealt with before. They have been sent in to cover the hard news stories of the day and don't like to get involved in the frills and features that so many public relations people are inclined to pitch.

With a story of any national significance you are going to attract outside newspeople who come in with a skeptical eye. It's nothing personal. That's their journalistic training and their style, which has been seasoned in covering news stories where they often get half the story from the participants and have to dig out the rest from a variety of sources. They expect to be told only part of the truth, and they expect that you want them to put your organization in the best possible light. And since reporters have to come up with news stories that sell newspapers or increase the viewing audience, don't expect to satisfy them with traditional public relations handouts.

THE LOVE-HATE RELATIONSHIP WITH PUBLIC RELATIONS

Experienced journalists don't always like it, but they know that the public relations people will be an important factor in their coverage of the story. "I'm on one end pressing for more information, and the people are on the other pressing back, so there's this dialectic," said Paul Raeburn, science editor of the Associated Press. "The PR person is the negotiator, and he will determine where this thing settles out. So the PR guy is out in no-man's-land between us and the people in the news."[82] But Raeburn and the other reporters know from experience that what they get will be what the organization wants to provide. They know there will be conflicting views about how much information should be disclosed, the approval process, and what latitude the public relations people are to have.

You find you get to know the reporters, producers, and photographers very quickly when they arrive—and vice versa. They will size up you and the other spokespersons to see how comfortable you are in dealing with the press. Anyone who has the job of working with the news media may be a little awed at first in talking to someone from a TV network or one of the national news magazines. That's understandable. The question the journalists will be asking themselves is, How knowledgeable and comfortable are the spokespersons in discussing what has happened? Are they forthright and candid, or do they seem uncertain of the facts, fearful, and close-mouthed? Every journalist has encountered public relations people who have been all too happy to work with them on a story that promotes the institution, but who have hollow excuses about why they cannot get involved if the story gets into anything negative or controversial.

Honesty

The single biggest problem that the news media has with public relations people is lying. That's a harsh word, but news reporters feel they often are lied to by public relations spokespersons who don't know how to respond, what to say, or are just carrying out the instructions of their superiors. Often it's not intentional. They get tired, frustrated, worn down by the incessant requests for information, or they just get careless in what they say.

The lying could even be well intentioned, as it was at Loma Linda when the public relations staff gave out the incorrect birthdate and also denied that Baby Fae had previously been sent home to die. Their intent was to try to protect the privacy of the family. What they did was destroy the credibility and integrity of the Medical Center and the Baby Fae experiment in the eyes of the publics who saw the story through the news media prism.

They may be accused of lying because they may not always get the most objective assessment from their sources when they are given the details for routine updates or the responses to questions the press has been asking. Fatigue, negative developments, or unhappiness with the media coverage can do a lot to warp the information coming from the scene of the story.

The best insurance policy against lying that a public relations spokesperson can take out is to understand as much as possible about what's happening from talking to others at the scene before getting together with the principals to go over the details. If a problem with the situation will make the update more sensitive, get a second and third opinion on the important elements in the disclosure, and your proposed information for the media, before going back for approvals.

An excellent technique to increase the accuracy of the information is to take along a tape recorder and interview the principals so you have it in their words. The comments in the interview can be the basis for a written update, but the principals also are likely to be more careful in what they say if they know it's being recorded and will be distributed to the news media. Once you have the tape, you can offer excerpts to the media as an actuality so they have a first-person interpretation of what has happened.

LIKES AND DISLIKES OF THE MEDIA

You quickly find that the journalists will have a number of likes and dislikes and that you'll never please everyone. KSL-TV's Ed Yeates commented, "Somebody is going to be grumped, but it's not that hard to satisfy the vast majority of the media covering a major story if you give them what they need to file their stories."[83] Most of their likes and dislikes in covering a story are logical and relate directly to the job they have been sent in to do.

A major source of contention will be in how you differentiate between the local and national news organizations. You probably will know some of the reporters, or at least the names of the local news media they work for, but suddenly you'll also be dealing with the major league news organizations—the television and radio networks, the prestigious national newspapers, and the weekly news magazines, all with circulation in the millions. Their reporters and producers know how to use that instant name recognition and the immense audience figures very persuasively in getting you to give them preferential consideration in interviewing the key participants when their availability is limited.

But what about the reporters from the local newspapers, radio, and television stations? There will be a natural tendency to give them short shrift, and that can be a serious mistake. First of all, they will cover your organization long after the national news media is gone. There will be times when you'll need their support and the benefit of the doubt that comes from maintaining a consistent working relationship, whether it's a big news story or a routine announcement. Another consideration is that they know far more about the background of the organization, as well as sources of important insights and details, than do their national counterparts. Too strong a preference for the national news media in providing access to the key people can result in local newspeople deciding to build a good story around their own sources, or taking an editorial approach that may not be to your liking.

A story that originates with your local newspaper or television stations invariably will get reworked and carried by the national news media. This doesn't apply if it's the other way around. What will result is anger and frustration among the local media, especially if the preferential treatment persists. "The Salt Lake City press noticed that DeVries, Jarvik, and the key players were appearing on the big news shows like 'Today' and 'Good Morning, America,' but if you were a local affiliate you somehow didn't have priority," Ed Yeates recalled. "That kind of unfairness really PO'ed the local media. . . Dwan was making a mistake to think that just because we were from Salt Lake, we should not get the same consideration as the guys from 'ABC Nightline.' Sure, the networks will give you more exposure, but you'd better be fair with the local press if you expect the press to be fair with you."

If you really want to raise the hackles of the journalists, show one news organization a little favoritism. There's nothing that will incite outrage in the pack faster than to have someone get a bone while everyone else goes hungry. Everyone will complain that they are not getting the same consideration as their competitors, but they take it for granted that some favoritism will be shown for their hometown media or (grudgingly) the national press. But look out if the preferential consideration is overt and comes from the public relations people.

Humana found that out when Phyllis George, the anchorwoman for "CBS Morning News," was granted an exclusive series of interviews with the Schroeder family and Doctor DeVries. Her questions were anything but penetrating, but those interviews enraged the other networks and the media as a whole. They questioned her journalistic credentials, much less her understanding of the artificial heart program. It didn't take long for them to conclude that George Atkins had set up the interviews because he had served in the cabinet of Phyllis George's husband, John Y. Brown, Jr., when Brown was governor of Kentucky.

Another major gripe of journalists is the stall—not returning a phone call or responding with the requested information before a reporter's deadline. The tactic frequently is used in dealing with media working on an unfavorable story. It is infuriating to reporters who are fighting deadlines, and they make a mental note when it happens. Tom Hardin, director of photography of the *Courier-Journal*, considers one of the most frustrating problems in working with corporate PR people to be, "May I ask who's calling, please? Well, he's out right now." "You know damn good and well he's sitting there chewing on the phone," Hardin says. "That creates tremendous credibility problems. People in my business laugh at that. They laugh at the corporate PR people who play dodge 'em."[84]

The stall often works because you have the upper hand—access to the information. But it also can backfire because you don't know what else the reporter has in the way of information and who he has been talking to. By not responding, you will not find out until the story appears, and you'll also lose the chance to make sure your organization's position has been clearly conveyed. There's not much you can say if the story is negative and you didn't do anything to try to balance it out. And if there's any benefit of the doubt to be had, you automatically lose it by not returning that call.

The press doesn't have time or patience for game playing on a major news story. If they feel they can't trust the spokespeople for an organization, they get angry, they get desperate, and they get ingenious. Within a few minutes they will have discounted their existing information source and will be looking for new, unauthorized, sources. At that point the finger of control has just been pulled out of the organization's media relations dike.

THE DIFFICULTIES IN COVERING A MAJOR STORY

Although reporters typically are skeptical, they are not vindictive. The most basic dilemma they have with any major story is how to cover it in a way that is intelligent, and critical if necessary, without alienating the participants and other sources that can provide what they need to continue reporting the story and to stay ahead of the competition. As we mentioned in Chapter 7, most of the newspeople will know very little about the story or its important details when they arrive to begin their coverage. Many of the print and broadcast journalists reporting on the artificial heart operations couldn't tell the difference between the left and right ventricles in the heart, and which pumped blood to what part of the body. A number of the news reports from the Wilberg fire described the "safe area" in the mine as if it were a little room where the miners could shut the door and be safe until rescued. In reality, it was a short, unfinished tunnel segment.

General assignment reporters will be looking for quick answers and solutions to the problems the participants have encountered, which Union Carbide's Jackson Browning noted in observing, "The press thinks the minute the cloud appears you're going to know exactly what's in the cloud and how it happened to be there and its potential for harming plant personnel and their neighbors over the fence. The world isn't that simple."[85] Most reporters are not going to report on the technical nature of your news story, nor do they have time to take an advanced course in all aspects of your organization's business. That information may be important to the special correspondents and investigative reporters, who are likely to get into more depth and detail if they cover the story. The general news people will want to get the immediate facts, write them up, or send them back to their newsrooms with some kind of edge or interesting angle that will keep them ahead of the pack.

PACK JOURNALISM

Ask any journalist about pack journalism, and he or she will tell you two things: they detest it, and they don't get involved in it personally or professionally. Then ask them how often they will step aside to let their competition get the edge. I have yet to find anyone who is willing to let that happen.

What pack journalism tends to do is adversely affect the judgment, sensitivity, taste, and accuracy of reporters and their news organizations in covering the story. Their professional sensibilities are influenced by the frenzy to file the story before the competition, to do whatever it takes to get it on the air or in the paper. And they are playing for keeps. According to several people at NASA, three veteran reporters were fired in the weeks after the Challenger accident because they were beaten too often by their competition.

The beat-everyone-else attitude tends to surface among many of the journalists, which results in the "how do you feel" questions being asked simply because they don't really know what to ask someone who obviously is in shock, but they need the visual and sound bite that will convey the human misery and set them apart from the competition. The pack journalism phenomenon also breeds the instant investigative reporters, who will focus in on anything that seems to have a tinge of controversy and will blow it out of proportion. George Strait of ABC observed, "There isn't a reporter in the world who hasn't overwritten a story for its drama to get it on the front page, or in the newscast, and that's wrong! It happens, and it's wrong, and what it takes is better journalism."[86]

Good journalism is necessary, and it will be practiced by a large majority of the news media in covering an event. But, as we've discussed, it also takes someone to set realistic disclosure guidelines and policies that will provide the media with sufficient information to get its job done, without excessively disrupting the activities of those involved in the story. That won't be easy considering the speed and the intensity of the media's efforts to cover a breaking story from the moment the first word is out.

HOW THE MEDIA COVERS A BREAKING NEWS STORY

If news organizations have any warning about an impending story, as was the case with the artificial heart, the local media will immediately get involved in some heavy research and editorial planning. The *Courier-Journal*, for instance, sent its medical writer, Mike King, to Salt Lake City the day after the announcement that Dr. DeVries was transferring the artificial heart clinical trial to Humana. King's interviews in Salt Lake City and discussions with the local reporters revealed the problems DeVries had with the Institutional Review Board at the University of Utah Medical Center, which monitors clinical trials and experimental procedures. The logical question was, How would the IRB at Humana Hospital-Audubon handle the artificial heart clinical trial in view of what went on in Utah?

King asked me for the names of the IRB members at Humana Hospital-Audubon, which I later refused to provide, not wanting the members of the IRB to be exposed to the scrutiny of the media while they reviewed the artificial heart protocol. That turned out to be a tactical error. The same day King was turned down, the *Courier-Journal* filed a request under the Freedom of Information Act for any information in the FDA files on the Humana Hospital Institutional Review Board. They not only got the names of the IRB members but also records of the government's review of their work, which revealed that the Audubon IRB had been cited by the FDA for having a number of deficiencies.[87]

You are likely to see much the same type of preparation among local television stations that will develop "News Specials" combining interviews, commentary, and file footage to provide extensive background on the subject. Ed Yeates, the medical news specialist at KSL-TV in Salt Lake City, had covered the development of the artificial heart at the University of Utah for nearly 20 years and had produced two 30-minute programs on the artificial heart prior to Barney Clark's implant. One ran the evening Clark's surgery was being performed and the second was broadcast the following night.

WAVE-TV in Louisville sent a camera crew and correspondent to Salt Lake City to obtain the background information and footage for a week-long series on the artificial heart, and then produced a half-hour special that was broadcast the day of Schroeder's operation. After his first stroke, Carol Grady, the station's medical reporter, prepared a 30-minute special report on strokes that explained through interviews with stroke patients and their families how the quality of life changes for stroke patients and what can be expected during their recovery period.

On the other hand, when a major story breaks suddenly and the national news media moves in to cover it, they are likely to have little more than the initial wire service copy that triggered the assignment. They are not, however, coming in cold, not in this age of data banks. Articles and information from hundreds of sources are now available in seconds to the print and broadcast news organizations. They are routinely accessed by newsrooms in developing information that might be needed to expand the scope of the story or just to fill in the background until the situation itself is more clearly defined. Al Rossiter, Jr., the chief science correspondent for UPI, knew when he headed to Louisville to cover Bill Schroeder's artificial heart operation that his wire service already had thousands of words on various facets of the artificial heart program in its computers, which could be accessed from any UPI bureau and used in the stories he'd be developing.

Often a number of bureaus will be pulled in electronically and by phone to combine their experience in coverage of a subject and contribute sidebar information. The information and insights of the wire services and local media in Salt Lake City that covered Barney Clark were a major part of the background information following the Schroeder announcement. Many journalists in Louisville later found themselves playing the same role in backgrounding the media in Tucson who covered the emergency artificial heart implant in Tom Creighton.

WHEN THEY ARRIVE

Reporters don't go shopping for sources when they arrive to cover a story, not with the time and competitive pressures they are under. Their first stop will be at whatever facilities have been set up to inform the press. They'll seek out whoever is responsible for working with the media to get the information and visuals that are available. Journalists will stick with their initial source as long as it will provide them with the information, interviews, and visuals they need to carry out their assignment to the satisfaction of their newsrooms. With dozens of news organizations arriving by the hour, there will be a never-ending job of providing them with background information, photos, video, or whatever you have to offer. Then there will be the constant need to answer hundreds of questions from individuals and groups of reporters, ranging from the correct name spellings and ages of participants to where they can get a hotel room. The more people you can pull in to help, the better.

At Humana, we had worked for two solid months to prepare the background briefing books and photos that were the backbone of the

Schroeder press materials. The briefing center—in the basement of the Commonwealth Convention Center in Louisville—was set up in 48 hours after it was necessary to abandon the briefing facilities at the hospital. Even though the first briefing was not scheduled until 9 P.M. on Saturday night, the media began arriving around noon to make arrangements for telephones and logistical needs and to get whatever they could in the way of informal updates to file before Dr. Lansing held the initial medical briefings.

THE INITIAL BRIEFING

The prevailing attitude of the initial wave of newspeople is usually neutral. They are looking for information and insights and are not ready to take an editorial position on what has happened. Their questions will range from incisive to appallingly ignorant and insensitive. Less than an hour after the Challenger explosion, while wreckage from the shuttle was still falling into the ocean, the president's press secretary, Larry Speakes, was being asked by the White House press corps how the explosion would affect the future of the space program.

Most of the questions, however, will have a human interest angle dealing with the situation, and they will focus on how the news story has affected the participants and their families. Many of the questions will have a time orientation in pushing the participants to forecast when specific developments are likely to occur.

The correspondents for national news organizations who have previously reported on the subject, or on the participants, will emerge as the leaders of the pack. They are the ones likely to ask the most incisive or all-encompassing questions. Their assessment of the most significant aspects of the story will likely provide the framework for a majority of the coverage handled by general assignment reporters.

It will be somewhat disconcerting for the participants to realize that often the criteria for what is reported will not necessarily be what is most important but rather what can be expressed in less than a minute. The print and wire service correspondents will be looking for the headline and lead paragraph material that can be slugged into their news budgets, "skeds," and feeds to subscribers. The radio and television correspondents and producers will be after the two- to three-sentence sound bites that will reinforce or illustrate the correspondent's analysis and commentary. If you want elaboration or explanation, you're going to have to wait for the next edition of your newspaper.

WHAT THE NEWS COVERAGE WILL BE LIKE

The general news media has a well-defined focus: what will rivet the attention of readers, listeners, and viewers and what will ultimately increase circulation or broadcast ratings. That can be frustrating to a scientist or physician. "They don't consider their real audience. They think only about their peers and don't see a need or a responsibility to report to the public, even though the public has paid for part of their medical education," George Strait added. "That's a basic source of conflict between the medical profession and the media. Doctors are interested in privacy and we are interested in exposition. Those really are opposite poles, and the challenge for both of us is to find the middle ground."

The primary thrust of the initial coverage will be to report what has happened in the greatest possible detail and to balance that by focusing on the personalities of the participants. The AP's Mark Knoller commented, "When you're the lead story the hunger that your newsroom has for material is bottomless. You almost can never file too much. There are newscasts at the top of the hour, at the bottom of the hour, and updates, feeds, or actualities being sent out on the quarter hour. There's always more that you can do, and they will welcome anything you give them when you are the top story."[88]

If it's a medical story, there's much more to it than the scientific news and the technical breakthroughs. There's the human interest story, which both the general press and the medical reporters consider just as important, even though the scientists may have a tough time understanding that rationale. The public was interested in the life-and-death struggle of Bill Schroeder, who had his life saved by the JARVIK-7, but they turned on their TV sets and radios or opened their papers to find out how he was doing, not to learn what was the status of the mechanical heart.

Factual information may get stretched by reporters who are looking for a distinctive human interest angle or who just don't understand the nuances of what was said. Chuck Zehnder of the *Sun Advocate* spent considerable time in the mines of Utah and felt that the "safe room" in the Wilberg Mine was a bad job of reporting. "The media gave the picture that there was a safety chamber in there with airlocks, oxygen, and the whole works," he recalled. "All those miners had to do was to sit back in their recliners and wait to be rescued. That just wasn't true. There never was anything like that."[89]

As long as there is hard news to feed on, the media machine will run smoothly. But if there's a lull, even for a few hours, the media will begin looking for new fuel in the issues and controversy. After the initial coverage the competitive trend is to broaden the coverage with a diversity of sidebar stories, which delve into the background as well as the broader questions and issues. The unpublished dissertation of Jan Quarles, a doctoral candidate at the University of Tennessee, dealt with the print and broadcast media coverage of Bill Schroeder's artificial heart implant from the day of surgery in November 1984, until he was discharged from the hospital in April 1985. Quarles, now a professor at the University of Georgia, concluded that for the first few months the story focused on Schroeder, and that the public policy issues regarding the artificial heart were overshadowed by that story—but would develop in later months after the Haydon and Burcham implants.[90]

And as the story wears on and the hard news becomes repetitive, reporters hungry for new facts to feed their newsrooms will branch out from the information you've provided and take their own paths to develop individual stories. At this point, the news disclosure is harder to manage because many of the correspondents have developed their own leads and cultivated their private informants within your organization. You may well be asked to comment on statements from within your organization that you know are true, but you don't know where the reporter got the information.

NEWS COVERAGE OF ETHICS AND ISSUES

Some reporters beat the pack journalism problem by addressing the ethical issues in a story because that's an area where anyone can take a stand on the subject and a debate can easily be developed. But even the practitioners will get involved. "There are a lot of ethical questions out there that need to be addressed," the *Courier-Journal's* Mike King said. "The person who first articulated that for me was DeVries. He indicated that there were ethical questions that none of us were dealing with."[91] Like journalists, there are no such things as licensed or certified ethicists. Some, like Dr. Arthur Caplan of the Hastings Institute, devote their professional careers to the "what if" and "who determines" types of questions in health care and other fields, which makes excellent ammunition for the media's cannons. Dr. Caplan noted rather wryly in addressing the FACS Human Heart Replacement conference, "When things are going well it is very unusual for someone to call me up or some other medical ethicist and say, 'What are the issues?' "[92] The problem all too often is that the participants don't have the same luxury of pondering the global questions and issues as the ethicists and journalists. Rarely will they have the time or the facts, much less the background, to be addressing philosophical questions that the story may have prompted. "I felt some of the ethicists were way off base in questioning the medical decisions," said Dr. Lansing. "Not one of them has ever had to make a decision about how you should treat actual symptoms. They pontificate but they never are in the front lines with us."[93]

Many of the reporters who covered Barney Clark and the artificial heart patients at Humana indicated that if they had to do it all over again, they would have gone into the ethical considerations much earlier and to a much greater extent. As the coverage of the artificial heart clinical trials has continued, the emphasis has shifted from the purely clinical and human interest considerations to the ethical issues and questions, both in the press and within the FDA, which held hearings in December 1985 to review the progress to date and establish additional reporting guidelines for scientific and medical information.

At the same time the ethics of the news reporting itself will be scrutinized closely by the public and by the press, especially when it deals with the personal privacy of the individuals involved in the story. The concerns of Father Gerald Lynch, the priest for the San Rafael Mission near the Wilberg Mine, speak for many people who were disturbed by the excesses they saw portrayed so often in the print and broadcast media. "Where are the ethics involved? Why would someone totally uninvolved go to a family?" Father Lynch asked. "When you get into that whole area of human tragedy and human feeling, and the media is trying to capture that 'human interest' angle, I don't know what the parameters are for that. Would any of them want the local news station to tell them their son was dead while they were being televised by a live camera? That to me is a total invasion of privacy."[94]

Those concerns were shared by many journalists including Michael Isikoff of the *Washington Post*, who wrote a story on how the television media disrupted a memorial service for the Wilberg miners in the tiny San Rafael Chapel. The same concerns were raised about the media coverage of Christa McAuliffe's parents after the Challenger accident, but they are nothing new to the journalism profession.

Reporters as a group don't like to invade people's privacy. Many, like Isikoff of the *Post*, hate having to contact people in grief, but he felt it was necessary to check details regarding the recovery of the Challenger astronauts when NASA refused to provide any information. Isikoff may not like making those calls to the astronauts' families, but he has to face an editor who wants a better story than the one in the *New York Times* and who wants any disclosures in Isikoff's article confirmed by reliable sources. This means that the reporter is going to have to work for any exclusive or for what he or she thinks is a unique angle on a story, even if it means tearing the fabric of someone's personal privacy.

CONSIDERATIONS REGARDING THE DIFFERENT MEDIA SEGMENTS

Television

There's also a problem of print versus electronic media. I have a very heavy pencil that has lights and takes two people to carry around. People think we are as we are portrayed, that we are rude and uncaring, that we are only interested in invading somebody's privacy. Doctors believe that. Salesmen believe that. So, while a doctor may talk to you on the phone, talking to you in front of a camera is something else. They don't understand that we are doing the same thing as the *New York Times*. The only difference is that Larry Altman can get the story over the phone and I can't.[95]

Whatever happened to the good old days of Huntley-Brinkley and Walter Cronkite, when we only had to worry about one news broadcast a day on the TV networks? Now you have to be prepared for news broadcast by the networks over a 19-hour day, and that doesn't include CNN's 24-hour-a-day news coverage. Then the local stations add an additional 90 minutes a day, primarily on their noon, 6:00, and 11:00 news shows, but with an additional 15–30 minutes of updates during the network morning shows and between prime-time shows in the evening.

TV camera crews have replaced flashbulb-popping photographers as the symbolic representation of media intrusion—and with good reason. A night doesn't go by where the American public doesn't get to see the cyclops eyes of the Minicam photographers, whose earphoned sidekicks wave shotgun microphones for the evening news.

My experience with the television news people who cover these stories is that they are especially sensitive about the intrusive nature of TV. Instead of being a pack of piranhas ready to pounce, the producers, correspondents, and camera crews tend to be among the most courteous and attentive of the media. They know they will be a burden on the participants at some point because their medium requires cameras, lights, and microphones. Rather than aggravating the situation, you will find they are ingenious at coming up with ways to get the story with minimum disruption. I was always amazed how fast a network camera crew on a pool could get in and out of Schroeder's hospital room on a pool assignment, or how easy it was to work out an arrangement to get one participant on four network morning shows in the space of an hour.

In the latter instance, Dr. DeVries agreed to be available for one hour after morning rounds at the hospital to answer questions on network TV. A pool meeting was held and the networks drew straws to determine which quarter-hour segment between 8 A.M. and 9 A.M. each would get. Since the networks had set up facilities in meeting rooms adjacent to the briefing area at the Commonwealth Convention Center, all Dr. DeVries had to do was walk a few feet from one room to the next every 15 minutes to appear "live" on a different TV network morning show.

Since there was no way of knowing what questions might come up or how DeVries would respond, we alerted the wire services and local media of the time for each network interview. This was a standard procedure and a frequent result was wire service news items being generated by the appearance of Humana's physicians on network television.

The field producers sent in by the TV networks are the ones who coordinate that type of live news coverage. "We're part logisticians, part journalists, part technicians, part hand-holding rabbis, part surrogate reporters," said Jon Meyersohn of CBS News.[96] The producers rarely are seen on television, but they are essential to the development of the news reports, working with the correspondent to hammer out the story angle, arranging interviews and covering media briefings while the correspondent is drafting a script or doing a standup in front of the facility. "On a major story the networks want to leave little to chance," said Roger Brown of NBC News. "In those instances a producer is provided as a second journalistic mind, as well as to coordinate the logistics of getting the story on the air.[97]

When a major story like the artificial heart is breaking, the networks often will have two producers working around the clock arranging to have tons of equipment flown in, coordinating airline and hotel reservations, and booking time for satellite transmissions. All that is done in addition to supervising the camera crews sent in to shoot the story and editors who get it ready to go on the air. "The cardinal rule in a producer's life is 'Make the Feed,' " Meyersohn added. "All else can be argued, even fudged, but you never miss that satellite feed to New York."

You quickly learn that producers, correspondents, and the camera crews have split personalities. They tend to be laid back, personable, often funny people who you'll enjoy getting to know over a cup of coffee or a beer. The other side appears when they are about to go "live." You'll see producers hunched over, holding telephone receivers to both ears, while the correspondents put something called an IFB in their ear and begin talking to someone who isn't there. It's almost like the *Invasion of the Body Snatchers*, in which the aliens from outer space implanted something in the peoples' brains that gained control of their personalities. The producers begin using a technical language you can't understand, and the correspondents' attention and allegiance is focused somewhere else via the camera in front of them. Often their conversations with the invisible people get interrupted or frustrated, to their consternation and the dismay of the person anxiously waiting to be interviewed.

Because of the immediacy and drama involved, the big push will be to "live" when the early morning, evening, or especially late-night news programs are on the air. CNN frequently tends to broadcast live during briefings because of its 24-hour-a-day live news format. You'll get used to that distraction.

You'll also have to get used to the ritual of stand-ups done in front of the place where the news event is occurring. Building signs are a natural. There you'll find correspondents memorizing a short commentary and then giving it over and over again to a camera until they get it right—or it gets too cold to stay out longer. When you add up the four major television networks and a host of local and regional stations, each doing their stand-ups and often shooting a 10-second promo as well for the evening or late news, you get a sense of how much activity television can bring to the front lawn of your headquarters building.

It's important to remember that the networks will service TV news primarily, but they also support their radio sides as well. The news of Schroeder's first stroke broke on ABC network radio news with the voice of David Cohen, who at the time was a field producer for ABC. Cohen was on the air from Chicago moments after I advised him of the change in Schroeder's condition. His first call was to alert the ABC network radio news desk. Then he began making arrangements to get ABC's TV news crews and correspondents back to Louisville as quickly as possible. David Dick of CBS News remembers looking for visual images of the cold and snow in the Utah mountains, which became word pictures for radio news updates on the Wilberg fire, which he handled in addition to his responsibilities as the network's television news correspondent over the Christmas holiday.

The dependency of TV news on its equipment and its ability to broadcast live result in those low-keyed news crews working under unbelievable tension several times a day. They are often racing the watch in trying to be ready at the designated "bird time" to feed segments via satellite to the network newsroom or to carry a live update from the scene. If it's an interview, the correspondent will appear very calm but from the cameras on back is a quiet tension that lasts until the field producer gets the word that the newsroom is done and has gone on to something else.

Of all the media, the financial stakes are highest for TV news. With all three networks locked in a neck-and-neck ratings race, their operating budgets reflect the potential payoff if they can get the edge and capture more of the viewing audience with their coverage of a breaking news story. The average operating costs for one of the television networks during the first 10 days of Schroeder's recovery was $20,000 a day, not including salaries. They had three crews working a 22-hour day to support their morning, evening, and late-night news programs as well as to provide updates. That may seem exorbitant, but it reflects the technology-intensive and profitable nature of TV news. Even if they are last in the ratings, no network or local TV station is going to cancel its evening news programs. It may change its broadcast sets or get another news anchor, but it is not going to drop its news programming. That's the one major calling card any TV network or station has with the viewer.

TV crews in the field usually don't have time to produce a "think" piece on a major story, but the networks do. Satellite hookups give them access to an infinite variety of people who can offer different viewpoints on the lead story of the day. But now, with the growing use of satellite transmission trucks by local TV stations, they also have the capability of providing the same type of live coverage from virtually anywhere. "Thanks to microwave and the 'birds,' I have the ability to have experts in my newscasts, be they local or national, discussing the same kinds of topics that used to be reserved for Ted Koppel or Peter Jennings," said Tom Becherer, news director for WLKY-TV, the ABC-TV affiliate in Louisville.[98]

Satellite debates are the essence of the "MacNeil/Lehrer News-Hour," "Nightline," and, to a lesser extent, the morning shows and Sunday news programs on network TV. It's always interesting to watch television news debates across the country or between continents, but satellite interviews are not without pitfalls for those who are involved. One is that they never are quite sure whom they will be debating until they're on the air. Program producers have a way of lining up several experts and then choosing those whose viewpoints are most divergent or whose remarks will be most colorful. Where is the objective standard defining who knows the most about your field? It's up to the network producer to decide because he or she is the person selecting the participants.[99]

Another problem is that any spokesperson for an organization involved in a news event is likely to be rather narrow in his outlook. All his time, thought, and energy are focused on what can be done to save the patient's life, or rescue the trapped miners, or determine what caused the accident. His specialty is surgery or mining or aeronautics, not television debates. It's easy for someone to second-guess him on national TV or talk about the ethics, the issues, and the financial considerations. They also can make grandiose forecasts and not have to worry about being held accountable for what they say.

The biggest surprise you may have in dealing with the TV news media is likely to come from the coverage provided by CNN. Their calling card will be a 12-foot satellite dish mounted on a truck and aimed skyward. Often the other networks will use the CNN satellite dish for transmitting their own stories if they don't have an uplink available, which was the case in Huntington during the Wilberg fire.

CNN differs from the other networks in that it will use its satellite transmission capabilities for live updates to Atlanta any hour of the day or night when an important new development is disclosed. CNN's satellite and 24-hour news format often will mean it is the first on the air with the news from the scene. It also means that its correspondents have more time available to develop their stories in greater detail. Many of the print media will use CNN as a way to cover news developments that are occurring thousands of miles away.

The coverage provided by any of your local TV stations will parallel the networks in many respects but also will have some distinct differences. Even if affiliated with a network, each will handle its own broadcasts and news segments separately. They are likely to do more "Live Eye" segments from the scene for their morning, noon, and evening news segments, taking advantage of their microwave transmitter trucks. They also will focus in on the impact of the news event on people from the local community in much greater depth and for a longer period of time. But don't get lulled into thinking that those stories will only be seen in the local area. In addition to feeding the evening news to its affiliates, each of the television networks also uses the satellite to send out a one-hour compilation of interesting news stories produced that day by its local stations. The "affiliate feed" often includes human interest or background reports on a major news story that don't fit the network's evening news format, but which will be broadcast by many of its affiliates across the country. "In addition to my deadlines for WAVE-TV, I had to make the affiliate deadline every day during the Schroeder coverage," Carol Grady, the station's medical reporter, recalled. "The story had to be written in such a way that any late-breaking details could be tacked on. Then when the network correspondents packed up and went on to other stories, we also fed the morning news shows and evening broadcasts."[100]

Finally, depending on the magnitude of the story, you are likely to have a number of TV crews from cities several hours away or even from other parts of the country. You may also find crews representing international news organizations arriving on the scene or contacting you to set up satellite interviews with their news anchors in another country. We did interviews on the artificial heart with TV news organizations in Brazil, Australia, Canada, Japan, France, Germany, Italy, and the United Kingdom.

Radio

> We are overlooked because we are very transient, just voices in the dark. But news radio to an important degree can set the tone of a story and can influence what people think and understand, because that's what they are hearing hour after hour after hour.[101]

While the total audience has declined in recent years, just as it has for most newspapers, it's easy to underestimate the power and pervasive nature of radio news. Radio correspondents may not have the star stature of a Rather, a Brokaw, or a Jennings, but they actually have a bigger audience. They also are a unique breed of journalists. Compared to print and television reporters, radio correspondents on an assignment have much more control over their reports because they usually have to do their own producing, writing, editing, and feeding of the material to the network, often with no subsequent editing in the newsroom before it goes on the air.

Radio reporters have to have sufficient understanding to tell the story in 40 seconds, which means knowing the details so well that they can compress it into its most important aspects and put it across with visual images. That's the real trick and the hard part for radio news, but that also sets it apart from the other media. A newspaper reporter may write one good story on what has happened; a radio correspondent may write a dozen. Each requires a new lead with different angles that will capture the essence of the story and catch the attention of the listener without repeating the information the same way it was used in the previous newscast. It's tough to write short, and it's tough to write fast, but that's the nature of radio news, where the demands are for immediacy in a story that can be used within a few minutes.

Radio news will not compete with newspapers, which provide a completely different journalistic service. The function of radio newscasts is to cover the highlights, to give verbal headlines several times an hour. If you want the in-depth reports, you can read the next edition of a paper. In the meantime, the radio reports will have much the same headlines and lead paragraphs on an hourly basis.

The network and local radio correspondents are electronic gypsies who can file their stories from virtually anywhere simply by unscrewing the mouthpiece from a phone and connecting their tape recorders directly to the line with two alligator clips. As with television news, it often will be the local radio reporters who handle the brunt of the national news reports during the first hours of a major story before their network counterparts can travel to the scene and begin filing stories.

For the public relations people who are working with the media during a news story, the most time-consuming part of the job will be in handling radio news calls. Hundreds of stations will take the wire service copy and network feeds to develop their stories. Hundreds of others will want to give their reports a first-person twist by including the voice of someone who is directly involved. They all want the latest information, which is just what the wire services have reported, so you wind up saying the same thing over and over to each of the radio stations that calls.

Unfortunately, it doesn't end at the end of the day. An overnight update may go out at 11 P.M., but you can expect to be awakened several times during the night by radio reporters, apologizing for the call at that hour but needing a voice that will give them the latest update. Most will come in between 4 and 6 A.M. Eastern time from networks gearing up for the morning news, but the call may also come in from the "Voice of America" preparing to broadcast behind the Iron Curtain. No matter how tired you are, you suddenly get very alert and articulate when awakened by that kind of phone call.

Wire Services

> We really are news wholesalers. We may not see the end product as an AP or UPI story, but you can be sure that we had some influence on a large part of what was reported.[102]

The cliche that journalists face a deadline a minute is an exaggeration that can be applied most easily to the wire services. The wires are always facing deadlines for morning papers, evening papers, and overseas papers, which come at 11 A.M. and P.M. Eastern Standard

Time. Meanwhile, information for broadcast is transmitted to television and radio stations 24 hours a day for hourly radio news updates and the all-news formats of some radio stations. Most wire service reporters' time will be spent writing and filing copy, but many also carry tape recorders on major stories and will file reports and actualities for the AP or UPI radio networks.

There will be no leisure time for the wire service reporters sent in to cover the story or for the nearest bureau, which becomes the ganglion for coverage of the story in transmitting copy, photos, and radio reports to the wire service headquarters for worldwide distribution. With Schroeder's artificial heart operation, the Louisville bureaus of AP and UPI stayed open 24 hours a day for the first two weeks, pulling in extra personnel from other locations in the state to handle their normal news distribution plus the extra reporting and photography overload caused by the Schroeder story. With the Wilberg fire, the *Sun Advocate* in Price, Utah, 26 miles from the mine, became the AP and UPI newsroom and provided a place for developing film as well as for filing stories via portable terminals and telephone modems.

Television news relies heavily on the wire services for information used by the network and local TV news anchors. Correspondents working a major story often will use wire service information to expand their own reports. With radio news, a majority of the copy in their news broadcasts originates with the wire services. In the many instances where a station doesn't have sufficient staff for editing and rewriting, wire service copy is broadcast word for word—the proverbial "rip and read" approach.

A newspaper usually will indicate when it is using a dispatch from AP or UPI; less so on television, and rarely on radio. What the public seldom reads or hears is the name of the wire service reporters who provided the information. Often their copy will be used word for word in the bylined story of another journalist. The converse also applies. Local reporters often have their stories moved by one of the wire services, which provides other news organizations worldwide with the insights of a journalist who has in-depth knowledge of the situation and the participants. The AP carried a number of stories written by the *Courier-Journal's* Mike King when King's research and investigative reporting resulted in important stories on the artificial heart. Chuck Zehnder, the editor of the *Sun Advocate*, was the AP's primary news source during the Wilberg fire. His knowledge of the Wilberg Mine provided the wire service with important insights in its coverage of the rescue efforts.

Wire service coverage also may include stories from its own specialized writers, especially if the focus is on science and medicine, aerospace, and business. With Schroeder's operation, both Paul Raeburn, the medical editor for Associated Press, and Al Rossiter, Jr., the science editor for United Press International, wrote the main stories dealing with the medical developments. Staff writers from their local wire service bureaus worked closely with them in developing the sidebar and human interest angles, which each wire service pursued to broaden its coverage. When the story had settled down to the point where Raeburn and Rossiter could return to New York and Washington, respectively, the reporters and editors from each wire service bureau were well attuned to all the aspects of the story and could easily handle the ongoing coverage.

Newspapers

While the most comprehensive coverage still comes from newspapers, many dailies are shortening the length of major stories and illustrating them more extensively with photos and computer graphics to compete with *USA Today* and the public's tendency to use the broadcast media as its primary source of news. Bastions of print journalism, such as the *New York Times*, the *Washington Post*, and the *Los Angeles Times*, can still be expected to devote inordinate space and resources to covering a major story, in part because they also have developed a secondary market for that coverage through their national editions and syndicated distribution to other newspapers and electronic data retrieval services.

Newspapers have the time and space to take greater advantage of data banks, wire service copy, and phone interviews to develop the sidebars, profiles, and background pieces that give the reader a full understanding of what has occurred. The front page of the *Courier-Journal* was a four-page color wraparound the morning after Schroeder's operation. The entire first section of *USA Today* was devoted to the Challenger accident the morning after the explosion.

The local papers will be the most sensitive, probing, and energetic in covering the story, and thus will be most likely to take editorial positions regarding what has happened. They also will become a source for the rest of the media since their reporters will be the most familiar with the people and conditions that precipitated the news story and the all important technical details. Gaby Jacobs, the reporter from the *Jasper Herald*, Bill Schroeder's hometown paper, was bombarded with questions from the other journalists about Schroeder, his family, and background during the first 48 hours of the story. Chuck Zehnder of the *Sun Advocate* spent hours straightening out misunderstandings among general assignment reporters covering the Wilberg fire about mining practices and terminology.

National newspaper reporters will know how to develop their own sources in a matter of hours, and they can be very persuasive in getting those involved to grant them the interviews they need to cover the story. They tend to be low keyed and laid back, sizing up the situation and the sources of information in terms of the deadlines they will be facing. Often they will provide the barometer for the other news coverage. Dr. Lawrence Altman of the *New York Times*, for example, is regarded as the most authoritative observer of the artificial heart program, having covered Barney Clark, the three Humana artificial heart patients, and the two Tucson patients. His articles on developments in the clinical trial were carefully scanned by participants and press alike and provided direction for much of the news coverage.

The approach of the print journalists in dealing with the problems of pack journalism will vary considerably from their competitors in the broadcast media and wire services. Knowing they cannot compete timewise, they will go for the exclusive, which usually comes from a one-on-one interview. That's far easier to do because the information can come via the phone, over a lunch tray in a cafeteria, or during a brief chat in the hallway. Mark Mayfield and Jack Kelley of *USA Today* were able to get the personal views of Ben Powers, the head of NASA's solid rocket program at the Marshall Spaceflight Center, by driving out to his home and explaining that they felt there was an undercurrent within NASA that was not being allowed to reach the surface. They were told to come back the next day, and Powers then leveled with *USA Today*.

MAGAZINES

The major news magazines like *Time* and *Newsweek*, and, to a lesser extent, the leading trade, scientific and industrial magazines, will go beyond what the reader saw in the newspapers, although the two print media will overlap in their coverage and editorial approach. The "Perspectives" or "This Week in Review" sections in the Sunday editions of major newspapers function in much the same way as the news magazines, while if the story breaks late in the week, the magazines can be just about as timely and competitive as a daily paper. "When your story is breaking on a Thursday, Friday, or Saturday, the news magazines will be behaving very, very much like newspapers," Morton Kondracke observed.[103] Even though President Reagan's meetings in Reykjavik, Iceland, with Soviet Secretary Gorbachev began on a Saturday, the *Time* cover story on Monday was on the summit. A combination of advance planning by their editorial staff with satellite transmission and computerized production of photos and copy enabled the magazine to have the story out of Iceland and on the newsstands across the United States within 48 hours.

The main effort of the news magazines will be to find and pursue a different angle on the story than the newspapers have taken to meet their daily deadlines. Their approach will be more analytical and tied into recent trends or other developments in the news. "We want to surprise you with information that goes beyond what you already know about the story," said George Raine of *Newsweek*. "Our job is to advance the ball, as far as the essential elements of the story are concerned, further than any of the daily news journalists have been able to take it. The task is to get beyond the obvious, to reach beyond the scraps that are the headline elements, and address the broader, more sweeping dimensions of the story."[104]

With the president's Iranian arms sale controversy, for example, both news magazines reported the important developments each week, but that was just their respective starting points. At the height of the crisis, the December 15, 1986, issues of *Time* and *Newsweek* carried the following array of articles and sidebar stories, supported by color photographs, charts, and cartoons:

Time

"Under Heavy Fire: Pressure builds on Regan and Casey to quit" A five-page analysis with seven photos of the president and his key staff advisors. Also included is a chart on "Reagan's Credibility Gap" displaying the official versions and conflicting accounts of important statements made by the administration.

"Pursuing the Money Connections: The supply lines to the Contras led through a maze of "cutouts" and middlemen" A four-page background article with pictures of Colonel North, the Contras air base in Honduras, and a cartoon of the president tied down like Gulliver in *Gulliver's Travels*. The second page includes a half-page box, "The Iran-Contra Connection," with photos and brief profiles of the people and companies alleged to have diverted the funds from the Iranians to the Nicaraguans.

"Backbone and Stature" A half-page profile of Frank Carlucci, the president's choice to replace Admiral Poindexter as head of the National Security Council with a photo of Carlucci.

"Hitting the Middle Octaves" A half-page article by Hugh Sidey on the problems of confidentiality surrounding the Senate intelligence hearings on the Iranian-Contras scandal, with a photo of Senator Sam Nunn.

Newsweek

Cover Photo: A concerned president at his desk talking to staff members out of focus in the foreground.[105]

Headline: **"Reagan's Role: His Secret Message to Iran—His Green Light to the CIA—His Attempt to Contain the Damage"**

"Reagan's Crusade: As the president digs in for a long siege, evidence mounts that his own diplomatic aims and concern for the hostages were the wellspring of the scandal." An analysis running over four pages with a large photo of the president during a television address to the nation on the Iranian-Contras problem.

Two half-page "boxes" accompany the text. **"A Rapid Decline"** summarizes a Gallup poll for *Newsweek* indicating the president has suffered a sharp decline in his approval rating and credibility among the American public. **"A Tangle of Contradictions"** summarizes the maze of conflicting statements from the Reagan administration that have worsened the damage done by the Iranian arms scandal itself.

"The Roots of a Brutal Bargain: From the very beginning the president was the driving force behind the secret overtures to Iran" A four-page background article with eight photos of the principal figures in the diversion of funds to the Contras, as well as key Reagan staff members and senators investigating the scandal.

"Some Hard Questions for a Tough General: Does Secord have answers?" A one-page article with photos of Colonel North, General Richard V. Secord, and a Southern Air Transport C-130 cargo plane.

"Recapturing the Magic: How a dug-in Reagan can salvage his presidency" A one-page article with photos of the president talking to Secretary Schultz and a worried Nancy Reagan.

"Politics: Running Away from Reagan: GOP presidential hopefuls and the Iran scandal" A one-page assessment with photo of Vice President Bush.

"Will There Be a Backlash?": The media play it carefully but love the chase" A one-page analysis with a photo of reporters and photographers staked out at the White House.

To achieve this type of coverage, the news magazines use a process called "group journalism" that involves having their correspondents in the United States and abroad submit two to three times as much copy as will be used to the magazines' editorial offices in New York. It then is written and edited by as many as three different levels of editorial staff before going on the presses.

The other distinguishing characteristic of news magazines is their aggressiveness in getting good color photography to support their stories. Their photo editors will use every possible source to get pictures including their own photographers, the wire services, and photo agencies, and they are willing to pay thousands of dollars if it means they can obtain excellent pictures on an exclusive basis. "The photo departments of the news magazines are the most competitive bunch of people I know of in the journalism field," Kondracke added. "Photographers will work incredibly hard for exclusive shots and if you are the PR man, you have to know who is really shooting for whom. If you make a mistake or show favoritism, then it's costly for the publication which loses out and someone may think about seeking revenge. It's a dog-eat-dog world."

Pressure is an inherent part of the news business, but with only 52 opportunities to satisfy their readers, it's especially heavy at the news magazines. Their correspondents often work all night as their weekly deadline approaches, and it's not unusual for them to call you at 2 A.M. to fill a hole in their copy before they submit it to New York. "Your adrenalin really gets going when you're on a big story—you really get pumped up," Raine added. "A story like the artificial heart was dripping with implications, both in Utah and at Humana. Now it's the Iranian-Contras affair. That's when we give the readers who are really interested in all the facets and ramifications of what happened the chance to get a solid understanding of the story."

THE PROBLEM OF ANONYMOUS SOURCES

There may be any number of participants, as well as executives and public relations people within your organization, who are well qualified to discuss the details of the situation with the news media when they move in to cover the story. But what about the people who supply information to reporters even though they are not authorized to speak for an organization, or who are not identified? An article in the 1986–87 Journalism Ethics Report of the Society of Professional Journalists, Sigma Delta Chi, noted that after the Challenger accident, "Ethical problems arose almost at once, as NASA went silent, not answering even noncontroversial questions." Mike Lafferty, the aerospace writer for *Florida Today*, was quoted in the article as saying, "Anonymous sources were widely used in those early days because NASA and industry employees feared for their jobs if they were named. News organizations were quoting each other, too, without being able to verify the quotes."[106]

Anonymous sources are one of the potential points of conflict between the news media and an organization, as illustrated in the following excerpt from the *New York Times* on Union Carbide's efforts to reach a settlement with the Indian government on the damage claims stemming from the Bhopal accident.

> Details of the settlement were provided Friday night and yesterday to the *New York Times* by people with close knowledge of the negotiations. They declined to be publicly identified because of the sensitivity of the case and instructions of the judge who is handling the case to keep the matter confidential.[107]

Did the article help or hinder the negotiations? As a matter of fact, they fell apart early the next week. According to Union Carbide, the breakdown was due in large part to the public disclosure of private discussions in the *Times* and in other papers that picked up on its revelations.

The anonymous source who leaked the details of Carbide's proposed $350 million out-of-court settlement with victims of the Bhopal disaster may have been a dissatisfied company employee, or maybe it was a court clerk. But then again, it could have been a janitor who empties the trash in the judge's office. The problem is that the public has no way of knowing. Partly as a result, a number of news organizations, including *USA Today*, have taken a stand that they will not use information provided by sources who refuse to be identified, while others like the Associated Press require approval of a senior editor before an unnamed source is used. That is a courageous policy, which puts them at a competitive disadvantage with the likes of the *New York Times* and the *Washington Post*, which do not hesitate to use anonymous sources and even indicate that they are going against the court of law in doing so.

What can be done to prevent anonymous tipsters from disclosing information to the press that results in your organization being blindsided? Not much. The best you can do to discourage the use of anonymous sources is to have a clearly stated policy that the organization will not provide one word of comment in response to any information in which the source is not revealed. Another way is to remember that you hold the high cards—access to the authoritative sources of information. Some organizations have set the record straight by arranging exclusive interviews for the competitors of any news organization that has filed a story based on anonymous sources. Some members of the press say that's retaliation. The organizations involved say it's a matter of personal preference.

POINTS OF CONFLICT

The incessant search for a new angle, a new visual, a new anything that will give one news organization a competitive advantage can cause some members of the media to take actions exceeding the limits of common sense. During the four-day Wilberg coverage, the road to the mine was closed to all but those involved in the rescue and firefighting operations. We mentioned in Chapter 1 that the response of some television news crews to the closing of the road to the Wilberg Mine was to charter helicopters to fly into the canyon to film the smoke and fire pouring from the mine, and that in one instance a low-flying chopper barely missed the high-voltage lines supplying electricity to the mine. On another occasion, a photographer posed as a deer hunter and tried to hike into the canyon to shoot photos for his news magazine. He was spotted by mine employees at a time when the last thing anyone at the Wilberg Mine needed was to go after an amateur mountain climber trying to scale a canyon wall in the ice and snow with his camera equipment.

Responsible journalists do not deny that questionable reporting techniques may be used, and they are sensitive about those actions that cast their profession in a bad light. But just let someone publicly criticize the reporting techniques of the news media. Then the news media's sense of self-righteousness surfaces. Chuck Zehnder was interviewed by Bill Moyers on the "CBS Morning News" during the Wilberg fire. He said during the discussion that he didn't see any sense in CBS interviewing a grief-stricken widow, that it satisfied absolutely nothing but the morbid curiosity of a few people who are not closely associated with the story itself. Zehnder got phone calls and letters from viewers all over the country who agreed with him, but he also recalls getting a hot response from the CBS correspondent who did the story indicating they had gained valuable information from the widow.[108]

Whether or not the interview was valuable is a matter of personal opinion. Actions of the news media that are disruptive are something else, and they need to be managed for the media's benefit as well as for the participants. Imagine the headline and the ensuing repercussions that would have come of Huntington out if that helicopter had hit the power lines and crashed in the canyon, killing everyone on board but also knocking out the power for the ventilating fans in the mine, where rescue crews were groping through the smoke and fire looking for the trapped miners.

MEETINGS OF THE MINDS

The best way to minimize the possibilities of disruption is to have realistic disclosure guidelines, but work with the news media in setting them up and maintaining them. You're asking for trouble if you try to tell the media what they can and cannot do in covering the story, which Loma Linda learned the hard way. On the other hand, the networks, national newspapers, and wire services are proud of their reputations and sensitive about their public images. They can do a lot to help you keep things under control if you seek them out and ask for their assistance on specific problems.

Humana and the news media had an understanding that either side could call a pool meeting if there was a problem to be discussed or if assistance was needed. Anyone could attend, and we'd get together as soon as possible, usually within an hour. The reasons for meeting ranged from our needing to set up a pool to interview Schroeder later that night to the media wanting to resolve the problem of how to get pictures of Schroeder going for a wheelchair ride outside the hospital without attracting a crowd and causing chaos in the parking lot.

It doesn't take long to figure out who the leaders are among the news organizations on hand. Get to know them, ask their advice, and establish a working relationship early on before things get out of hand. That step would have saved NASA considerable travail with the news media in the months after the Challenger accident and would have lessened the adversarial relationship that developed after the initial disclosure delay.

THE DIFFICULT QUESTION OF PERSONAL PRIVACY

A major potential problem that needs to be addressed very early in your discussions with the press is the personal privacy of the participants. The individuals involved in the story will be the single most important element in the news media's coverage, and the media will want access to them. Those who are involved in the situation itself may be too busy or preoccupied and not want to talk to reporters. The families may be anxious or grief stricken and apprehensive about being interviewed. In this instance, some realistic guidelines are needed to reduce the necessity of the media to get in touch with people who do not want to talk to them.

A great deal can be done to lessen the tension on both sides. First of all, the organization needs to find out who does and does not want to be interviewed and to make that known to the media. For those who are willing to talk to the press, provisions should be made so they can be interviewed in a way that will be most comfortable for them. It may be a meeting with the media at the briefing center or a pool interview with a few reporters. The media can be very helpful in working out a way to keep the participants' uneasiness to a minimum.

Reporters understand that many people don't want to be interviewed. They frequently get that response on routine stories, so it's even more natural on a major story where people are under major stress. The important point is to make it clear to the press with more than a response from the public relations staff. The participants or family members may want to provide a personal, handwritten statement expressing their appreciation for the public interest and concern and requesting that their privacy be honored until the situation has stabilized. Another option is to have someone who is not directly involved in the story represent the participants or the family members. An articulate relative or a member of the clergy can be an excellent alternative and, in the process, take the pressure off everyone.

In considering the options it's critical for the organization to retain the proper perspective regarding the news media. "The tension comes from not establishing a working relationship with the press so that the needs of both organizations are satisfied," Barbara Dolan of *Time* said. "There will be some elements of cross purposes on both sides, but nastiness, the cold shoulder, feeding the competition, and things like that can destroy the trust needed to get the job done for both the PR folks and reporters alike. What you have then is war, and in a war I'd put my money on the journalists any day. They rarely, if ever, lose out once they have the scent of a story. President Reagan is finding that out in trying to cope with the Iranian controversy."[109]

When the News Coverage Turns Negative

Dealing with the news media is difficult enough under the best of conditions. When the press turns hostile, however, you and your organization will have an entirely new set of problems. Now, rather than giving you the benefit of the doubt when there are discrepancies in the news updates, they will be more inclined to look for holes in your information, the damaging statement, or the small chink in your organization's armor that may be interpreted as a significant problem, even if it's only based on rumor or innuendo.

The safest assumption you can make is that you will be attacked by somebody during the course of the news story because nobody is perfect, and the media knows that. Reporters are always on the lookout for discrepancies that may provide the startling revelation that gets their story on the front page or lead position on the evening news. Even if your information is consistently factual, some journalists are going to break loose from the pack to interview former employees, union officials, local residents, politicians, environmentalists, or other "experts" who don't necessarily share your interpretation of the situation.

Look at the news event as if it were a series of battles within a larger war. This point of view will enable you to see that although the reputations of your organization and the participants may be nicked by negative news coverage in their daily engagements with the media, the primary job is to ensure that they are not seriously damaged by unfavorable news reports. Their response to those stories also should not cause the media to focus more on the bad news than on the story as a whole. Your organization usually will know where the problems are and can anticipate the negative media coverage. At that point, it's a question of how far you and the other members of management are willing to go in admitting that the organization has a problem because its people have erred.

The Baby Fae experiment, the Challenger explosion, the Bhopal disaster, and the Reagan Iranian-Contras scandal are all classic examples of organizations which have had to contend with negative news coverage partly because of the story, but also because of the way the press relations were handled.

ARE YOU REALLY BEING ATTACKED?

In the preceding examples there was no question that the organization was being attacked by the news media, but in most instances management has a difficult time understanding the difference between legitimate investigative reporting and yellow journalism. Even the most media-wise executives work in a communications world where the object is to convey a perception that will favorably affect sales, stock price, fund raising, legislative support, or whatever they need to survive. If it's necessary to discuss the problem, it will be couched in carefully worded statements that bear no resemblance to the heated conversations during management meetings when it first came up. Rarely will any executive or employee be singled out for criticism. That simply is not done, even if the mistake or misdeed costs the organization millions of dollars.

After existing in a rose-colored world of corporate communications, it's no wonder many executives are uncomfortable relating to the press, knowing that they have no control over what will be reported. Nor is it surprising that they get angry when the media coverage tends to focus on the problems and unfavorable aspects of the situation rather than reporting what management has emphasized in interviews, backgrounders, and briefings.

Executive wrath in response to negative news coverage has a disturbing irony when you consider that these are highly paid, intelligent people, many of whom work in a world measured by return on investment. Yet they will waste hundreds of executive hours, and cost their organizations hundreds of thousands of dollars, seeking redress for statements in a news story that struck them as offensive. And what do they have to show for it a year later? Nothing more than a lot of unpleasant memories and hard feelings on both sides. You don't get in a fight with the guy who owns the printing ink. He's equally proud and sensitive, and he has a lot of friends in the same business. They may be competitive, but when there's a fight, you know whose side other news organizations are likely to take.

Even without the Iranian imbroglio, imagine how the president of the United States would fare if he took the same kind of umbrage with every critical statement made by the White House press corps, and what effect it would have on his daily work schedule, much less the subsequent news reports. The press secretary and his staff get involved in a lot of jawboning with specific reporters regarding their coverage, and that's expected because there are legitimate differences of opinion or interpretation. However, you don't find the White House launching counterattacks against the news media, at least not since the Nixon administration tried it with "The Enemies List." They know they must work with the press corps and vice versa. The same is true for your organization.

WHAT CAUSES THE NEGATIVE NEWS REPORTS

The mistake that executives tend to make all too often is to take the negative comments in a news story as an insult to themselves and their organizations. Rather than adopting a Watergate mentality, they'd be much better off accepting the fact that critical comments, allegations, and innuendos will be made by reporters editorializing on what has happened. Again, that's the nature of the news business, and there's nothing you can do about it. It's also compounded by the fact that reporters get tired, frustrated, and whipsawed in trying to cover the story, which will influence their attitudes. That's where you can have an impact that can lessen the extent of the negative news stories.

We've already pointed out that reporters heading for the scene of a breaking news story won't be trying to figure out how to embarrass or discredit whomever is involved. Their only concerns at that point are to find out what has happened, what caused it, and what the results are, so they can begin filing updates and full news reports as soon as possible. Their coverage will turn negative if they encounter any one or more of the following.

Controversy

There's nothing that sends a pack of journalists into a feeding frenzy faster than the scent of controversy or scandal in a news story. After all, they regard investigative reporting as the epitome of good journalism. That's what wins Pulitzer prizes! Robert Woodward and Carl Bernstein, the *Washington Post* reporters who exposed the Watergate scandal, are the folk heroes of the fourth estate.

The controversy at NASA resulted when the press learned that NASA had overridden Thiokol engineers' recommendations to cancel the launch because of the effects of cold weather on the solid rocket booster (SRB). Thus, within hours of the first indications that the SRB might have caused the Challenger explosion, the media had its teeth into solid controversy. This was happening after NASA had been accused of mismanagement of its budget, and the administrator had been indicted by a grand jury.

When NASA didn't respond within the hour after the accident, the negative momentum in the media's attitudes and resulting coverage began to snowball and build to the point where an attack by the press was almost unavoidable and would color the rest of the Challenger disclosures. The Thiokol story turned out to be only the first of many controversial stories in the Challenger aftermath, and the members of the press were off and running.

With Baby Fae, reporters discovered that Dr. Bailey had not even tried to find a human heart transplant for the infant before grafting the baboon heart. That disclosure led to a chain reaction of other revelations in the news media, including one by NBC News that Baby Fae's parents were not married, not living together at the time the baby was born, and both had criminal records. Bob Bazell of NBC later observed, "The chairman of the surgery department, Dr. David Hinshaw, said because of my story, 'The whole basis of medicine in the Western civilization is challenged and attacked at its very roots.' "[110]

Reporting Roadblocks

During the initial coverage of Baby Fae, Challenger, and Bhopal, the news media was shut off from getting the additional information it needed. In each instance the reason was different, but the media reaction was the same. The principal physician in the Baby Fae experiment, Dr. Leonard Bailey, chose not to be available to the press after the initial briefing in the hope of maintaining the scientific integrity of his experiment. NASA's senior management concentrated on impounding the data from the Challenger launch and refused to allow anything to be disclosed to the press or the public for nearly five hours. Union Carbide could not provide additional information beyond the news reports coming out of India since its Bhopal plant managers were under arrest and the phone lines through Bombay to Bhopal were simply not available. Each organization had its own very valid reasons for not responding to the media's demands for more information, but when pack journalism is involved, there is little, if any, benefit of the doubt.

Most observers of the Iranian-Contras scandal, including the media, agree that President Reagan helped himself by trying to get all of the information on what happened out in the open as quickly as possible so the Congress, the American people, and the press would have the details. Admiral Poindexter and Colonel North, on the other hand, quickly became the villains when each sought protection under the Fifth Amendment and effectively blocked both the United States Congress and the news media from getting all the details on the arms sale and diversion of funds to the Contras.

Errors, Omissions, Inaccuracies, or Outright Lies

A hostile reaction from the news media is guaranteed for anyone who discloses information that turns out not to be true. There may be logical reasons for misstatements, but they won't find a sympathetic ear among journalists covering the story, especially if they have reported the first disclosures as factual information.

NASA's revelation that three of the Challenger crew airpacks had been activated and that the last words on the intercom were "Uh oh" came 10 days after the space agency had announced that the crew had not been aware of the impending disaster. That reversal led to some derogatory editorial comments. An example from the *New York Times*:

> The agency has so long depended on currying its public image that it has forgotten how to tell the exact truth. Yet, especially when disaster

strikes, that's the best way, indeed the only way, for an agency to maintain the public's trust. Tell everything you know as soon as you know it and be the first to admit error if you turn out to be wrong.

NASA let fly the convenient belief that the Challenger's crew died instantly. It kept close the knowledge that one of the crew, even in those last terrifying seconds, had thought to save another's life. A grieving public would have deemed that a truly noble death, had NASA's image makers seen fit to describe it sooner.[111]

The problem at Loma Linda was that information was disclosed that turned out not to be true. The editorial results were the same.

Loma Linda's public account of the course of events leading up to the landmark surgery has been one of confusion and, at times, outright misstatements of fact.

When researchers like Dr. Bailey decline to talk directly to the press and delegate the task to others who do not know the facts and who answer questions by guessing at the answers or by making factual mistakes, then the absent principal investigators are responsible for the mistakes and distortions, if not sensationalism, that result.

For instance, Dr. Hinshaw opened one news conference by saying he had just come from the intensive care unit, where the mother was nursing Baby Fae. In fact, she was not nursed. Dr. John W. Mace, the chairman of the Loma Linda pediatrics department, later said the medical center usually discouraged mothers from nursing infants who may die.

One of the most serious misstatements occurred when Loma Linda officials denied a report that Baby Fae's parents had taken her home to die before the operation. Later, after repeated questioning, they admitted it was true. Loma Linda officials have declined to provide details about the circumstances. But the incident has added to the many questions critics have raised about what the doctors told Baby Fae's parents before they consented to the operation.

Further confusion has come from information contained in the Loma Linda press release. It stated Baby Fae's age as 14 days at the time of the operation. Officials later admitted that they had stated the age incorrectly as a means of protecting the family's privacy, and the infant's true age remains unknown. Steps to protect confidentiality are laudable, but lies by medical school officials are not. Confidentiality and accuracy could have been maintained by properly wording the news release.

News briefings about medical research do not necessarily reflect the quality of the research and medicine practiced at a hospital. But sometimes they do, and they also often provide insights into how thoroughly researchers have thought through the implications of their work.[112]

Even before the Iranian arms scandal, the Reagan administration had planted the seeds of skepticism within the news media and the American public with its statements regarding the potential threat posed by Libyan leader Gadhafi, which actually was a carefully planned program of disinformation ("lying") coordinated by the National Security Council, and approved by the president. The disinformation campaign prompted Bernard Kalb, a respected former journalist, to resign as assistant secretary of state for public affairs and chief spokesperson for the State Department.

The negative impact of the Iranian arms deal on the administration was escalated by a number of contradictory statements from the president and his staff, which gave the journalists covering the story ample opportunity to question their credibility. The fact that both *Time* and *Newsweek* would focus in on "Reagan's Credibility Gap," and "A Tangle of Contradictions" in their December 22, 1986, issues is a good indication of how the news media will react when their information proves to be incorrect or untrue. When "a quantity of arms that would easily fit in a single cargo plane," turns out to be 2,000 antitank rockets and 235 antiaircraft missile systems, you can't blame journalists for being hostile.

The Lack of Hard News

The press is not going to sit around waiting for an organization to provide them with something to report. The minute they begin to sense they will not be getting any solid information or pictures, the news media will begin to seek out anyone who can provide them with personal insights, controversial angles, or comments on the ethical issues involved in the story. The television networks were lining up a variety of retired astronauts and aerospace "experts" for interviews during the first few hours after the explosion when they couldn't get anyone from NASA to discuss the Challenger accident. The media even had former NASA officials and engineers from Morton Thiokol speculating on the possible causes of the explosion and the management procedures at NASA that would have prevented vital information from reaching the launch decision makers. NASA didn't provide any spokespersons—and rightly so—knowing independent experts could theorize as much as they wanted, while its representatives would be held accountable by the media for every word they said.

Double Standards in Dealing with the Press

Journalists by nature have a strong sense of fairness and impartiality, and they will react with anger whenever an organization appears to play favorites. The biggest bone of contention will be the competition between the local and national news organizations for the few interviews that can be set up. If the local media feel that preference is being given to the television networks and national newspapers, you are going to hear about it on no uncertain terms. Some may go further and fill the gap in their coverage with behind-the-scenes stories based on insights and innuendos from their local sources.

A worse situation will develop if the organization finds itself involved in a checkbook journalism situation, which effectively shuts out the rest of the media from the primary news sources. You may have no control over that decision, which ultimately has to be made by the participants, but the consequences had better be considered. "The worst thing you can do is take a story that has worldwide interest and sell it on an exclusive basis to somebody and reject everybody else," Ed Yeates of KSL-TV observed. "Then the press gets mad, and when they get that way the feeling is, 'OK, let's start looking for the underlying stories here that are not so favorable to this institution. Let's look on the dirty side.' The press doesn't start out that way, looking for dirty linen in the closet, but if they feel they are being treated unfairly, that's where they are going to head. Realistically, that's how a lot of exposés get started."[113]

If the participants are considering a financial offer, determine what control the organization has over the pictures and information so that some provisions can be made for the rest of the press. The story undoubtedly is on the organization's premises, and its employees will be directly or indirectly involved. That's worth something and should give you some leverage.

Journalists are trained to look for balance and any mitigating factors in the news story. Paul Raeburn of the AP observed, "The press often will start on the neutral or favorable side in covering a story and then pull back and say, 'Now wait a minute, what's the bad news?' After the initial wave of enthusiasm it's almost inevitable they will become more critical."[114] As a result, most good journalists will quickly discount the credibility of the spokesperson if all they get are the favorable details. If that is all you intend to provide, think again. You will simply force the reporters to look for counterweights to the Pollyannaish news that you are disclosing.

Stalling and Stonewalling.

We've already talked about the media's attitudes about "the stall" —not returning a reporter's calls when he or she is developing a story and needs the information. The public relations people in some organizations may carry that tactic one step further by trying to delay or divert the reporter in pursuit of the story, if they think it's not favorable to the organization. That's their right and their job, and often they will be successful. But the same applies to the reporter.

The mistake often made is that the organization tries to shut off the story by refusing to provide information or even respond to the reporter. That doesn't discourage good journalists; it just frustrates them and angers their editors. The question reporters will ask themselves is, "What are they trying to hide, why, and whom do we know who might give us the inside story?" All of a sudden you will have lost control, because you won't know what information a news organization has until it suddenly appears on the front page or as the lead story on the evening news.

HOW THE NEWS MEDIA DEVELOPS HOSTILE INFORMATION

In addition to its anonymous sources and various types of "leaks," a news organization that senses it's onto something you'd rather not divulge will have its reporters, librarians, and researchers digging through news reports, government records, and other sources to find out anything they can about the organization and the people involved in the news event. In the process they often will come up with difficulties the organization had had in the past, as Mike King of the *Courier-Journal* did when he requested information on Humana Hospital-Audubon's IRB. So did many journalists digging into NASA's management and engineering problems. In both instances the details were obtained under the Freedom of Information Act.

The media also will use news morgues and computerized databases to uncover information about similar problems the organization had in the past, but which might be linked to the possible cause of the situation. And they'll have a lot of help from disgruntled employees, union officials, environmentalists, and politicians, who will seize upon the problem to gain visibility for themselves and the position they are advocating.

The artificial heart program was criticized by the president of the American Medical Association, a number of heart transplant specialists, medical ethicists, and even the governor of Colorado. Emery Mining Company found itself being attacked by some of the trapped miners' relatives, officials of the United Mine Workers (who flew in to hold a press conference), and even by the Eastern coal establishment. "Once the media is present, a symbiotic relationship occurs when the media needs new controversy, a new angle, a new line." Bob Henrie observed. "They are willing to play ball with people they normally would be leery of. The people who want to go on the attack exploit the news media and the media exploits them. They become strange bedfellows, but for the time being they are serving each other's purposes."[115]

RESPONDING WITHOUT OVERREACTING

You may have to deal with members of the news media who seem to want to tack your organization's hide on their newsroom wall. There's no way you can avoid it if reporters truly want to go after you, but you can lessen the effects their negative reporting will have on the overall coverage of the news story. These are the most time-tested damage control techniques that you can apply.

1. Have Your Defenses Up

The first contact will undoubtedly come by phone so make sure your switchboard knows where to route calls from the news media and have people answering those phones who know what they can say and how far they can go in responding to the media's questions. It's imperative that you keep your phone people informed of developments in the news story and how they should be handled so they know when to respond to the media or get someone else to take the call.

Union Carbide's Ron Wishart and Walter Goetz still bitterly recall the "Heard on the Street" column in *The Wall Street Journal* three days after the Bhopal accident which dealt with the possibility that Carbide could be facing potentially staggering damage claims that would exceed the limits of its insurance coverage. The stock was already under pressure because of Bhopal, but it dropped nearly eight points in the 48 hours after the column ran. The Carbide executives feel that the right people in the company were not contacted by the reporters, even though the article carried the following statement in the fourth paragraph:

> Union Carbide officials don't believe the company's liability is likely to reach that magnitude. "We discussed the issue of potential liability today," said William Kelly, a Union Carbide spokesman. "And we do not believe the company is likely to go under."[116]

That press call probably should have been handled by someone else, but the fault that it wasn't rests with Union Carbide, not *The Wall Street Journal*. It's the organization's job, not the media's, to decide who will respond when a journalist calls, and what information will be provided. Work that out in advance so foul-ups like the one at Carbide can be avoided.

2. Do Some Digging of Your Own

The natural reaction to questions with negative overtones is to adopt a defensive stance and try to dissuade the reporter from going further. You can try that approach, but if you sense persistence you'd better take the initiative. Get all the questions and ask a few of your own to explore the rationale for asking them. Find out where he is in developing the story. He may be in the initial stages or just about done and looking for some information to fill holes in the story. Ask if he's considered these points, and mention your organization's position on the question. Have somebody see if they can get some of the stories he has done previously to see what his reporting style is like and the types of stories he tends to write or broadcast. Then decide whether it's in your best interests to have him talk with others in your organization. "There's no law that says you have to talk to the media," Denny Brisley of the White House said. "You may not like the reporter personally, but it's always wise to give him your input on the situation so it's on the record even if it isn't used, or if it has to be a politely stated "no comment." Also suggest people who you think he should talk to. That can't hurt, and in some cases it can make a bad story better."[117]

3. Approach Any Probing Question with the Right Attitude

The problem with too many spokespersons and corporate executives is they lose patience and get indignant when anyone starts digging into subjects they are sensitive about, usually because they know that's where they are vulnerable. They may not say it while they are figuring out how to respond, but their initial reaction is "Who does that s.o.b. think he is, asking a question like that?" Even though the subject may be sensitive, this is not the time to get belligerent or holier-than-thou. All that does is signal the reporter and other journalists that they may be onto a soft spot in the organization's armor.

If the reporter wants an interview, ask for the questions in advance so you have time to decide what the responses will be. You also need to decide how to handle topics you don't want to discuss so polite, appropriate responses can be developed for those subjects. If a tough question comes up during an interview, it's a good idea to step back and take a hard look at the line of questioning when you are framing a response because the question may be legitimate, considering what has happened. Accept the fact that you are dealing with a tough competitor and adopt the same approach you would use if this were an IRS audit rather than an interview. Start with a smile to let the questioner know you appreciate his or her resourcefulness. Then respond carefully and be sure you can back up whatever information you present.

For example, consider the people who have really impressed you on programs like "60 Minutes" or "20/20." The ones who come out ahead in the tough interviews never seem to lose their composure, even though their stomachs undoubtedly are churning. They are always pleasant, even in discussing a problem or mistake. They also talk about it with sincerity and a smile, which conveys genuine confidence that they did what they considered best at the time, regardless of what the interviewer thinks. Good eye contact, the right body language, and a sincere smile can mean as much or even more than what you actually say, especially when you're in trouble in responding to tough questions.

Then think about the people on those programs whose actions and answers have been appalling. Invariably they have been evasive or even combative and have appeared to be guilty of something, even if it is nothing more than not being able to handle tough questions. They may have started out with good answers to what they believed was right at the time, but they cave in under the incessant pressure of repeated questioning until their answers are confused and contradictory. You feel sorry for those people and wish they had never agreed to be interviewed. Nobody likes to see anyone being massacred by the news media.

Remember who the person on the street is rooting for when someone is subjected to difficult questioning by the press. It isn't the media. The participants in a news story are the underdogs, and the public likes nothing more than to see someone smile and politely respond to a reporter with a solid answer that halts that line of questioning in its tracks.

4. Watch Out for Wishful Thinking

It's human nature in a crisis for both the participants and the news media to look for anything positive or hopeful that will help to offset the negative aspects of the story. That's when statements need to be weighed most carefully. The press will use them, but then will flail you with them if they turn out to be even slightly inaccurate.

Jesse Moore, NASA's associate administrator of spaceflight, stated at the initial briefing after the Challenger accident, "There was absolutely no pressure to get this particular launch up."[118] The next day Jay Green, the launch flight director, told a media briefing, "There were no requirements waived in either the systems area or the weather area. It was probably one of the better weather days we've ever experienced."[119]

At the initial briefing after the operation, Baby Fae's surgeon, Dr. Leonard Bailey, talked about the infant attending college and referred to the procedure as therapy rather than an experiment.[120]

After the Bhopal tragedy, Jackson Browning, Union Carbide's chief spokesperson, told a Congressional hearing that it was "inconceivable" that a similar accident could occur at the company's facility in Institute, West Virginia.[121] Seven months later the Institute plant experienced the toxic gas leak that sent 135 people to the hospital. "That hurt us more than Bhopal," Carbide's Warren Anderson recalled. "It hurt us because one of the questions that had been asked at the Congressional hearings in Institute was 'Could this (Bhopal) happen here?' We said, 'No, it couldn't, Bhopal could not happen here.' After the Institute gas leak, they said it *had* happened even though the product involved had about as much toxicity as kerosene smoke."[122]

Each spokesperson meant well and thought he was right, based on what he knew when the statement was made. But this is no time to be using words like "inconceivable" when you could be saying "that I am aware of" or "to the best of my knowledge." The reputations of the spokesperson and the institution ride on every public statement. Spokespersons should speak with authority and provide any factual information that has been confirmed. But they also need to recognize the limits of what they know and assume there is much they are not yet aware of.

Journalists do not have to hand down indictments for perjury. They can convict spokespersons and their organizations far more quickly and effectively through their news stories if they find out they've been provided with information that isn't true, even though the people thought it was accurate at the time.

5. Beware of the Wolves in Sheep's Clothing

Some reporters will request an interview to discuss a specific subject but will use the opportunity to zero in on especially sensitive or controversial details that you may not want to discuss. How do you get out of answering the line of questions gracefully, especially if the TV cameras are rolling? The best approach is to have good mantra statements worked out for any touchy topics before you sit down for any interview and use them as often as necessary—but always with a smile.

Bill McAda of FEMA had a more novel solution. A television reporter had requested an interview on the cleanup operations after a hurricane, but started off by asking instead why an elderly woman had been refused disaster assistance funding. McAda knew he was in trouble. The woman had complained to the media after she was turned down, but funding applications are confidential so he couldn't even admit she'd applied. His response with the cameras rolling was to walk over to the reporter and give her a big kiss, which stopped the interview cold.[123]

You also need to beware of being baited, especially during briefings when you may not know everyone in the room who will be asking questions. If the query sounds inappropriate or uncalled for considering the focus of the news story, your best response is to get to know the person. Ask their name and the news organization he or she represents. It may turn out you're dealing with a union official, animal rights activist, or someone else trying to take advantage of the news media's presence to push their viewpoint or discredit your organization. The best answer is you'll be happy to meet with them and discuss the question later, but your time is limited right now and this briefing is reserved for the news media.

6. Fess Up When You Mess Up

Any journalist appreciates receiving a call to correct or clarify something that was said. They also respect a spokesperson who starts off a briefing by acknowledging a mistake or clarifying a point that was misunderstood at the most recent briefing. If the error is not acknowledged or explained, however, the organization is leaving itself wide open for a barrage of criticism from the press.

NASA knew it had erred within hours after announcing that the preliminary analysis of the Challenger intercom tape indicated the crew was not aware of the impending disaster. The examination of the airpacks had been completed several days earlier. Then came the further analysis of the tape, which picked up Commander Smith's final comment. "Uh oh" had a double irony. It was a tragic indication of what the crew was aware of and a prophetic statement of NASA's dilemma in explaining it.

For some reason the space agency did not anticipate the outraged reaction of the media to the disclosure of the airpacks and the reversal of its position on how much the Challenger astronauts were aware of before the explosion. The *New York Times* editorial, "Nobility and Knowledge in Space," on July 30, 1985, referred to earlier in this chapter, prompted NASA to call a press conference to explain the chronology of the airpack and crew tape analyses. NASA's Shirley Green also used the occasion to accuse the news media of giving the space agency a "bum rap" for suggesting that NASA had known about the airpacks since March but had chosen to withhold that information from the news media and the public. The ensuing news reports carried the agency's explanation of why the communications foul-up had occurred. Most included Green's "bum rap" comment, which under the circumstances seemed rather Nixonian. The *New York Times* went one step further. Their story was illustrated by a picture of Christa McAuliffe training for the Challenger mission in her spacesuit. The caption pointed out her emergency airpack.

The same intransigence was one of the major problems for President Reagan in overcoming the impact of the Iranian arms scandal. "If the press had heard the words, 'I made a mistake,' I think the thing would have cooled down right away," said Morton Kondracke of *The New Republic*. "There would have been investigations of Oliver North and things like that, but if the president had done this ritualistic thing of accepting responsibility and said that they had erred, he would have been 50 to 70 percent better off."[124] Many of the president's statements in the first few days after the initial disclosure subsequently had to be reversed or recanted, further damaging his credibility with the news media and the public's confidence in his ability as a leader.

LESSENING THE DAMAGE

Very rarely will a news media attack come as a complete surprise. When it does, the spokesperson certainly is entitled to say the organization is not aware of the details and will respond when it is. In most instances you will know the onslaught is coming from questions being asked by reporters, or by that feeling in your stomach that someone has said something that will give the news media a major opportunity to penetrate. In these situations the best defense is a good offense. You can lessen the seriousness of the media criticism, and the damage it can do to the reputation of the organization, if you get your information out first so the news media will understand what happened and why a communications foul-up occurred. It's tough for reporters to be too critical of an organization that has leveled with them, but very easy when it tries to finesse or disregard its error.

NASA's public affairs staff had ample time during the 10-day interval between the first and second disclosures to develop an explanation of why the preliminary analysis of the crew tape had been released to the media. A fact sheet with a chronology of the separate analyses of the crew tape and airpacks should have been prepared, with a written explanation and cover letter apologizing to the media for the earlier miscommunication. Distributing that background information at the press conference when the airpack and "Uh oh" disclosures were made would have blunted much, if not all, of the criticism in the news media. It also would have eliminated the need for the subsequent "bum rap" media briefing, when Admiral Richard

Truley, the former shuttle astronaut, had to explain what happened. That gave the media one more opportunity to do a story on the tragic disclosure, and how it was mishandled by the space agency.

You also can lessen the chances of criticism by recognizing when you have a problem and seeking advice from respected members of the news media on how the participants and the press can work together to resolve it. Humana's "pool meetings" with a group of the journalists covering the artificial heart patients allowed us to set up pool interviews on short notice, but they also provided both the press and the public relations staff with a way of airing their gripes and problems. The discussions always were constructive, although they sometimes got heated until we understood each other's positions and came to a meeting of the minds on how we could resolve the dilemma.

RECOURSE WHEN THE MEDIA MAKES A MISTAKE

Even when you have a good working relationship with the media, it's very important to point out reporting or editorial errors. However, don't expect news organizations to bend over backward to make readers or viewers aware of the mistake. The wire services will send out a correction to their members or subscribers. If it's a newspaper, you'll get a correction in a small box, along with any other errors that occurred in the previous edition. News magazines may ask you to submit the error in a letter for the letters to the editor section. The chances of any correction being made on network television are slim.

A common gripe is with headlines that do not correctly convey the gist of the news story. However, that can be just as maddening to the journalist who filed the story since he or she did not write the headline but will be the one who will catch the brunt of the wrath from the participants or spokespersons. The problem lies with a headline writer in the newsroom who will skim the first few paragraphs and then develop an informative phrase that he or she feels is appropriate for the story, considering where it will be in the paper and the space the story will take on the page. Most of the time the headline people do a very good job, but every so often you'll see one like:

"Heart Man's First Words: Gimme a Beer!"

The real problem comes in the interpretation of details. Some news reports of a chemical gas leak at Union Carbide's plant in Institute, West Virginia, indicated that 135 people were hospitalized.

You would assume that 135 people were admitted to the hospital, when in fact only 15 were kept overnight for observation while the remaining 120 people were examined in the hospitals' emergency rooms and released. Carbide made it a point to contact any news organization that conveyed the wrong impression and to get that figure corrected, but subsequent stories on the Institute gas leak still mention that 135 people were hospitalized.

In some cases the news reports can be truly damaging, such as an article in *The Wall Street Journal* during GAF's hostile takeover attempt of Union Carbide that said, "Warren Anderson had made it clear that Carbide was for sale."[125] When the misstatements can actually damage the value of the organization in the eyes of its important publics, it's imperative that you follow up first with the individual reporter and, if necessary, with his editor or news director to set the record straight and see how the misimpression can be corrected with readers or viewers. This is no time to relay the emotional outbursts that are occurring within the organization as a result of the story. It is a time for a one-on-one discussion with the reporter to point out the errors and the resulting problems it has caused and to find out what will be done to correct the mistake.

A good technique for illustrating the relative balance and accuracy of a news story is to color code the newspaper or magazine article. You can do the same with a transcript of the broadcast with the visuals summarized beside each paragraph. Use green for favorable statements, red for unfavorable, and leave the neutral sections white. Number any paragraphs with major inaccuracies and attach a sheet with the correct statements beside the numbers corresponding to the inaccurate paragraphs.

You'll see very quickly just how balanced and accurate the story in question is, and so will the reporter and his editor, although they may not necessarily share your interpretation. Send them the color-coded copy with a cover letter and ask for their assistance in setting the record straight. It's also a good idea to let them know you're interested in working with them to ensure more balanced and accurate coverage in the future.

When there's a real problem with the story, contact the journalist who filed it and then follow up in writing. The reporter can talk to his editor about the points in your letter, which also will provide them with something to use if they choose to correct the error. At the same time you will have documented your position and can use the letter as background information for other journalists if they bring up the points made in the inaccurate story.

It also has to be done quickly. You won't have the luxury of a normal media relations situation, where the problem can be worked out with phone calls and letters over several days. With hundreds of journalists on hand, the last thing your organization needs is to get tied up with one member of the news media in a dispute that can easily spur some of the other news organizations to pick up the idea and do their own versions of the same story.

EXPECT TO BE CRITICIZED

One way or the other, you are going to be criticized by some members of the media in their coverage of the story, if only because you cannot possibly satisfy all of their demands. Your game plan needs to establish priorities for responding to the press, knowing that some of your decisions will not sit well with the media but will help your organization to achieve the most important long-run objectives. The primary corporate objective for Union Carbide since Bhopal, for example, has been to reach a reasonable settlement of the claims stemming from the accident, and that objective has often influenced its disclosures to the news media, even if it meant being criticized in the ensuing news reports. "The news media wants confrontations, they want issues that bang you, and I was trying to stay away from that," Carbide's CEO Warren Anderson added. "I was very conscious of the issue of settlement as being the real game that we were playing, and if you want a settlement then you don't want to antagonize the people you want to settle with. To blow up all the deficiencies in India—and there are lots of them—would get their backs up and push us into complications that we didn't need."

Union Carbide also decided it would hold all media briefings on the Bhopal accident at the Hilton Hotel across from its corporate headquarters on a 640-acre tract in Danbury, Connecticut. Its public rationale was that with an average of 500 phone calls coming in a day, the company did not have people available to accompany television crews and reporters around the headquarters complex. However, one only has to drive along the beautiful roads and cross the curved bridges leading into the modernistic buildings hidden in the trees to quickly grasp another reason. Television crews would have had a field day shooting the spectacular facilities in their pastoral sur-roundings. Their editors would have had a visual bonanza contrast-ing Carbide's architectural award-winning headquarters with scenes showing hundreds of bodies and animal carcasses in a Bhopal slum killed by the gas from a Union Carbide plant.

Another Carbide decision which angered some reporters was to limit interviews to specific print media and to decline many of the interview opportunities on the network news programs and morning shows. The company's rationale in this instance was that the Bhopal accident or its causes couldn't be easily discussed in a few minutes on a television program and that television news film showing the hor-rors in Bhopal probably would be used at some point, overwhelm-ing anything a Carbide spokesperson could possibly say about the accident.

The company also knew it would have no way of knowing who else might be interviewed on the same segment of the news program. A number of politicians, environmentalists, and government officials in the United States and India were taking advantage of any opportu-nity to use Bhopal to gain visibility and support for themselves or the legislation they were trying to push through. It wasn't difficult to envision satellite interviews on network news programs bringing together on a split screen an Indian official in Bhopal, with its thousands of casualties, and Warren Anderson or Jackson Browning of Union Carbide.

On a practical level as well, the company also questioned whether setting aside several hours to prepare for a few minutes on a network television program was the best use of management time in the midst of the crisis, and whether this was the optimum way to get its message across to the publics that really counted. "A lot of people on the outside don't realize that when an accident like this happens, some-body just doesn't get on the tube and say something," Anderson observed. "It's not that simple. There's a lot of homework and an awful lot of preparation." At the time Carbide had consumer prod-ucts, including Eveready batteries and Glad Wrap, but Union Carbide was not part of the brand name. Consumers thus were not as im-portant an audience as were government officials, stockholders and investors, community leaders, and Union Carbide's 100,000 employees in the U.S. and abroad.

The reaction of the news media to both decisions was predictable. Union Carbide was called secretive and uncooperative for not allowing the press into the corporate headquarters. The terms of endearment and persuasive techniques used by frustrated producers of the network news programs were far more extreme. After several minutes of telephone arm wrestling with a producer for "60 Minutes," Walter Goetz, Carbide's director of corporate communications, was put on hold. When the conversation resumed, Mike Wallace was on the line. It's easy to come away from that kind of discussion with the feeling that you have betrayed the public trust in freedom of the press, and you can be sure that reporters and producers will do nothing to discourage that impression.

Those are always agonizing decisions, but you have to trust your instincts if you are going to protect the organization and the participants in the news story. At other times you may have to fight for full, prompt disclosure for the same basic reasons. Six years of remarkably successful press relations were demolished by one ill-conceived management decision that was then aggravated and inflated as much by the Reagan administration's communications inconsistencies as by the unwillingness of Poindexter and North to explain their actions. "If the administration had disclosed the whole story in the first week it would have been a huge story right then, but then it would have lost its news value," Barbara Dolan of *Time* observed. "In terms of the number of stories or the length of time it has been dragged out, there would have been far, far less to report."[126]

Watergate cannot be compared with the Iranian controversy, other than in the way both scandals consumed so much of the administration's time and attention when it was badly needed for much more important matters. The legacy of Watergate, as far as the news media is concerned, is that it honed the appetites of journalists for investigative reporting. For the American public, Watergate developed a miniseries mentality regarding presidential scandals that the Washington press corps is now very capable of satisfying, with daily installments that run for months.

Before the Iranian scandal, the Reagan administration's press relations had been extremely successful because Larry Speakes and the press office staff were constantly planning ahead to take maximum advantage of every opportunity, big and little, to gain favorable media coverage for the president and his position on the important issues. A good example is the president's weekly five-minute radio address each Saturday. It's only carried by a fraction of the nation's radio stations on a regular basis, but notice how often it's picked up and quoted by the other news media.

The White House press office also had done an excellent job of anticipating what the press corps would want to know and the information and visuals that would be needed, regardless of whether the president was in the White House or Walla Walla, Washington. "They are very well organized. They communicate well with the news media and provide good information on who, what, when, and where—where credentials are available, the names and phone numbers of those in charge, and so much more," Tom Hardin of the *Courier-Journal* observed. "They are up front with you 95 percent of the time about planning. That's all the media needs, even when the answer is a straight-out 'no' to your request."[127] Denny Brisley commented on the White House approach by saying, "We responded to the media when it was most beneficial to be seen and heard. I wasn't always in the perfect position to get my points across, but the press understood that I was going to do the best I possibly could for the president. That might go against what the media wanted to hear, but the questions they ask often went against what I wanted. I guess that's adversarial in a way, but it doesn't have to be a nasty professional relationship."[128]

Errors obviously were made in the Reagan administration's press relations after the Iranian arms deal was revealed, but they emanated from decisions made in the Oval Office, and thus provide some interesting lessons for any executive to consider. The president may well have believed that his policy goals toward Iran were well founded and that it was a high-risk gamble that the circumstances warranted. That's a management decision that any executive is entitled to make. The problem was that he didn't give adequate consideration to how it would be reported by the news media, and the resulting public reaction, before he authorized the initial arms shipment sometime in 1985.

The inconsistent and contradictory statements by the president and his administration over the ensuing weeks after the disclosure fueled the controversy and the media's negative reaction as they sought to get the story straight. An article in *Time* titled "The Tower of Babel" described how at a November 19, 1986, press conference "reporters, using words like 'duplicity' and 'deception,' peppered the president with the most skeptical—at times downright hostile—

questions he has had to face since taking office. His answers were at best unconvincing, at worst contradictory of what other government officials had said, and sometimes self-contradictory."[129]

If there's any lesson to be learned from Reagan's mistakes, it's that if you want to avoid or lessen negative press coverage, you'd better have your facts straight from the start, stick to them, and make sure that everyone else in your organization agrees before anyone starts talking to the news media. Your story will only be newsworthy as long as the media has something new to report, so get everything negative out in the open as quickly as possible, take your lumps, and look ahead. "News simply moves faster nowadays. The same elements that helped this scandal become so big so fast might combine to make it flame out more quickly, if it doesn't burn the house down first."[130]

CHAPTER TWELVE

Who Shall Speak?

During most major news stories the events themselves, whether they are a major disaster or a remarkable breakthrough, will determine the content of the news media's reports. Yet you will influence *how* they report those facts, and whether their coverage is accurate and objective. More specifically, it will be determined by the effectiveness of your spokespersons, whose attitudes and character will influence the way the media perceives your organization. Their actions and reactions in informing the news media will largely define both content and context of the news coverage, and thus the perceived value of the organization in the eye of the public.

What the presidential press secretary will say on behalf of the administration each day is a primary means of communicating the intentions of the U.S. government.It has a profound impact on the stock market, businesses, and government agencies, as well as the policy decisions of foreign countries. As the Iranian arms scandal has shown, one misstatement or position change by the spokesperson or any other senior officials can create a chaotic situation for the administration with the same audiences it wishes to inform or influence.

For any other spokesperson in the midst of a major story, however, the intensity and pressure of determining how to handle routine announcements and important disclosures will be just as important as it is for the White House press office. It takes a coordinated effort by different types of spokespersons with different levels of responsibility within the organization. It takes people with the right personalities, who are informed and articulate, but who also understand the limits of their authority and can respond to the media without damaging their credibility or the integrity of the organization. The spokespersons, therefore, have a critical role during a major news story, which is too often underestimated by top management until it is too late. This chapter analyzes that role.

WHO AND HOW MANY SHALL SPEAK?

The natural tendency is to think that one person should be the primary spokesperson for the organization. A solitary spokesperson, such as Bob Henrie during the Wilberg Mine fire, can do a remarkable job but that person also has significant limitations, especially if the story lasts for more than a day or two. On the other hand, an organization can have dozens of spokespersons, as NASA did during the investigation of the Challenger explosion. The space agency's charter stipulates that anyone within NASA can speak out to the press or the public without fear of retribution. That policy, however, has led to confusion in communicating with the public via the news media on more than one occasion.

The optimum number of spokespersons is three, with their authority to speak determined by their rank in the organization and their level of responsibility for disclosing information to its different publics. The president speaks for the U.S. government. His press secretary or other "senior government officials" speak for the administration when the subject does not require the president's views to be expressed directly. The deputy and assistant press secretaries in the White House press office handle the brunt of the media relations activities on a daily basis. They are authorized to speak for the administration on certain matters or at specific times when the press secretary is not available.

This three-tiered alignment has also worked well outside government. It has been used effectively during the artificial heart program, by Union Carbide in the aftermath of the Bhopal tragedy, and by Johnson & Johnson in response to both Tylenol poisoning crises. It's effective because it allows the organization to convey its major points regarding the news event while also providing a mechanism for keeping the news media informed of specific developments. It can work against an organization, however, if the principal figure in the news story is not interested in getting involved with the news media or if the people supporting him in the ongoing press relations activities are not well-suited for their responsibilities. The notable case where the three-tiered alignment did not work was during the Baby Fae experiment where Dr. Bailey refused to meet with reporters after the initial briefing and several ill-informed spokespersons were used.

Not every principal figure in a major news story is interested or well-suited to get actively involved with the news media. Those who are have to be willing to give up their personal and professional privacy for the life of a public figure who will be inexorably linked by the print and broadcast media with the news event itself. They have to convey the impression—in the glare of television lights—of being relaxed, confident, and in charge of the situation, no matter how good or bad it is. Regardless of how difficult or innocuous the questions asked by the dozens of reporters who ponder every statement, they have to respond patiently and convincingly.

That's not an easy task for most top executives, who might be used to breathing fire during management meetings and telling their subordinates exactly what they want done. On the other hand, if the principal figure is a natural leader who has the presence and self-confidence to handle himself effectively in meetings with large numbers of reporters, or in one-on-one television interviews, he can be a major asset in helping your organization convey the important messages to the key audiences it needs to reach if it is to maintain and enhance its perceived value in the aftermath of the news story.

SHOULD THE TOP PERSON BE INVOLVED?

For the artificial heart program, Dr. DeVries agreed to an occasional interview or media briefing during the course of Dr. Clark's 112 days of life with an artificial heart. He expanded his media involvement after the Humana artificial heart implants on Bill Schroeder, Murray Haydon, and Jack Burcham, making appearances on the network television morning shows and granting interviews with a number of national and local journalists.

On the other hand, Dr. Leonard Bailey, the surgeon for Baby Fae, wanted to avoid that kind of exposure and only met with the media twice. The first briefing came immediately after the operation, before some of the national news media had arrived from the East Coast, and the second was after Baby Fae died. In the 20-day interim, he only granted one interview, to the *AMA News*, a tabloid distributed by the American Medical Association. Bailey felt this was the publication that would be most widely read by physicians.

The degree of involvement of corporate chief executives is even more divergent. In the case of the Wilberg fire, the top management of Utah Power and Light, the owners of the mine, or Savage Industries, which operated the mine through its Emery Mining Company subsidiary, had nothing to say in public about the tragedy. The same was true of David Garrett, Jr., the chairman and chief executive at Delta Air Lines, after the crash of Flight 191. It seems to be traditional for the chief executives of major airlines not to make public statements when a crash occurs, even when their customers and employees have been killed.

The last few years have seen a growing willingness among the chief executives to get involved and take a public spokesperson's role when their organizations are in the midst of a crisis. James Burke at Johnson & Johnson was highly visible during the company's two Tylenol tampering crises and was credited by many as being one of the major reasons that J&J engendered so much public support for Tylenol during and after the investigation. Warren Anderson, the CEO of Union Carbide, took public responsibility for the Bhopal tragedy. Anderson's decision surprised many of those in the chemical industry, who knew him to be a very capable executive but a reserved man rather than a public figure.

Anderson had the option of designating any one of several members of Union Carbide's top management to take personal charge of the Bhopal aftermath. That would have allowed him to direct the efforts from the secure position and relative privacy he had enjoyed during his tenure as Carbide's chief executive. Instead, he designated Carbide's president, Alec Flamm, to run the corporation's ongoing businesses so that he could take personal charge of the Bhopal Team and address the complexities of how the company would deal with the worst industrial accident in history.

Anderson's public statements and his trip to India gave Union Carbide a face, a personality. It conveyed the personal concern of a major corporation about a tragic accident and demonstrated its willingness not only to shoulder the blame for what happened but also to get going on correcting the physical and emotional damage it had caused. The trade-off was that Anderson became the personification of the Bhopal tragedy and the series of aftershocks from Wall Street and Washington that trembled through Union Carbide. After the

Bhopal trip and after the Institute chemical plant leak, only one person was sought out to speak authoritatively for Union Carbide at congressional hearings about environmental safety. That was Warren Anderson.

However, even though he believes he made the right personal and corporate decisions, Anderson admits that not every chief executive or principal figure in a major news story should step forward to represent the organization in its communications with the public via the news media. "So much depends on the circumstances," Anderson noted. "The rule should be to get involved rather than don't get involved unless you have to. There should be a preference for involvement."[131]

Some CEOs may be reluctant to get involved publicly or to speak out on behalf of their organizations in the midst of a major news story for fear of not having all the answers to the questions reporters may ask. They should not be expected to have all the details. That's the job of people in the organization. Top management's role can be limited to speaking for the organization as a whole and introducing the people who will be best qualified to handle specific areas of activity, including press relations.

The principal spokesperson for Delta Air Lines the night of the Flight 191 crash was Matt Guilfoil, the airline's marketing manager in Dallas. Delta's president, Ron Allen, was not heard from even though he arrived in Dallas several hours after the crash. Allen could have spoken briefly to the news media on behalf of the Delta organization, expressed the feelings of its management and employees regarding the tragedy, and indicated how the aftermath would be handled.

Allen chose not to make a statement, so Guilfoil was the personification of Delta Air Lines that night. He did a highly effective job, but it's hard to see how he could be as believable as Delta's president in speaking for the entire Delta organization. The company's flight crews, ground personnel, and other employees, who are noted for their sense of loyalty to the Delta organization, certainly would have felt better about the tragedy had they heard from their president and known he was on the scene.

THE CRITICAL ROLE OF THE CHIEF SPOKESPERSON

Even if the principal figure is willing to respond to the news media, there will never be enough time to satisfy the demand for interviews and appearances on television news programs. Nor should there be. The highest priority will be the situation itself, and the CEO should have an important reason for meeting with the news media. Daily press briefings and interaction with reporters is important and should continue in the meantime, but that's the job of the chief spokesperson, not the CEO.

From an organizational standpoint, the chief spokesperson needs to be actively involved with the participants in the news event, so he has a firsthand perspective on what is taking place. He also needs a professional background, which will allow him to speak with authority and provide background and details for the many reporters who will not understand the underlying elements of the story. If it's a medical story, he should be a physician, although there are differences of opinion about whether he should have specialized in the subject area that is the focus of the story. It's very easy for a doctor to find himself giving second opinions in response to questions from reporters. "A doctor who's the medical spokesman is going to get pushed by the media, who see him as a doctor, and he's going to have to give medical answers, even if he's not a cardiac surgeon," said Dr. Allan Biegel, the medical spokesman during Tom Creighton's artificial heart operation in Tucson. "You need a very well-trained doctor who knows how to deal with the press but, even more important, knows the limits of what he's going to say."[132] In recalling the news media who covered Humana's artificial heart operations, Dr. Lansing observed, "This was an extremely knowledgeable press. They wanted detail and if we hadn't provided it they would have been out in the hospital finding someone else who would give it to them off the charts. What we were doing was meeting their needs and demands to be sure they got information from someone who knew firsthand what he was talking about, rather than misinformation from some secondhand source."[133]

One need only consider how Larry Speakes came across in the televised briefings with the White House press corps to know that you don't have to be glib to be effective. Speakes would never make it as a game show personality, but he had considerable clout with the press corps because he left no doubt what the position of the administration was in his statements to the press or his response to questions. It does help to have a spokesperson who can come across as being relaxed and confident, but Speakes wasn't concerned about that, knowing the impression his boss could make in public.

IMPORTANT SELF-ANALYSIS

Anyone being considered for the role of chief spokesperson needs to go through some careful introspection and analysis to be sure he or she is the right person for the job. They and the organization both have to recognize that this responsibility is going to consume their life during the duration of the news story and for months afterward. The role must be accepted willingly. Nobody should ever be forced to take the job, because they may destroy any chance their organization has with the news media if they reveal a negative attitude. If, on the other hand, you have people in your organization who badly want the job, take a look at their egos and consider what will happen after a few interviews on network television. "They become everyday actors," Dr. DeVries recalled. "When they get up in front of the bright lights, they suddenly are changed by the roar of the greasepaint and the smell of the crowd."[134]

They may not volunteer for the job, but the people who accept it had better be willing to take on this burden because they believe in the importance of helping the media understand the facts about the story. That means being knowledgeable about the subject, but also aboveboard and willing to answer any question, pro or con, and no matter how stupid it may seem. He or she also has to be unflappable in the alien, pressure-packed environment, which will emerge the first time they step into the glare of the television lights.

Dr. Chase Peterson at the University of Utah is still remembered by the news media as an outstanding spokesperson for the artificial heart program. Peterson was candid with the press and provided detailed information on Barney Clark's condition, sometimes too detailed for Dr. DeVries. He also is an enthusiastic teacher who enjoyed educating reporters with illustrations on a blackboard to explain important details.

Jackson Browning, Union Carbide's chief spokesperson, was known as "Cool Hand Luke" to members of the Bhopal Team. Ronald Wishart, Carbide's vice president for public affairs, recalled that "Browning would sit in a meeting for an hour and a half with 16 guys offering all kinds of opinions and not take them. He'd walk out of there in front of the press and in lucid English, declarative sentences, without undue embellishment, tell the facts. He had a great gift of being faintly amused by it all, and that was very helpful."[135]

THE ROLE OF THE PUBLIC RELATIONS SPOKESPERSON

No chief spokesperson can respond to the hundreds of daily phone calls from the media in addition to his other duties, but somebody has to. That's where the third tier of spokespersons, the public relations staff, becomes so important. By working closely with the chief spokesperson and the participants, they can respond to the brunt of the media inquiries as well as issue press advisories and interim updates that don't warrant having the chief spokesperson call a media briefing. In many instances the public relations spokesperson will release an important disclosure so the news media is aware of what has occurred and will indicate when a briefing with the chief spokesperson is scheduled to provide additional details.

Public relations spokespersons will be the ones heard most often on radio, reiterating over the phone the most recent update or development for hourly newscasts. In some instances they may brief the news media when the chief spokesperson is not available, but most often they are a secondary source, without their answers or clarification of specific details being quoted by newspapers and wire services. Because information will flow in two directions, they also will serve as an important conduit of concerns and opinions from the media to the organization. The public relations spokespersons thus are the principal eyes and ears of the organization in knowing what story angles are developing and the questions the chief spokesperson or the principal figure are likely to get at the next briefing. One of their most important jobs, therefore, should be to brief the spokespersons before their next meeting with the press, so they can develop answers in advance to the most probable questions.

John Dwan, the public relations spokesperson at the University of Utah, and Dr. Chase Peterson routinely met before Peterson briefed the press to review details in the update on Barney Clark and work through questions that were likely to be asked. "Often I'd play devil's advocate with Chase for as much as 45 minutes," Dwan recalls. "I'd ask the questions I thought he'd get, and he'd answer them. He was spontaneous and extemporaneous in responding to the media's questions, but he rarely got one that we hadn't anticipated and worked through before the briefing."[136]

THE IMPORTANCE OF HOMEWORK

Regardless of the approach taken in updating the news media, the relevance and effectiveness of what is said will largely be determined by knowing how the press is reporting the story. You and the other spokespersons can then take that into consideration in determining what will be disclosed. You cannot avoid knowing what the news media is saying. Anyone who tries is doing himself and the publics who are important to the organization a real disservice by adopting that kind of ostrich-like attitude.

Some physicians, such as Dr. Bailey at Loma Linda, made a conscious effort not to be influenced by news coverage and would walk out of the room when a press report was broadcast. Dr. DeVries tried not to read the newspaper reports on the artificial heart. They heard reports just the same, via radio news headlines in their car, over the television in another patient's room, or from the comments of another doctor or nurse in the halls.

The opposite approach was taken by Carbide's Jackson Browning. He made it a point to immerse himself in the latest print and broadcast news reports each day before he walked in to brief the news media so that he would be as knowledgeable as possible. The same applies to the president's press secretary. He is provided with a summary of all relevant newspaper articles and wire service stories before he goes into the presidential staff meeting each morning and then is kept updated with wire service stories throughout the day.

You must know as much as possible about the news coverage so you can correct any errors and inaccuracies, and anticipate what the press is likely to ask during the question-and-answer sessions. If a story is not accurate, you need to set the record straight in your remarks without indicating the offending news organization by name. That's the only way you can point out that you're aware of news reports that are not completely accurate. Then give the facts. The press is responsible and will appreciate having the record set straight. In that way you will have much less chance of that erroneous information being picked up and used by other news organizations for weeks, months, or even years to come.

Doing your homework involves following the ongoing news coverage in newspapers published nationally, like *The Wall Street Journal*, the *New York Times*, the *Washington Post*, the *Los Angeles Times*, and *USA Today*. You and the other spokespersons also need to know how the local papers are reporting the story because that will be what the participants, their families, and your employees are most likely to see. In addition, make sure you know how the three networks' evening news broadcasts covered the latest developments, as well as the softer news approach taken by the three network morning news programs. Then there will be PBS to consider and also CNN's ongoing coverage of the story. That's going to take a lot of time, which you or the other spokespersons won't have. As we mentioned in Chapter 3, it can be handled by professionals who make a business out of monitoring print and broadcast news reports, if you have the budget and time to set it up, or it can be done by people you know who are nearby and want to help. Whichever approach you take, make sure documentation is an ongoing part of your media game plan.

The danger is that any spokesperson is liable to get complacent or even a bit cocky after the first few briefings, especially if they have handled the updates and reporters' questions without much difficulty. That's when they begin to think they can get up to speed a few minutes before a briefing. The problem is that the press will sense when any spokesperson isn't prepared, just as you could tell when one of your teachers was not ready for a class. The toughest questions will then be asked, and gaffes or regrettable statements are most likely to be made. The only way that can be avoided is if you make it a standard policy to meet ahead of time with whomever will conduct the briefing to be sure he or she has the latest information, knows how the media is covering the story and is ready for the most likely questions.

If you're the person who will be on the spot, give yourself at least a half hour to prepare with one of your staff. Start out by discussing the basic details that will be disclosed to ensure they will not be misconstrued. Then review the transcript of the most recent briefing so you both know what was said. Take a look at any significant newspaper or magazine articles, with important paragraphs highlighted, and, if you have a VCR, any noteworthy TV news coverage. Have a list of the 10 questions most likely to be asked, and practice answering them.

If that seems like overkill, you're missing the point. It's no different than doing warm-up exercises and running passing drills before a football game. The spokesperson who is mentally prepared will go into each briefing informed and ready. Most important, he or she will have the right information and attitude for responding to any question the media will ask.

ATTRIBUTES OF A GOOD SPOKESPERSON

While a personable appearance is an asset for any spokesperson, it is not the most essential factor in making someone effective in this job. A number of important criteria can, however, make all the difference in representing an organization to the media, and these will apply to both primary and public relations spokespersons.

Having the Right Attitude

Many spokespersons have little understanding of how to relate to the media covering a major news story. That's a problem because their first encounter with the press can get the relationship off on the right foot or start it in the wrong direction, never to return. "The relationship between Loma Linda University and the press was strained from the beginning. It was clear that the university officials did not expect the attention, nor did they know how to handle it. The first press conference was opened by Edward Wines, the university's vice president for community relations. 'Allow me to tell you what the order of service will be,' he said, and then explained that he was used to running church services, not press conferences."[137]

You have to go into this new job with the attitude that you like what you're doing and you believe it's essential for the organization that it be handled correctly, because it is. "I think that if the bedrock of your belief is that your organization is worthwhile and important, that's got to be a great foundation to work from," said NASA's Shirley Green. "I really think NASA is an extraordinary agency. They've done great and wonderful things for this country, and that's why the Challenger experience hurts all the more. When you believe all the criticism is not accurate and well founded, it gives you the feeling 'By God, they're worth fighting for.'"[138]

It's much more than briefing the news media. It's informing the public, serving as the voice of the organization, and communicating on behalf of the participants so they can concentrate on what needs to be done. It also means recognizing the influence the news media can have on your operations.

Give the Impression of Assurance

You may well be apprehensive at first, but believability comes from spokespersons being well prepared and then able to convey the impression of being relaxed and confident to the mob of reporters who will be taking in every statement. It comes from walking into the glare of the television lights with a quiet, confident smile and then taking a moment to size up the audience before beginning to brief the journalists on the situation. A spokesperson who pauses to reflect before answering a question tells the news media a lot, and also allows the answer to be framed so he is sure of what he wants to say and is less likely to stumble through the statement.

The last thing anyone should do is act like he is a graduate of the Larry Speakes Spokesperson School. Remember that you will be in the eye of the beholder, better yet, in the eyes of millions of them. You have to come across as confident, relaxed, assured. You need to speak in an interesting manner, varying the pace of your comments, pausing, changing the level of your voice. You need to give the impression you are sure of every word you are saying and you believe in the importance and integrity of your organization.

Speakes could get away with acting like he was a defendant being cross-examined because he had "The Great Communicator" in the wings; but too many spokespersons appear worried, unsure, or angry, and that impression has far more impact on reporters and television audiences than anything they may say. Consider it from the media's perspective. Ed Yeates believes "The press is universally skeptical until proven otherwise, so this imagery, even if it's just nervousness because he's not used to all this, can be lethal and kill the effectiveness of a spokesperson for the company then and there. No matter what he says after that, it's liable to be misconstrued, misquoted, or, more likely, read between the lines."[139]

Barbara Dolan added an interesting perspective based on 10 years of experience in reporting for *Time*. "The press is always keyed up when they're on a big story, and the last thing you want to do is give them your crisis mentality. That will happen if you're very nervous—reporters will interpret that as your having something to hide. Before you ever deal with the press, deal with the situation internally so you're not terrified by it."[140]

Some people recommend confrontation training for anyone who will be the spokesperson during a major news story, or just in case they may be interviewed by a reporter. While it may seem useful at the time, in reality the ambush interviews and being grilled by "the world's most obnoxious anchorpeople," which seem to be a standard part of confrontation training, are rarely, if ever, seen during a major news story.

Training and practice for spokespersons is a good idea, but they should spend less time getting verbally abused in the equivalent of Kung Fu Communications School and more time learning how to be clear and precise in making statements to the press, and how to respond to questions on touchy topics. "One of the biggest difficulties is that doctors aren't trained to talk to us, and they need to be," George Strait of ABC News said. "They need to know that they must be precise because we are going to take them at their word. And they have to be precise in more than a scientific sense. They have to know when they are speaking to the mass media, they're speaking to the general public."[141]

Having a Good Grasp of the Important Elements in the Story

As the principal information conduit, a good spokesperson needs to understand where the media's primary areas of attention are likely to be and then play to those areas. "I thought they would want to talk about the project and where it was going," Dr. DeVries said. "They wanted to talk about everything. They had this vociferous, voracious appetite for information." The story will be much more than factual details. The primary focus of the media will be on the possible causes, the potential outcome, the future implications, and the human interest aspects of the story, which can include everything from what the first words were to what someone had for breakfast.

It's also going to take good judgment in deciding what should be disclosed without jeopardizing the integrity of the organization and people involved. Personal privacy is a major consideration, and most members of the news media respect that. But disclosures need not be a yes-no situation. Often there may be options that will allow relevant information to be provided without jeopardizing the working relationships with the participants and the news media.

Spokespersons at the White House frequently will go off the record to make a point or clarify information. Many of the background briefings are conducted under the condition that the press refer to "senior government officials" as their sources. That's a dangerous route for novices to take because once the precedent has been established, the news media will expect you to maintain it. A safer option is a written statement. This can be very effective when a spokesperson doesn't want to brief the media and then have to respond to questions that may be difficult or impossible to answer at the time.

Having a Penchant for Accuracy

Any spokesperson is going to be surrounded by information and often may think he has the answer to the news media's questions. This is no time to "think" about anything. The spokesperson has to be as sure as possible about the information he is giving out because his personal and professional credibility, as well as the reputation of the organization, are riding on everything he says.

Part of the spokesperson's problem will be that the media often will have more information than he has. Accept that as a fact of life for one basic reason. They have more sources. Even if it means feeling stupid and uninformed at the time, it still doesn't mean there has to be a response until those details have been confirmed and the organization has decided what it wants to say, which may be nothing at all.

NASA's public affairs staff at the Kennedy Space Center was often told by the media what the ships were bringing in during the recovery of the Challenger crew compartment. The media was getting its information by listening to the ship-to-shore radio communications. NASA chose not to respond because it wasn't monitoring the radio messages and, more important, because of its decision not to reveal anything about the recovery of the astronauts' remains until the families had been informed.

Jackson Browning of Union Carbide was questioned repeatedly by journalists, and criticized by some public relations professionals, for not responding to a series of extensive articles in the *New York Times* on the causes of the Bhopal accident. Browning didn't respond to specific points in the *Times* stories because he didn't have the facts. The company's investigation of the accident had not been completed. If he had and the company's analysis came to a different conclusion, his dilemma would have been no different than NASA's with the Challenger crew tape and airpack disclosure.

Journalists are going to report whatever details you disclose as factual information, so you can't rely on someone else to verify the accuracy. Their credibility will not be on the line—*yours* will be. In the controlled chaos that's a part of any major news story, the information you get often will have small but significant flaws because your sources have other responsibilities besides keeping you informed. Rather than relying on what you're told about specific details, get the report that has that information, or have someone copy it down over the phone. Then check it yourself. That may take a few more minutes, but it's the best way to be sure your disclosures are accurate, and that you are well informed when you make them.

Understanding the Relationship with the News Media

Spokespersons need to realize that a marriage of convenience occurs between the news media and their organization when that first disclosure goes out. It will last only as long as the media continues to cover the story, which could be days or months. It's also going to be tough and unpleasant at times, but this is the way these relationships have to work during a major news story. "So many people get involved in these things for the first time, and they just freak out," says Paul Raeburn, science editor for the Associated Press. "The participants and the PR people are always going to be at cross-purposes with the press. They have different jobs to do, so there's always going to be tension between them. They shouldn't conclude that reporters are out to get them, and they should not get nasty and try to close things up."[142]

Reporters know that any spokesperson has more information than is being disclosed. They often will pepper and pound a spokesperson with questions, hoping to chip away until they find out something additional that probably has more news value because it wasn't supposed to be disclosed. When they succeed, it's because the spokesperson doesn't know how to handle the stress that a barrage of questions can generate and just wears out.

Going Off the Record

One option is to agree to disclose the information to a reporter on condition that your name will not be used. That technique goes by different names including, "off the record," "not for attribution," "background," or "deep background," depending on what is being disclosed, how sensitive it is, and how often the spokesperson uses the technique. The terms often mean different things to different people, which can cause confusion and misunderstandings with the members of the media.

No matter what you call being an anonymous source, it's dangerous and invariably will cause harm to somebody or the organization as a whole because people don't go "off the record" if they have something positive to say to a reporter. "The reality is that we're usually forced to rely on anonymous sources when we've got a sensitive story, especially in government," said Michael Isikoff of the *Washington Post*. If you look at the Challenger coverage and knock out the information that was provided by sources who refused to be identified, there would have been very little that we could have reported."[143]

Going off the record sets a dangerous precedent in your relations with reporters, even though most will keep their word in order to get the information—although you can never be sure. What you can be sure of is more probing questions to get more off-the-record information. Morton Kondracke of *The New Republic*, suggests that the rule should be "don't ever tell any reporter anything 'off the record' because very little is ever kept truly off the record, unless you know the person extremely well and mean it to be a genuine secret for history."[144] A reporter's business is to get things into print and on the air, and you're just winding them up to find out more whenever you're "off the record."

Another problem is that enterprising reporters can take your statement and use it to corner someone else and get them to comment by disclosing how much they already know. Once the reporter has and uses your off-the-record comment, he can get it on the record by finding an informant who will either quote you indirectly or by corroborating another source for the same information. That defeats your entire purpose of going off the record.

A more satisfactory and less stressful solution to the pestering problem is the mantra, the phrase that can be stated repeatedly in response to questions that you don't want to answer. The basic mantra for U.S. combat troops taken prisoner is clear and simple—your name, rank, and serial number. Mantras can be somewhat more expansive for a spokesperson, but the intent is the same. You also will find that the news media will pester you less about things you won't discuss once reporters begin to realize they will only get a smile and the same basic response, no matter how many times they ask you. It's always tougher to maintain it when you're tired, but by knowing the disclosure limits and what your mantra will be, you're less likely to come out of a briefing or one-on-one conversation with a reporter with that awful, gut-wrenching fear, "Did I say too much and will they use it?"

Sticking To Your Disclosure Limits

The major concern for the spokespersons will be maintaining a limit of disclosure that is acceptable to both sides. Guidelines may be established at the outset, but that's the same as telling teenagers they can't be out after 9 P.M. on a school night. The good reporters will be pressing the limits to gain any information that will give them a fresh angle for their stories, the edge on their competition. This is where the spokesperson has to have a will of steel and simply refuse to cave in to the demands of the individual reporters. Those demands will not simply be straightforward requests to exceed the limits of disclosures; they will be couched in the form of "We have a source that has informed us that . . . " or "So-and-so told the AP in an interview an hour ago that . . . Can you comment on that?" or "Can you confirm or deny that . . . ."

Dr. Allan Biegel, chief medical spokesperson during Thomas Creighton's emergency artificial heart implant in Tucson, faced the same dilemma and found himself consistently sandbagged by reporters who approached him with varieties of baited questions. "I got uneasy when I had to deal with badgering reporters because I was tempted to overreact in responding," said Dr. Biegel. "Part of what threw me at the first briefing was that the media said they heard from other people. That could very well have been true. I was caught between saying I don't know, that's not true, or saying more than I wanted to reveal."

For many spokespersons the biggest difficulty will be in having a courteous way to say *no* to persistent reporters without getting in what seems to be an argument. The key is knowing in no uncertain terms the limits of disclosure before talking to members of the media. Then it's knowing how to respond, because if the media senses that a spokesperson isn't sure how much he can say, they will pepper him with questions on that subject until they break through.

During an interview for this book, we subjected Denny Brisley, who was then an assistant White House press secretary, to the type of questioning that she and her colleagues in the press office had to deal with every day so she could show how a spokesperson should respond to a reporter when very little can be said.

Reporter: I'm calling from Springfield to confirm that William Birnes, one of our prominent citizens, is being considered for the post of commissioner of the Glockenspeil Regulatory Commission.

Brisley: I'm sorry, but I can't confirm or deny that. As a policy the White House does not discuss presidential appointments until the president has made a decision and announces it.

Reporter: What do you mean? We have it from a number of sources!

Brisley: We don't discuss people who are being considered or a timetable or the reasons for a selection until it's announced. I'm afraid you'll have to just wait and see.

Reporter: Well, can you confirm or deny that he's being considered?

Brisley: We won't discuss it.

Reporter: We know he was at the White House today.

Brisley: We do not discuss personnel matters.

Reporter: You have to understand that Mr. Birnes has been very important in Springfield's political scene and had a lot to do with the president carrying this part of the state in the last election.

Brisley: I simply do not have anything more to say beyond what I already told you. The White House does not comment on personnel matters before they are announced.

Reporter: Can you confirm that Birnes was at the White House today?

Brisley: The president's public schedule is available to the press every day. However, he usually has other meetings and appointments that are not on the public schedule. I'm sorry, but I've told you everything I can, and that's it.

Reporter: Well, when will you know more so I can plan to do the story?

Brisley: As I've said several times, the White House has a policy of not discussing personnel matters or timetables or presidential appointments until the announcement is made. Here's the phone number you can call to check every day to see what the announcements are.

Reporter: What's your comment regarding the statement from Senator So-and-So's office that Mr. Birnes is being considered?

Brisley: Can we go off the record?

Reporter: Sure! You can trust me!!

Brisley: You're wasting your time. We are not going to discuss this. That's a matter of policy. You're not going to get an official response from the White House, and that's all there is to it.

Reporter: Well, we have it from a source within the White House that he is being considered.

Brisley: We won't comment on anything from an unofficial source. You have our policy, and that's all I will tell you. Thanks for calling.[145]

You won't have more than a few seconds to meditate, but you can use your mantra, your prepared statement that can be repeated over and over again in response to stressful questioning. Brisley's mantra was, "The White House policy is not to discuss personnel matters until they are announced." She said it several different ways, but she said it over and over again and never went beyond that statement.

Maintaining a Level of Consistency

The news media can and will react in a hurry in covering the developments in a breaking news story, but they also expect a reasonable degree of consistency in what is disclosed and in how information is provided. Reporters are going to examine the details the spokespersons provide to see if they detect any discrepancies and also to compare the disclosures with information that the news organization's research or other interviews provide. The spokesperson's credibility will stay intact only as long as the discrepancies can be explained.

Steve Lyons, the medical writer for the *Louisville Times*, noted that Dr. DeVries said in a speech that Humana Hospital-Audubon had checked with two transplant centers about the possibilities of a heart transplant on Murray Haydon before he proceeded with Haydon's artificial heart implant. Dr. Lansing mentioned at a news briefing that they had checked with one hospital, in Indianapolis. Lyons checked and was told by the only heart transplant hospital in Indianapolis that it had not been contacted by Humana about Haydon. When he asked Dr. DeVries for clarification at a subsequent press briefing, DeVries refused to discuss it further, and Lyons began to suspect a cover-up. "The inconsistencies in Humana's statements on where they had looked for a transplant, and their refusal to clear up the matter, made me wonder if they really had looked at all," Lyons recalled. "Another reporter on another paper might have run a story with the headline, 'Humana Caught in a Lie'—if only to pry the truth out of the artificial heart team. I was reluctant to do that because there was still a possibility it was a simple mixup between Lansing and DeVries that they stubbornly refused to straighten out. In that case a story about a coverup would have hurt the Haydon family and embarrassed the paper by blowing a simple misunderstanding out of proportion."[146]

There will be a natural tendency for the participants to hold off on negative or embarrassing disclosures as long as possible. That inclination will increase as the fatigue factor begins to set in, or when the participants have been criticized in the media. But it needs to be resisted. The spokespersons have to step up and make the disclosures, good or bad, on a timely, consistent basis if they are to keep the organization's credibility intact.

The same holds for changing the information guidelines in midstream during a news story. NASA's decision to impose a news blackout on the recovery of the crew cabin and the remains of the astronauts added insult to injury in the space agency's already damaged press relations. Michael Isikoff, who covered the crew recovery phase of the Challenger story for the *Washington Post*, recalled that assignment with considerable anger. "We were reduced to things I'm not proud of," said Isikoff. "I don't like calling families and asking what NASA has told you. 'Have they found the remains? Your husband, your son, what have they told you?' It was a demeaning experience because NASA wasn't putting out any information. There was a clear interest, the public wanted to know, and NASA was only telling the families."

The problem is that the media will discount the hundreds of good briefings and interviews and focus on the errors and inconsistencies in their assessment of a spokesperson's credibility. Dr. Lansing maintained an extremely busy schedule as an open heart surgeon in addition to serving as the chief medical spokesperson for Humana's artificial heart procedures, and he didn't always take the time to get a full medical update on the artificial heart patients before heading for the briefing center. The medical reporters quickly picked up the inconsistencies and requested a pool meeting to discuss their concerns with him. Two months later, when he responded to the question about Schroeder by mentioning the concerns about depression and suicide, the media declined to give him another chance. "Familiarity breeds comtempt," said Gary Schwitzer, the medical correspondent for CNN. "When Allan I ansing started getting cute and when he put on the Hollywood smile, he didn't come across as a scientist then so much as a guy who really got caught up with seeing himself." That's what made that inconsistency look like the Grand Canyon.[147]

Dr. DeVries, upset with Lansing's comments regarding Bill Schroeder's depression, added to Humana's inconsistency and further aggravated the situation when he unilaterally announced that detailed information on the artificial heart patients was going to be cut back and that the press would have to get its information from articles in medical journals. "DeVries got great press at the beginning, and most of us still respect him for what he's trying to do for his patients," said George Strait, medical correspondent for ABC News. "But you can't blow hot and cold with the media. You're better off if you choose a temperature and stay there."[148]

Patience and a Sense of Humor

A good spokesperson is not going to take himself, the news event, or his responsibilities too seriously. No matter how bad it may seem, it's not Armageddon. The spokesperson who can maintain his patience and sense of humor in the midst of the incessant pressure and frequent frustrations is going to make the news media feel more relaxed and comfortable.

Union Carbide spokesperson Jackson Browning handled his responsibilities with a great deal of nerve, presence, and aplomb. The *New York Times* provided an interesting insight into Browning's qualities as a spokesperson. "In his handling of the press, Mr. Browning maintained a calm, measured, and confident composure while declining to divulge technical information about the Bhopal plant. When reporters raised their voices, the Carbide spokesman responded in warm tones, and when reporters asked questions out of turn, they simply were ignored. Still, like Mr. Anderson, Mr. Browning has been dealing with a presumption on the part of reporters that the company, if not negligent, must bear some guilt for the profound suffering in Bhopal that has been portrayed nightly on television."[149]

Browning recalls that at news briefings it seemed like he was asked the same question 20 different ways by reporters. "If you start thinking about it, there's only so much time and if you've already answered that question and you know you can handle it, well, why not do it again? The clock's running and the next one you get might not be that easy to answer because you might not have the facts at your command. So, if they keep lobbing that question up there, why not knock it out of the park!"[150] Rather than getting impatient in having to respond to something he already had covered, Browning actually looked forward to the repetitious questions because he knew what his answer would be.

Browning also emphasized the importance of not venturing outside the previously determined limits of disclosure—of having the mantras clearly defined and of sticking to them regardless of the question or reporter's reason for needing to know. Even if you rephrase the answer to the question, there's always the danger the reporter will consider it to be a different interpretation and therefore an inconsistency to be wedged open.

Sincerity

Spokespersons have to know they don't have all the answers, even if they have been on national television, but are going to do the best they can to inform and help the reporters covering the story. They also need to convey the impression that they personally believe in what they are doing and are involved for that reason. That's something that will be sensed by the press.

Bob Henrie, the Emery Mining Company spokesperson, got high marks from the national media as well as the local and regional press covering the Wilberg Mine fire because of how he related to the journalists during the long hours of uncertainty. "Henrie empathized very well with the situation," said Chuck Zehnder, editor of the *Sun-Advocate*. "He did not remain aloof from it and was not the hard company official disseminating information. He was greatly affected by the whole thing and he shed some tears himself. That was admirable."[151]

There's nothing wrong with expressing personal feelings, or even getting emotional with the media. Matt Guilfoil, the Delta Air Lines marketing director at Dallas-Fort Worth, did more to convey the spirit of his company and its feelings about the Flight 191 tragedy when he choked up while disclosing the names of the flight crew, and then explained his emotions by stating, "We are all one family."

WHAT THE MEDIA EXPECTS FROM THE PUBLIC RELATIONS SPOKESPERSON

The press is going to rely on the chief spokesperson as the principal source of information in their news reports, but will turn to the public relations spokespeople for information and assistance in getting their stories out. The reporters who were interviewed for this book expressed the same informal criteria for judging the effectiveness of the public relations people they know they will have to deal with in covering a major news story. The criteria include:

Access to Information

How fast can the PR staff respond with firsthand information and answers to questions from the principals? The president's press secretary can go down the hall to the Oval Office or check with other members of his staff when something comes up during briefings of the White House press corps. Bob Henrie could pick up the phone and call the mine to get a response, but that wasn't as effective as if he could have talked with those involved in the rescue operations and provided their firsthand perspectives directly to the press. If the media briefing center is not at the scene of the news event, the good public relations spokesperson will spend time at the scene talking to the people who are involved and getting a sense of what is happening so he can speak with authority and provide firsthand examples.

Availability and Accessibility

The news media needs to be able to get to the public relations staff frequently and in a hurry for answers to questions, to request information, photos, or an interview, or just to get a sense of what is happening when there's a rumor or news report that someone doesn't understand. That need will be at all hours of the day and night because of the complexities of the news media's deadlines and world-wide media coverage from different time zones.

The White House system is to have rotating phone duty among the assistant press secretaries, which means that any press calls between 11 P.M. and 7 A.M. that week are routed to his or her home. If a reporter in Europe wants a direct response from the White House on a statement by a terrorist leader, he will get it, even if it is a bit groggy. NASA staffed the briefing center at the Kennedy Space Center 24 hours a day for more than a month after the Challenger. They responded to thousands of phone calls from media all over the world wanting information, the answer to a question, or a statement that could be used as a part of their news stories.

Delta Air Lines did the same thing for a week after the Flight 191 accident. Bill Berry recalls being surprised at the extent of the world-wide news media interest. "In the 1970s the press attention was intense, but the exposure after the Dallas crash made us aware that the media has ceased to be domestic and now is worldwide. Because of the different time zones, the continuous media need meant that you were dealing with the world, that you had no opportunity for a rest spell. The media did not go to bed at midnight and get up at 6:30 in the morning. While the domestic press was getting some sleep, the European press was calling."[152]

Availability also can come from being close by. Humana's press relations benefited by having its working space and telephones in the same large room at the Convention Center with the media, who thus could get any information or assistance we could provide just by walking a few feet from their work tables to ours. The same approach is used in the west wing of the White House, where the press corps briefing area and cubicles for filing stories are next to the assistant press secretaries' offices. The interaction that results can have a lot to do with knowing the mood of the news media and being able to anticipate what information they will want. At the same time, they'll get to know the public relations staff personally, which can make a difference when either side has a problem or something that needs to be worked out and requires a cooperative effort.

Ingenuity

In most instances there will be middle ground between disclosing anything and everything the media wants at the time and providing enough to satisfy their needs. What it takes is ingenuity on the part of the public relations spokespersons in determining how the organization can work with the media to get them the material they need. NASA's technique of having press conferences from space can easily be adapted for earthly news stories by placing a speaker phone in the briefing center. Reporters could then have a conference call with participants at the scene who are willing to spend a few minutes on the phone briefing reporters and responding to questions.

There are many options, and the public relations spokespersons don't have to be creative geniuses to figure out what can be done to accommodate the media with minimum disruption of those who are involved in the news story. All it takes is an open mind and the willingness to listen to the reporters and broadcast journalists. Their collective experience in covering hundreds of stories has spawned many techniques for gathering the information and visuals they need.

Some will say the White House is staging the news when the press office staff meets with representatives from the White House press corps before the president will be in a major news story to discuss how the needs of the news media can best be accommodated. More accurately, it is helping the press cover the story. How the press corps reports what happens is up to them, not the White House or any other organization.

It's important to remember that reporters are human beings working under terrific pressure. They appreciate being given a hand when it helps them get their jobs done. Human nature being what it is, you're likely to get more favorable consideration if you go out of your way to help the news media than if they have to fend for themselves.

Integrity

We mentioned in Chapter 9 that reporters will arrive to cover the story with a natural distrust for any public relations people who are on hand. It's part of their journalistic training to question the motives of their sources, and unfortunately they have had to deal with public relations people who have been ill-informed, evasive, and in some cases, dishonest in what they have said about the situation or people involved.

What the news media is looking for are public relations people who will be consistently truthful and open with them, regardless of what has happened. The dilemma all too often gets down to a public relations person who works for the organization and would like to keep his job. He knows that a majority of the questions reporters are asking are legitimate and that the major obstacle is with the paranoia of the participants, not the press.

If the organization expects to have objective news coverage, the spokesperson has to spend a lot of his time working in the no-man's-land between the participants and the press. Both sides sometimes will be distrustful and angry with him, but the single most important part of the job during and after that major news story will be in getting each to listen and understand the other side's viewpoints.

Often the spokesperson will be trying to get the decision makers to understand why it's important to clear up a discrepancy that nobody wants to discuss because they don't agree with each other, or how a specific interview will increase the chances of more accurate coverage, knowing that other journalists will follow the lead of that reporter. At other times, he's going to have to tell a reporter he's checked and the participants are not willing to be interviewed or to answer that question. Journalists tend to be good judges of character. They will discern very quickly if the spokesperson did what he could to get the information or just looked for a convenient excuse for not responding.

COMMON MISTAKES AND HOW TO AVOID THEM

Reporters also are quick to point out the mistakes the chief spokesperson or the public relations people backing him up are likely to make. With a bit of care and advance preparation, these mistakes can easily be avoided.

Not Having All the Facts

It may seem like a given, but the only people who should talk to the press are those who have been thoroughly briefed on the latest developments or who have been actively involved in the story itself and are willing to meet with reporters. "The worst thing you can do is put someone out there who doesn't know what's really going on or is not knowledgeable in discussing what the story is all about," said Ed Yeates, who's been a medical news correspondent for nearly 20 years. "You see that very quickly when they start to field questions.

The answers just aren't there. Then the press feels its old skepticism setting in."[153]

Overstating the Good News and Bad

With major news stories involving anything new, there will be a natural sense of excitement and a tendency toward enthusiasm, especially with medical spokespersons who are used to meeting with family members and saying something to boost their spirits.

The pattern seems to be with medical breakthrough stories that the doctors are supremely confident that they have an answer before they have had any real experience with the experiment. Then they find out it's much trickier than they thought. The problem may be compounded by the news media, who will pick up the enthusiasm of the participants in a good news story. They also will look for anything positive in a disaster that can help to offset the ominous situation they have been sent in to cover.

It's human nature to want to be optimistic and upbeat, especially in responding to a question with favorable implications, but that's the time to be thinking worst-case rather than best-case if any predictions are to be made. If it's worst-case and the spokesperson is wrong, the situation will be better than was predicted. If it's the other way around, he can be sure the news media will flail him later with what was said.

Another thing the media is likely to jump on are the absolutes and colorful phrases that many spokespersons like to use in their statements to the press to convey certainty. Again, it's human nature to want to give the public a sense of assurance, especially if you're a physician or a politician, but the press is going to report exactly what was said and hold the spokesperson accountable if it doesn't hold up. "Comments like 'a brilliant recovery' come to mind," said George Strait of ABC News. "Sure, it was a brilliant recovery from a surgeon's standpoint, but the public doesn't understand that, especially when the patient dies 10 days later."

It's equally important not to lose perspective on the whole project when there has been a reversal. Negative developments may seem all-consuming at the time and you'll feel as dejected as the participants, but you cannot come across that way when you meet with the press because you are going to have to live with whatever you say.

The best approach to take when a setback has occurred is to state what is known at the present time and not get caught up in any particular aspect of what happened. The spokesperson should keep the comments short and let the information speak for itself. Jesse Moore, NASA's associate administrator of spaceflight, did that well at the first briefing after the Challenger accident. It's unfortunate those comments were not made several hours sooner.

Letting the Press Get Your Goat

There will be many, many times when you'll want to scream in anger and frustration—when you've been jousting for hours with a reporter over a legitimate difference of opinion or after a long day filled with petty problems and stupid questions. But do it in private. The last thing the press needs to know is that you're angry. When they get that impression they don't back off, they start probing to find out why and just how hot under the collar you really are. Remember you're working in an adversarial environment, and some members of the media will pull the tiger's tail if they think it's mad.

There will be inaccuracies in the news coverage that will seem to be anything but fair and objective. That's upsetting, but that's the way it is. In many instances you'll understand the reasons better than the participants, who will want equal time or the equivalent of a full-page retraction. Their anger can easily spill over on the spokesperson if you allow that to happen, and it will come at a time when you need to keep your composure. The last thing any organization needs is the kind of combative mentality that existed in the Nixon White House during the Watergate probe.

THE NEED FOR MORE THAN ONE SPOKESPERSON

Bob Henrie is living proof that one spokesperson can handle a news event single-handedly for 72 hours, but Henrie feels he would have been better off if he'd had help during the height of the Wilberg Mine fire news coverage. "At the time of the fire, having two people working in tandem would have been much better," he observed. "In the subsequent weeks and months, I had more time to stay on top of things. I never had a reporter call me and say, 'So-and-So from the company said that, while you've been saying this. How do you explain the difference?'" Managing the press relations, as well as staying on top of the story and coordinating the logistics of briefings and interviews during the height of a story will be more than a full-time job for at least two people.

One reason Humana's media relations worked so effectively in the early months of the artificial heart program was the "twin towers" setup of its public relations spokespersons.[154] During the three heart operations, for example, George Atkins handled the hourly updates at the briefing center while I supervised the editing and selection of photographs. On other occasions one of us would be at the hospital getting the latest information and preparing updates, while the other was responding to the hundreds of media calls coming into the briefing center.

Atkins' experience in politics made him highly adept at knowing how to deal with the egos and conflicting personalities within the Humana Heart Institute. My strength in planning and coordinating press relations lent itself to handling the hundreds of details that had to be considered each day in maintaining the flow of information and visuals to the media. The other benefit of having two pivot people was that it allowed us to compare notes on sensitive situations to decide what approach to take in disclosing them to the media. We also could cover for each other if one was out of town, which was the case when Atkins was in New York the night that Jack Burcham died suddenly.

At the other extreme was NASA, which had too many spokespersons after the Challenger accident, due primarily to provisions of its charter which encourage freedom of expression. After the explosion, public statements were made by any number of space agency officials because no spokespersons were designated by NASA to be the media's primary source of information regarding the investigation. Some of its managers and employees felt no compunction in meeting with the media and providing them with hundreds of details and insights regarding the causes of the accident and management problems within NASA. Others wanted no part of the news media after seeing the coverage of the Challenger accident and aftermath.

Important lessons have been learned from the Challenger accident, as they are from any major tragedy. From the standpoint of the press relations, nothing stands out more clearly than the importance of making an informed spokesperson available to the news media as soon as possible and then designating one spokesperson whose primary responsibility will be to direct the media relations regarding the story as it evolves and until it dies out.

If it was anything, the Challenger explosion was a catastrophic problem which required decisive press relations. But in that respect it was no different from Bhopal, Delta 191 or the Wilberg fire. Better decision making about the news media could have been achieved by NASA, as well as more accuracy and consistency in its disclosures to the press, if they had been coordinated through one person with the job of being its chief spokesperson regarding the accident and investigation.

While there were some difficulties in each instance, all of the organizations in this book which handled the news media effectively invariably have had a chief spokesperson. Where the organizations have had considerable difficulties with the press, nobody had that job or it was assumed by many people, as in the case of NASA.

CHAPTER THIRTEEN

Battle Fatigue

Managing a news event is like racing an eight-oared crew shell. The winner is not determined as much by team strength as by who can continue the intense pace throughout the race and still maintain their balance and precise timing even when they're dead tired. And they have to do it without having any way of knowing how much further it is to the finish line.

The same considerations apply to the crew of an organization as it surges through the evolving news story. The participants and public relations people will be straining to coordinate their disclosures to the press without throwing the priorities of the organization out of balance. Physically and emotionally, they will never work harder than during the brunt of the media siege, but they also have no way of knowing how many days or weeks it will continue. As the news coverage wears on, stress fractures begin to appear in the organization façade, fatigue will wear on the patience of the participants, and spokespersons will get careless or, worse yet, thoughtless in what they say to the press. The strongest of people can wear out during a lengthy media siege, causing them to make mistakes that can upset the best game plan and can even cause the undoing of an organization.

This chapter deals with the physical and mental fatigue that affects everyone in a news story. It will discuss what the most likely causes will be, how to avoid burning out, and what can be done to lessen the mental and emotional errors that fatigue can cause.

THE GROUNDS FOR EXHAUSTION

The participants and public relations people learn very quickly that news events are an exhausting ordeal. The immensity of the situation itself and the stresses it causes are difficult enough, but there's also the frightening knowledge that dozens or even hundreds of newspeople are milling around outside, looking for information, pictures, and anything else they can use in covering the story.

People who are suddenly thrust into a news story generally are awed at first by all the lights, television cameras, and general media interest. They are private people who will be worn out by their concerns about what's happening at the scene of the news story. The relentless interest of the media will be difficult to understand, especially when their friends and neighbors are urging them to get some rest rather than asking how they feel and what they think about the way the situation is being handled. The intense media interest will be an added, awkward burden because for most first-time participants, the last thing they want to do is talk to reporters. The problem is they are courteous by nature, and it's difficult to know how to politely decline to be interviewed.

Even if they liked the media exposure at first, most of the participants and the top management of your organization soon will get tired of the presence of the news media and the relentless publicity. Tempers will get short with some of the news reports, where they often will see or hear only the headlines. They will have a hard time understanding why the news media covers the story the way it does and the reasons it seems to place so much emphasis on the seemingly negative aspects. Before long they will be asking how you can get them to go home.

Mel Schroeder, the spokesperson for Bill Schroeder's family, described the constant media coverage as like being at a party where someone shows up who wasn't invited. "Any time you made plans, one of the first things that came up was how to handle the press," Schroeder said. "You always had to have a place to put them so they could get their shots.[155] For the public relations people, that attitude will add to the stress of an already chaotic job, which is like a never-ending election night at one of the television networks. As a news event evolves, fatigue becomes more of a problem than the news media itself. The phone becomes an enemy that must be lived with day and night. Months later a feeling of dread will still crop up and you will find the members of your family looking at each other with a painful expression whenever there's quiet and the phone begins to ring. It's not bad news; it's just the news media wanting something, but the feeling is the same

THINGS THAT WILL WEAR YOU OUT

First is the sheer volume of those phone calls and personal contacts with the newspeople on hand to cover the story. That number probably will reach the thousands during those 18- to 24-hour days, although there's no way to know for sure because you'd never have time to count. Each conversation will have an intensity that reflects the reporter's concern about the pack journalism environment and the imminent deadlines they so often will be facing. Every reporter will want to interview the participants, and they'll quickly submit interview forms or follow whatever procedure you've established. They know you have hundreds of requests stacked up, but only one really is important, and they'll check with you several times a day to find out. Some will be polite, others will pester you and insist on an answer, which you probably can't provide because no decisions on any interview requests have been considered, much less made.

The network program producers tend to be the most insistent and convincing people you will run into when they are trying to line up guests for one of their shows. The problem is that several hours of the participants' and public relations staff's time can be consumed in making the arangements and getting ready to appear for two minutes on live television, which is what the networks prefer. And it may come at some oddball hour like 4 A.M. if it's one of the morning shows and you're not on the East Coast.

Next, you may find yourself having to deal with the media gunslingers, the investigative reporters who come riding into town and are going to get the story behind the story at all costs and no matter what you say. Everyone gets worn out in the effort to give them the same consideration as the rest of the news media while also trying to anticipate who or what they will dig into next and how to respond most appropriately.

The real problem with investigative reporters is they may know how to probe and ask intimidating questions, but all too often they know very little about the subject when they show up. That means you, and any participants who get pulled in, have to explain everything with extra patience and care, knowing they are looking for any opportunity to take a hunk out of your organization's haunches, preferably quoting you to make their point.

The exception is the television news magazines. Dr. DeVries recalled that Barbara Walters had a file about eight inches thick when she came to Louisville to interview him for "20/20." "She showed me the file but wouldn't let me go throught it. I'd love to have seen what was in it just to see the criticisms. They'd really done their homework, and she probably had every piece of relevant information, positive or negative, on artificial hearts."[156]

Then there will be the complex decisions that will take hours of meetings and discussions, while you know all the time there never will be an easy answer, and everything is piling up in the meantime. It took nearly a week to decide that Bill Schroeder was too weak from the stroke and fever he had suffered to be safely transported to Jasper, Indiana, for his son's wedding. What made it even more difficult was that Dr. DeVries had told the Schroeders after the surgery that Bill would be on hand, and the *Life* magazine contract stipulated that $10,000 would be paid for exclusive coverage of Schroeder at the wedding.

Getting the appropriate people involved with the media also will be time consuming and stressful, especially if interviews are to be arranged. The efforts of Union Carbide's Ron Wishart in convincing Warren Anderson to be interviewed by Stuart Diamond of the *New York Times* are typical. "It was hard as hell to get him to do that interview, but we needed to have our situation personified. We needed to get out of that faceless, corporate, noncaring group," Wishart recalled. "You know, he's a proud man, but he's not an 'I' person. . . . It's easy for a Congressman Waxman, but hard for a Warren Anderson."[157] It may have been hard, but the feelings that Anderson expressed in that article conveyed the personal concern of the company, as well as the man, for the Bhopal tragedy.

On the other hand, you may be dealing with extracurricular situations involving the news media when public figures like the president of the United States suddenly get involved. Or there may be people in your organization with armor-clad egos who insist on media exposure, regardless of the impression they are likely to make. Humana had one whose wardrobe and behavior quickly became the butt of some nasty jokes among the reporters and television crews. Later she enraged the television networks when Bill Schroeder took a wheelchair ride outside the hospital, which was being pooled for the benefit of the media. In spite of his weakness, she insisted on wheeling Schroeder down to the corner and back so there was no way she would be missed. Then, even though his speech was severely impaired, she prodded him to say something, making Schroeder and his family very uncomfortable and herself look ridiculous.

That type of situation creates a great deal of stress for the news media, just as it does for spokespersons and the public relations staff, because you can't help but get personally involved with those who are in the midst of the story. You, the journalists, camera crews, and photographers become a part of their family. You laugh with them when there's some good news to report and weep when it's the worst. "I'll never forget when I had to announce that all parts of the mine that could be searched had been explored, and that we had determined there were no survivors," Bob Henrie recalled. "It was an extremely emotional situation because I and all of the media had always maintained a hope that we would find survivors. You saw very quickly that they weren't just reporters anymore. They were concerned people who hurt just as much as everyone else because of what they now knew."[158]

Even though they have covered tragedies before, it gets no easier for the news media each time they are sent out to cover a disaster. CBS correspondent David Dick, now a professor of journalism at the University of Kentucky, was there when Henrie announced that all of the Wilberg miners had died. "It was that God-awful news that as a human being you dread to hear," Dick said. "But as a professional you have to get it right, and you have to make sure he really said what he said and that you don't screw it up. But that doesn't make you feel any better. I felt a hurt as a human being, but I felt that my hurt should not, cannot, must not stand in the way of doing a professional job in reporting what had happened."[159]

THE EXHAUSTING LIFE OF THE NEWS MEDIA

While the emotional strain affects everyone, the exhausting hours the media keep will exceed even those of the participants. It will be especially tough on the reporters and camera crews who have flown in to cover the story and are in another strange town in their endless sojourn in search of the news. They are used to the long hours and can sleep on straight-backed chairs in a briefing center, but they don't enjoy the hardships any more than anyone else. "For Schroeder we were up at 5 A.M., or at 4 A.M. if we had something going on 'Good Morning America,' and usually didn't finish until the 'Nightline' segment was done," said David Cohen, now the St. Louis bureau chief for ABC News. "We had two crews, one at the hospital and one at the briefing center, and averaged 22 hours of coverage a day during the first 10 days. Many nights you didn't sleep or you slept for an hour and you could never guarantee anyone time to eat. That's why we bought the small refrigerator and coffeemaker for the trailer."[160]

The workdays for CBS correspondent David Dick ran from 3 A.M. to around midnight during his coverage of the Wilberg mine fire since he was covering for both the network radio and television newscasts. The day would begin with editing and updating the most recent television news reports for "CBS Morning News" and would continue without letup doing the hourly radio news broadcasts as well as television reports for "CBS Evening News." It would end in the motel room phoning in radio segments for the next morning "World News Roundup" before grabbing some sleep and starting again. "Whether it's a hurricane, tornado, coal mine disaster, or actual combat, you reach a point where you don't need as much sleep as you normally do," Dick observed. "Your sensory and spatial relationships are altered, and it's incredible what human beings can do. Obviously, you'll need a break later, and when it comes you'll fall flat on your face."

All-nighters will be commonplace for many journalists covering the story, especially the news magazine correspondents when they are on deadline and the network television crews, who have to be ready for a live feed at the specified time, regardless. Both the print and broadcast media also will be contending with the excessive demands from their newsrooms, where the distance and authority often insulate an editor from the realities at the scene of the story. "The fact is that the people back in the newsrooms who are running the story don't have any sense of the situation. You not only have to deal with events as they are occurring, and the press you're competing with, but you deal with a news organization that wants you to do the impossible," remarked Barbara Dolan of *Time*. "It's a highly pressured situation and in many instances the journalists aren't given any choice as to what they have to do."[161] Journalists tend to give you the impression of being easy-going, but as the hours and days drag on, you'll see some of the most low-keyed newspeople you've met shouting into a phone and slamming down the receiver.

RELIEVING THE PRESSURE

Stress is an integral part of any news story and is going to build up in direct proportion to the magnitude of the media coverage and the length of time it continues. Stress is also degenerative; it saps your strength and your resiliency, making you unable to bounce back from knocks you will continue to take from all sides. Knowing that, there's a lot you can do to keep the news media from shouting at you, and vice versa, even though you're going to get tired and before long the patience on all sides will be in short supply.

Get Help and Delegate Assignments

It's human nature for the public relations spokesperson to act like a duck in a shooting gallery, going in a different direction every time somebody wants something, whether it's an update, an interview on the noon news, or an answer about where to park the microwave truck. The first and third requests should be handled by someone other than the spokesperson and can easily be delegated to people who do not necessarily have a strong public relations background.

The same holds true for the middle-of-the-night media calls. Network radio newscasters are not looking for earthshaking disclosures at 5 A.M., but they do need a voice that will give them the latest update, even if it's six hours old. Take a tip from the White House and set up rotating phone duty among your associates. They can handle the calls, and the spokespersons can get some much needed, uninterrupted sleep.

Give Everybody a Break

Considering the intensity and long hours, everyone is going to need some time off. The White House has the answer when it puts the "lid" on so that the news media and the press office staff can get a break from each other. The optimum times are when the news deadlines will be the lightest, from 11 A.M. to 3 P.M. and 11 P.M. to 7 A.M. Eastern time. Everyone needs and can use that time. It will give the public relations staff a chance to find out what's happening at the site of the news story and talk about how to disclose upcoming developments. The news media will use it to work on stories.

And every so often there may be a chance to sneak in a quiet lunch or an hour's nap somewhere without having phones ringing. That's not to say that the phones will stop when the lid is on. They never stop, but they can be handled by whoever has phone duty. That person can provide information from the latest update and get the names of any reporters who need more information for a return call later.

Make it a point to get away from the briefing area or wherever those long hours are being spent. Get some fresh air for an hour or, better yet, some exercise. Go for a walk or do something strenuous if you're into physical fitness. The demands on everyone will be exhausting no matter what you do, but you'll have more endurance if you've had a chance to clear the cobwebs out of your brain—and with something besides a cup of coffee.

Those breaks will become especially important if the story is likely to continue for an indefinite period, as it did at NASA, Union Carbide, and Humana. Then those periods away from the action will need to be extended for more than a few hours. You and the participants probably cannot get away and take a real vacation from the situation, but you can take one from the news media. Have someone step in and cover for you for several days in providing information to the press.

Have a Realistic Interview Policy

A major stress point for the participants, the public relations staff, and the press will be the dozens of interview requests that will come flooding in, primarily for the principal figures in the news event. They need to be funneled through the public relations staff, or else the participants are never going to have a moment to themselves, much less for what has to be done. At the same time, decisions should be made on whether interviews are going to be granted and what the procedure will be for conducting them so everyone can plan accordingly.

It's tough to give a firm answer to each reporter when there are hundreds of requests and the people they want to talk to have very little, if any, time to talk to the press. The best approach is to get as much information as possible on what the interview will deal with and the reporter's deadline and to say when you hope to discuss it with whomever has been requested. But be realistic. It's easy to raise false expectations when you know the chances are next to nothing. Give them an answer. The sooner they have a response, the less stress will be on you and the reporter in advising his newsroom of what to expect.

You can do a lot to reduce the stress on the participants by setting up the initial interviews so they will be relatively relaxed and everyone in the media has equal access to the information. The biggest obstacle will be participants, not the press, since they will be anxious already and the thought of being interviewed by reporters and television cameras will just add to their anxiety. What they need to know is that the first interview can be done in a way that is most comfortable to them. They can meet with a small group of reporters who will be the pool for the rest of the media, and one television camera can supply the rest of the media. It can be done in their home or wherever they will be most at ease.

You also can reduce the stress of the news media if the participants cannot or are not willing to be interviewed by coming up with some good alternatives. Who else involved in what has happened would be interesting to talk to? What's their background? How comfortable would they be in being interviewed by members of the news media? "It has to be somebody who is intimately involved in knowing what is going on as a member of the team, not just designated because he has an M.D. and wears a white coat," observed Dr. Lawrence Altman of the *New York Times*.[162] You may well have some very interesting and articulate engineers, nurses, technicians, executives, or others who can fill the gap and do a superb job in representing the organization.

The alternate's participation has to be voluntary. They also should have a chance to check with the principal figures to ensure that what they say is consistent with the latest information from the scene. Then let them be in a setting that's comfortable for them, which may be a pool interview or a series of one-on-one interviews. If they are willing to brief the media as a group, but are not used to public speaking, the thought of standing behind a podium in the glare of those lights may be too scary. A good alternative is to have a draped table where they can sit and be more relaxed. The public relations spokesperson can open and conclude the briefing and spot the reporters with questions so everyone will be recognized and the person conducting the briefing can concentrate on the answers.

Avoid Getting Overextended

Who will talk to the investors, the customers, government officials, community leaders, and the press? They all want to hear from the principal people, and their requests are legitimate and important. In its efforts to help the organization make the best impression on the people it needs to convince, the public relations staff may overextend the principals and wear out the most valuable asset the organization has. Warren Anderson, the chairman of Union Carbide, contacted Charles Locke, his counterpart at Morton Thiokol, after the Challenger accident. "Everyone was interested in whose fault it was, and I knew they had him on that rat race from Cape Canaveral over to the Houston space center, then up to Washington," Anderson recalled. "They had him on the circuit, so I dropped him a note and talked to him on the phone. I said to be careful and don't let them do it to you. The organization is trying to help, but when it comes to how much the CEO can do in any given period of time, only *he* can judge that."[163]

We fell into a similar trap by not scheduling any periods when Dr. Lansing and Dr. DeVries would be completely free of the news media. Two months after Schroeder's surgery, medical briefings had been discontinued, but we were still working down the backlog of interview requests. Neither physician had any time off from reporters and television cameras, which was evident in how quickly their interest and enthusiasm waned when the news media returned to Louisville to cover Murray Haydon's artificial heart operation.

"I think if there's any message for executives, it's for Christ's sake don't let them push you," Anderson added. "Your people mean well, but they won't let you alone. They'll want you to be on "Face the Nation," and "Good Morning America," They'll have you in New York for meetings in the morning, Washington in the afternoon, Charleston the next morning. You've got to get somebody to sit by your side and say 'Don't let them do that to you.'"

Bring in People off the Bench

You'll find the media will be sending in relief crews and backup reporters if the story will be prolonged. Your organization should do the same thing by using backup people who can take over the press relations activities. That gives the first team a much-needed break and provides their alternates with the valuable experiences that only can come from having to handle the situation in their absence. How effective your press relations are in the long run will be determined by the strength of your bench. The sooner you begin to get the capable people involved, the more effective they can be in taking over in your absence.

Reach Out and Touch Someone

It's easy to lose track of the rest of your life in the midst of the mayhem. The days become a blur, and weekends are meaningless. It's always dark when you finally get home at night. In the morning, nobody is up yet when you head back to the briefing center. That will be the spokesperson's normal working situation for days, which may stretch into weeks, and you quickly lose perspective of what else is happening in the world, your regular job, or at home. But those are the things that really count; they will still be there long after the situation has settled down and the media has moved on.

When you are handed a wad of phone messages from the media and sort through to see who called, you may find one that's not from the news media, but from an old friend. They will be calling to let you know they heard you on the radio going to work this morning or saw you on television and wanted you to know they were thinking about you. Those are the special calls. When you take a few minutes to return them you'll find they provide an emotional boost that will help you for hours.

It's vital to stay in touch with those who mean the most to you, so give your loved ones a call to let them know you're surviving and have been thinking of them. If you have been interviewed and know it's likely to be used by one of the television stations or in the local newspaper, let them know so they have something to look forward to. In turn you will find them providing the encouragement, support, and understanding of what you are going through that can help you to keep a positive attitude. You also will know you have something to look forward to when it's all over.

Your spouse or a close personal friend can be immensely helpful in the support and encouragement he or she provides. My wife, Becky, often gave me a unique perspective with her "innocent bystander" reactions to how the news media was reporting specific developments and to how the Humana spokespersons had come across in explaining the details. She also became very adept at fielding media calls in the middle of the night and whenever I was not home. Most important, she knew the participants, and she provided the safety valve for venting frustration when the politics and power plays within Humana and Humana Heart Institute International complicated the already difficult job of being consistent with the news media.

Have a "Hideout" away from the Action

After the initial shock of the onslaught, the daily routines will become established and you will lapse into a kind of trench warfare with the reporters. It will become more intense as their deadlines approach and will seem to die down when the lid is on. Barring any unforeseen disclosures or sudden events, the days will conform to a schedule much like the coming and going of the tides. You will be constantly in demand, and people will be pulling at you from all sides, but the immediate needs of the press and the national audience can easily be satisfied. Once you have established this schedule, find a "safe house," a secure location where you know you will not be disturbed. It should be a place where, for about 15 to 30 minutes, you can sit back, close out the world, and let your mind refresh itself.

Warren Anderson recalls going to see the company doctor during the prolonged stress after Bhopal, to make sure he was physically OK. The doctor said he was fine, but gave him a key to a room with a bed in the dispensary. "I put the key in my desk and didn't think much about it until about two weeks later," Anderson recalled. "It was one of those days where I felt like crawling *under* the bed. So I went down and spent about 45 minutes by myself. That's the only time I used that room, but I knew it was there. That made a difference."

KEEPING THE FATIGUE FACTOR UNDER CONTROL

The duration of some major news stories is predictable, but with others there will be no way of telling how long they will continue. When it's an election campaign or a bicentennial celebration, you know when it will end and that everything will then return to normal. But what about a story like the Challenger accident, the Bhopal tragedy, or the artificial heart clinical investigation? Chapter 14 will cover what an organization should do if the news story continues for weeks or months. The message in the meantime for anyone who may be involved in a major news story is to pace yourself. Even if it may last for only a day or two, handle it as if you were running a mile race, not a 100-yard dash.

The best way to learn how to run that marathon is to take a lesson from the journalists themselves. They will be under just as much pressure as the participants, but you'll rarely see one of them getting hyper, unless they think their competition is being given an unfair advantage. Most of the time they will seem rather laid back, even when they are working intensely. They know they can't afford to burn out and miss something significant. Neither can you.

Develop a routine for the daily activities that will allow time to step back from the situation to size it up. There may be hundreds of calls to be returned, but that doesn't mean they should bury you to the point where you cannot stay in touch with the situation or the people involved. Somebody else can handle the less important details so you have time to catch your breath and chat with members of the media and people at the scene who have the best sense of what's happening. Those contacts, as well as the insights they can provide, can make all the difference in you having the right perspective on the story, as well as a fresh attitude and outlook when it's time to make the tough decisions that invariably will come up.

When you know you will have to be in the trenches for some time to come, the best answer to battle fatigue is to pace yourself. Resist the compulsion to respond immediately, unless it can be done easily and you are absolutely sure of the answer. The situation that has attracted the media's attention will not be resolved at the next news briefing or by what is said in response to the next question a reporter asks. It could, however, be severely damaged by an ill-thought-out answer that is prompted by exhaustion or having no patience left. How well your organization comes out in the media coverage will depend on you being as calm and consistent as you possibly can for an indefinite period of time.

CHAPTER FOURTEEN

Managing a Marathon News Story

Most news stories run their course in a week to 10 days. There may be a few blips of media coverage when government investigators report their findings, lawsuits are filed by the victims or their families, or the first anniversary occurs, but it won't approach the intensity of those frantic hours and days at the beginning. Any story, however, has the potential to continue indefinitely. Some will go on for months or even years because major questions are still unanswered, important new developments occur, or reporters dig up revelations that add a controversial angle to the situation

After those first few days, an organization will become increasingly vulnerable to criticism and outright attack in the press and in public. "There's some benefit to a short-duration crisis story," said Ed Yeates. "When it happens, the press comes and covers it and then they leave. But the longer it goes on, the more vulnerable the organization is to the skeletons in the closet."[164] The change in the tone of the news coverage as the story drags on may come as a surprise, but it will quickly give way to shock at the realization that all those reporters who were interested in what was happening now have completely different reasons for wanting to know. Then comes a feeling of hostility, aggravated by fatigue and the ever-present microphones and narrow spiral reporter's notebooks. Finally, a profound sense of despair sets in when you begin to think this situation may never end.

If you have done your job well and have the foresight to see the realities of the situation, you know your organization will have to change its ways if it is to accommodate a news story that has become a media siege. Like the White House, it will have to accept the fact that the news media onslaught will be a part of its daily routine. It will have to develop capabilities to service the needs of the media who will continue to cover the organization, whether it likes it or not. This chapter deals with how you and your management team can size up the impact that a news story can have on your organization if the media coverage is likely to drag on for who knows how long. It discusses the important decisions and steps that need to be taken so a new organization emerges that can survive and succeed in a media siege, no matter how long it lasts.

HOW LONG WILL THOSE NEWSPEOPLE BE HERE?

That question will be on the minds of management and the participants as soon as the awe of being covered by all those reporters and television cameras begins to wear off, which usually begins within the first few hours. Who's to say? If another major story breaks that has more news potential, most of the national media will be gone the next day. The story would, however, still be covered by the local media and wire services. If it's a slow news time and nothing significant comes up, they are likely to be there until all of the news possibilities have been picked clean.

If the story occurs near a metropolitan area where it can be serviced by reporters and television crews from a nearby bureau, the networks and national media can afford to cover it longer, even if it means driving an hour and a half each day to get to the story. However, if the news media has to travel to the location and set up shop for the duration, the expenses can become a consideration in weighing how soon to pull out—as long as the competition will be doing the same thing. The television networks remained in Louisville for four weeks covering Bill Schroeder's artificial heart operation and initial recovery. Several newspaper reporters were in town for two weeks on the story. Dr. Lawrence Altman of the *New York Times*, remained for 45 days, writing a series of in-depth stories on the artificial heart and working on the manuscript for a book.[165]

The media will cover the story as long as new disclosures give reporters fresh news angles to develop. The Schroeder story was unusual in that the news media had an endless stream of favorable news developments to report for two solid weeks, and a sense of euphoria developed in the press, just as it did with everyone at Humana. Most stories will go the opposite way and get more negative because most of the journalistic emphasis will be on one question—what caused it? Interviews with critics and experts and the history and safety record of the organization will be among the dozens of considerations explored by the news media as possible factors. The more detailed and tangible the revelations, the longer the siege is going to continue and the darker the shadow it will cast on the reputation of the organization. The Challenger accident and Iranian-Contras scandal continued to be major news stories for months because of the subsequent developments reported by the news media.

SIZING UP THE SIEGE POTENTIAL

Executives often make the mistake of assuming the media is out on a witch hunt whenever it covers a story. Unfortunately, that impression is likely to get reinforced during the initial encounters with reporters, when the majority of the questions will focus on what happened, what caused it, and who is responsible for what occurred. After getting questions along those lines for a few hours, it's easy for anyone to get defensive, especially if the organization seems to be guilty, if only because it was involved.

Those first few hours are the critical time when you need to filter out the noise and consider the most likely duration of the story. Also look closely at the substance of the situation as quickly as possible to see just how vulnerable the organization will be to a media siege. Those two factors will give you a rough idea of how long and how much media coverage you can expect. Then it's a question of management anticipating how the media is likely to react as soon as it settles in and starts to map out its coverage plans for the story. What's the organization's track record with situations like this? Who in government, the community, the media, has attacked it, and on what grounds? What information exists that would support their contentions? The longer the list of answers you can develop, the more likely the media siege.

Consider Delta Air Lines' excellent reputation in the industry, exemplary safety record, and high employee morale. The company's reputation may have been dented by the crash of Flight 191, but it has not been damaged, even though the NTSB concluded that pilot error was the probable cause. Delta's only major press relations problem began a year later during the trial of the first lawsuits, which brought up the past sexual activities of a widow and a dead passenger. The investigations into their private lives were widely reported by the news media, and later by "60 Minutes." After its attorneys refused to allow an interview with "60 Minutes," Delta wound up with a black eye because the 45 million CBS viewers never were told that the personal investigations actually had been prompted by claims in the lawsuits.

THE IMPORTANCE OF BEING PROACTIVE

Every organization has its weaknesses and vulnerabilities. Top management gets into that subject in no uncertain terms when annual operating budgets are being reviewed. But these executives will shy away from discussing those problems publicly when they could affect the price of the stock, relations with potential investors, efforts to raise funds, or government support—much less their own personal and professional reputations.

One of the most difficult jobs you'll have in a protracted news story is getting the other members of management to understand the importance of taking the initiative when their organization is faced with the prospects of a media siege. In reflecting back on what has been learned since the Bhopal tragedy, Carbide's director of corporate communications Walter Goetz commented, "The corporation now is proactive, but then it was reactive in media-related situations. What needed to be done was handled by the business divisions selling a product. It wasn't a corporate need. But if we had the knowledge and depth of experience we do now with some particular media folk, it would have been a lot different. . . . This is realized now. We don't just put the chemical plant manager in to run the chemicals. He's got to be more capable of being a spokesman and managing assistant managers who run the plant. He's more of a community relations manager than he is a plant manager."[166]

The message the chief executive needs to get is that the organization has a difficult situation now, but it could become impossible unless management adopts a policy of being forthright with the news media. President Nixon could have finished his second term in office had he not decided to play "Beat the Press," a game nobody wins. The best way of conveying that message is to provide a rational assessment of the story's news potential, along with a realistic scenario of how the media coverage is likely to develop as the problems related to the situation are uncovered by the press.

If the organization takes the initiative in getting its facts out, the press will be better informed and have details to back up its reporting of the story. They also will have more respect for the organization and its management for being forthright. If, on the other hand, the organization and its management get off on the wrong foot with the media, the attack will begin when the first whiff of anything negative is smelled by reporters. You may never regain control of the situation. Anyone who doubts that should consider what has happened to NASA since the Challenger accident.

One way or the other, the press is going to find out if there have been problems. The organization is under no obligation to disclose them, but it had better be ready and willing to discuss the details and provide facts to back up its position without getting defensive, abusive, or belligerent when the subject is brought up by members of the media. Even though the media coverage will get more negative as time passes, providing authoritative information from the beginning can do a lot to lessen the extent of the damage by building rapport with the reporters covering the story, who then will be more inclined to seek out the organization's side of the story.

THE ROLE OF THE CEO

For it to be effective in a siege situation, the forthright approach will have to start quickly and be more than a written plan or philosophical statement. The organization has to make its most authoritative spokespersons available to the news media. The sooner they begin briefing the press and responding to questions, the better shape they will be in to handle the tougher topics that will develop as the story progresses. Whether top management should take on a spokesperson role with the news media should be determined by their personal preferences and persuasive skills.

The chief executive personifies the organization and can be a substantial asset or a major liability in a media siege, depending on how comfortable he is in responding to tough questions from reporters and how easily and naturally he relates to the public via the news coverage. "It goes with the territory," Carbide's CEO Warren Anderson said. "If you're willing to accept the checks that they give you, then you have the responsibility and you have to accept the accountability that goes with it. That means getting into the forefront of a very unpleasant environment. . . . Jim Burke [CEO of Johnson & Johnson] got involved in Tylenol, and it made a tremendous impact. He projected well, showed their concern. He's the organization. He's the guy. That's hard to delegate, that really is."[167]

The role played by Warren Anderson during the Bhopal and Institute news stories is an example of what the top executive can do in a crisis. Anderson, a quiet, reserved CEO, was anything but a public figure. The multinational chemical company he led had traditionally been conservative and low keyed in its relations with the news media, granting occasional interviews to business publications but doing no corporate advertising and shunning the news media limelight as much as possible. Yet Anderson correctly understood that the CEO has to step forward and represent the corporation in the midst of a major news story. In an industry that had previously created a public awareness of chemical accidents and toxic wastes with incidents like the Love Canal problem and the kepone contamination of the James River, his corporation was virtually unknown. Anderson grasped the importance of giving a personality to the corporation in the eyes of its many publics.

Just the opposite approach was taken by Delta Air Lines, as it seems to be by any company in its industry when a major accident occurs. "It's our feeling that the way the public would view the chairman or president saying how sorry he was and how the Delta folks are doing the best job they could, just doesn't fit into this type of situation," said Bill Berry, Delta's director of public relations. "This was a straightforward reporting job, and we never felt the need to call on our chairman or president to say something. They were available to us, but we were providing straight news, and we really didn't feel it was proper to have someone involved in informing the news media just because of his title."[168]

As mentioned earlier, Ron Allen, Delta's president, was on the scene in Dallas soon after the accident, along with Hollis Harris, Delta's senior vice president for operations, and other Delta executives who would be involved in the Flight 191 crash aftermath. Harris was the senior executive designated to direct Delta's emergency accident procedures. Allen would spend much of his time visiting passengers, relatives, and members of the flight crew in hospitals in Dallas-Fort Worth. He did not meet with the media, even though

Delta had numerous requests for interviews. "We never asked him," Berry added. "We felt our plan was in place, and that it was working well, and that there was really nothing he could add."

Even if he chooses not to be interviewed, the CEO needs to be actively involved in helping the organization inform its other important publics. Even in the midst of the most negative news disclosure, the CEO should remain visible. He may never make a public statement during the event, but his presence on the scene and his acknowledgement that he is actively concerned for the participants or the victims can be a "crisis breaker."

THE BROADER IMPLICATIONS

If the aftermath of a situation that has the attention of the media will be prolonged, the news coverage is going to have a much broader and more serious impact throughout the organization and among the important external audiences. The Bhopal accident has generated thousands of stories worldwide in the newspapers, news magazines, trade journals, and on radio and television over a two-year period. During that time, Union Carbide's debt rating was lowered by Standard & Poor's, the company went through two congressional hearings, and it was named in lawsuits seeking more than $15 billion in damages for the victims of Bhopal. It also was the target of an unfriendly takeover attempt by GAF corporation and had to sell off $2.5 billion of its assets to resist the takeover and to establish reserves to pay the expected expenses stemming from Bhopal.

Bhopal also is a classic example of how a news story that becomes a siege will spread beyond the limits of the organization to affect an entire industry. "The incident at Bhopal," *Industry Week* reported, "exploded much of the confidence the public has in industry's ability to operate plants safely. But what is only now beginning to be grasped—and what may have a more dramatic impact on the long-term health of all industry—is Bhopal's shattering effect on the executive psyche. Bhopal has grabbed many executives by the lapels and shaken them—and not just in the chemical industry. Since the tragedy, users and supporters of chemicals—especially those in electronics, pharmaceuticals, steel, autos, paper, and computers— have been reexamining the hazards associated with their products and controls."[169]

When you know the story will be in the news for more than a week, the organization is going to be faced with an ongoing, monumental communications effort to maintain the support of its key internal and external audiences. Most important will be its own board members, management, and employees, whose level of support while the organization is being scrutinized in the news media will determine how well it can survive and succeed in spite of what has happened. Customers and suppliers also need to know its position on developments being reported in the news, as do the segments of the financial community and government officials who follow the organization closely. The communities where it has facilities will need to know, considering how much the organization's future affects the local economy.

Communications with each of these audiences is essential in its own way, and it can be handled by different areas of the organization. What's most important, however, is that the messages be consistent and timely. Often they need to be disclosed immediately before or at the same time as they are conveyed to the press. That requires careful planning, with clearly defined priorities and a well-coordinated organization to handle the internal and external communications as one important element in resolving the overall situation.

PLANNING FOR A LONG-TERM MEDIA SIEGE

If the media relations plan is to be workable, it can't be unwieldy. Its basic objectives and responsibilities have to be an integral part of the overall plan for managing the situation, but they also have to be carefully defined so the specific responsibilities are easily understood by those who will be directly or indirectly involved with the news media. Hundreds of details can be considered by specific members of the team as part of their responsibilities, and need not involve top management. What your CEO does need to understand is that an ongoing news story is going to put a significant dent in the organization's resources, primarily its personnel and operating expenses.

Working with the news media during a siege can't be a "while you're at it" responsibility. It will be a full-time job for some public relations staff, and it can easily chew up 50–100 percent of the chief spokesperson's time as well, in addition to the heavy burdens imposed by the other responsibilities with the situation itself. John Dwan recalls that after the first month of the Barney Clark media siege in Utah, Dr. Chase Peterson wanted to extract himself and lower his profile by handling fewer news media briefings. He was tired physically, but he also was aware of criticism from the medical school deans and other officials at the university for having to put 80–90 percent of his time into being the medical spokesperson for the artificial heart program. Bob Henrie recalls having to spend 100 percent of his time dealing with the news media for several months after the Wilberg Mine fire and spending at least half his time during the first year on media relations regarding the fire.

Warren Anderson turned over the day-to-day management of Union Carbide's businesses, which were generating $9.5 billion in sales at the time, to Carbide's president so he could devote whatever time and energy were necessary to resolving the Bhopal aftermath. "I really, honestly thought we could have a solution to this problem in six months if you really had compassion and wanted to accomplish something," Anderson commented. "But if someone wants to place the blame or wants to litigate, that's a different story. So here we are, 21 months later, and we're still at it."

Anderson knew what the participants in a major story soon learn—forget your regular job. When management gets immersed with the media, their daily schedule will be jammed, and "must do" jobs may be overlooked in the chaos. Perhaps people can be brought in from other areas or outside help used to fill the gaps until the situation subsides, whenever that will be. If the news coverage looks like it will continue for more than two weeks, the media relations plan had better make provisions so that additional personnel can take over for the key people for a while.

THE COSTS OF PRESS RELATIONS

Operating expenses for the organization also are going to take a pounding, although the amount spent for public relations is likely to be a fraction of the legal fees, insurance, and other expenses that seem to be a part of any newsworthy disaster story. With average workdays running well into the "teens" and weekends meaningless, the overtime costs for the public relations department secretaries alone will be astounding. Photography and video are expensive propositions, and if it's necessary to rent a facility for briefings, that bill, with all the side expenses, will be in the thousands of dollars.

What are these side expenses? You can start with telephones, electrical power, coffee and sandwiches, Xeroxing, phone machines, and dozens of other items, all the way up to printing and postage. NASA's public affairs department responded to 240,000 expressions of sympathy after the Challenger accident on behalf of the space agency and the astronauts' families. That's a lot of postage and duplicating costs. And it doesn't stop when the news story finally subsides. The University of Utah and Humana still get dozens of requests a week for information on the artificial heart program from students doing school reports, but also from journalists who may be pursuing a new story angle or including the artificial heart in a more extensive article on medical technology.

Executives may feel their anxiety can be lessened in dealing with the media onslaught by bringing in crisis management consultants to advise the organization on how to deal with the media. While that may seem expensive, don't arbitrarily rule out public relations consultants until you consider the strengths and skills of your own media relations capabilities. A consultant who's been through other crises and media onslaughts often can point out the broader implications and longer-term considerations. He or she can assist with important details and decisions in dealing with the media when an organization has all it can do in trying to anticipate and respond to the dozens of reporters and television cameras. When compared to the long-term damage and expense that a media siege can inflict on the organization, the consultant might be a good investment at twice the price.

The chief executives also had better understand that the public relations budget will be enclosed in brackets if duration of the news story cannot be determined. The expenses can be carefully controlled and management kept informed, which should help, but there will be no way to predict how much money will be required for media relations and related activities during the course of the news story. Humana's public relations budget for the artificial heart program cost $325,000 during the first six months, not including salaries or overtime.

The costs may seem high, but consider what is at stake. Management and employees will closely follow the news coverage because they will have a personal interest in what is happening to the organization. The same holds true of investors, government officials, customers, suppliers, and people in communities where the organization operates. They are the publics who will determine the future value of the organization, and they will be influenced by what they read, see, and hear via the news media. Any executive who doesn't buy that premise needs to consider what adverse news coverage did to the Nixon administration, to the owners of Three Mile Island, and more recently to NASA and to the Reagan administration. Then look at how Johnson & Johnson has been affected by the two Tylenol crises and at what has happened to Delta Air Lines since the crash of Flight 191. The latter two instances were major, costly problems for the corporations, but, if anything, their reputations were enhanced by the media coverage. That didn't happen by accident.

If your organization feels it has to win a major legal battle, its attorneys are not told they only can spend so much money to fight the case. They'll be told to watch the expenses but to do whatever it takes to win. The same logic should be applied to an organization's public relations staff. You have to look very carefully at how much adverse news coverage can cost an organization if its credibility and reputation are damaged with the people who really count, and what it will take to make sure that won't happen.

THE APPROPRIATE LEVEL OF RESPONSE

Personnel and money by themselves will not ensure accurate and objective news coverage. What will increase the chances will be if the organization establishes a consistent level of response at the beginning and maintains it throughout the duration of the story. That means sticking to your guidelines for disclosures to the media to ensure timeliness and accuracy in what will be provided and consistency in the level of details to be disclosed.

The organization needs that kind of policy in any onslaught but especially if there's no way of telling how long the story will continue, or if it looks like the news media will be living with the organization for more than a week. It should be developed by laying out the most likely scenario for the situation. Consider the milestones in the story that will elicit significant media interest and when it will reach a point where ongoing news coverage will die off.

Within the first few hours, NASA knew that the story would continue for months until the cause of the explosion was confirmed, the fate of the astronauts was known, and the future of the shuttle program had been determined. With a medical news story, it's a question of how long the patients will be alive, which will be anybody's guess. Utah's planning for the artificial heart was based on the premise that the first patient would either die in the first few days or be discharged from the hospital. They did not consider the possibilities that Barney Clark would remain in the hospital for 112 days and that the media coverage would continue.

Humana's media relations protocol for the artificial heart program anticipated that news coverage would continue indefinitely, but it made no provisions for a consistent disclosure policy that would be in place from the beginning and maintained until Dr. DeVries had operated on the remaining six patients and submitted his data to the FDA. We also did not take into consideration the most likely scenario for the clinical trial and how the news coverage would change if the patients ran into the complications outlined in the patient consent form, which had to be signed twice by each patient before the artificial heart could be implanted. That was a mistake on our part which became apparent after Bill Schroeder's first stroke, when it was necessary to switch to weekly updates on his slow progress in recovering. The problem was that the media had been used to twice-daily medical briefings and regarded the change in disclosure policy as an indication of a cover-up.

When the duration is unknown, you need to establish the disclosure guidelines in the beginning and stick to them as long as the story continues, regardless of what happens and whether the news is good or bad. They should be realistic and in writing so everyone, including the news media, knows who's responsible for disclosures and what type of information and level of detail to expect. Chapter 8, Feeding the Bears, has a number of points that need to be considered in determining how much detail will be provided, who will handle the disclosures, and the timing considerations.

Periodic briefings, even when there is nothing significant to report, are one way to maintain a good working relationship with the media during a long-running news story. An informal monthly briefing for members of the press interested in attending and asking questions will make it clear that the organization is maintaining its open line of communication with the news media. It also will allow reporters to stay current on the situation and be better prepared for significant developments when they next occur. At the same time, this paves the way for a smooth transition to a crisis situation, should the news story heat up again.

As the story drags on, the participants will become increasingly reluctant to meet with the media unless it's absolutely necessary, which is understandable considering the physical and mental toll an ongoing news story can have, as well as the preparations that are required for any news briefing. At the same time, it is vital to maintain that line of communication, which is why presidents meet periodically with the White House press corps. That approach would have allowed NASA to review developments in the Challenger investigation, including the fact that the airpacks had been recovered in April, rather than in August when the press first found out. It also would have allowed Dr. DeVries to maintain contact with influential members of the medical press who had been so supportive in the early days of the artificial heart. As it was, little was heard from Dr. DeVries during the last year of Bill Schroeder's life, prompting many of the news media who had been early supporters of the clinical investigation to attack the program when Schroeder died.

Your organization also can benefit if it's consistent in its willingness to listen to the suggestions of the media throughout its coverage of the story, not just at the beginning when everyone is fresh and knows so little. Once again, the problem will be patience and fatigue, as well as the adversarial relationship that gradually develops between the participants and the press as the news story drags on. However, maintaining those lines of communication can be invaluable. It may be an informal, off-the-record meeting every so often or just a chat over a cup of coffee, but the participants need to be willing to listen to the thoughts and concerns of the news media so they can understand the directions the news coverage is taking. Some of the suggestions in those conversations will be self-serving or impractical, considering what the organization has to contend with. Others will spark an idea or a small change that can make a big difference for the organization in the accuracy and objectivity of the ongoing news coverage. If nothing else, the news media will know and respect the organization for its willingness to listen.

WHEN IT'S ALL OVER

You have to assume that the longer any news story goes on, the more negative it's likely to get and the greater the chances that the organization will be criticized at some point by stories in the news media. They may be severe, and even if they aren't, after the first few days they are likely to seem that way. The patience of the participants and public relations staff will be worn thin by then from the fatigue and constant pressure of having to deal with the news media as well as the situation itself. But there are battles, and then there's the war itself.

The facts rarely change. Two thousand people died in Bhopal when gas leaked from the Union Carbide plant, the Challenger was destroyed by a faulty solid rocket booster, and Bill Schroeder lived for 620 days with an artificial heart, 602 of them as a stroke victim. But what will the publics who really count recall two years later? And how will their reactions to what they read, saw, and heard in the news media have affected their support of the organization? Those questions should be the central focus of management's long-term plan for a media siege.

The publics will have mental pictures from the initial news coverage: the explosion of the Challenger, gasping victims in Bhopal amidst the bodies of those who died, Bill Schroeder's surgery and recovery, and his long struggle as a stroke patient. The subsequent major developments are likely to be less visual and will be remembered more on the basis of how they were reported by the news media. The publics may not remember all of the details, but the tone of the reporting will give them an impression, a perception of the situation, that will influence their attitudes whenever the subject happens to come up in the future.

The members of the press who covered the story will have far more vivid memories. They'll recall the excitement and intensity of the initial news coverage, but they will also remember the ensuing days and weeks and what it took to get information for stories that were acceptable to their newsrooms. They know that human frailties are intensified for those who are involved in a long news story and that things happen which are difficult to control, much less to explain.

What they will remember most will be the personal involvement and candor of the spokespersons and how consistent they were throughout the days and weeks of the story. They'll also remember the statements that didn't hold up and commitments in the beginning that weren't being honored in the end. The key to successful media relations over the long haul is to do everything you can to maintain that candor and consistency, as well as the commitments, regardless of how long the news coverage continues.

The Best Laid Plans

We all know about what happens to the best laid plans of mice and executives. Remember the seemingly effortless rise of Challenger on that cold January morning at the Cape, with the nation's first schoolteacher astronaut aboard? Who—except for a tiny cohort of engineers at Morton Thiokol—could have guessed that only seconds later the worst disaster in space exploration history would engulf NASA in full view of millions of television viewers, including the family and pupils of Christa McAuliffe. Similarly, it could be a call from a mine supervisor that there's been a fire and the 27 miners on the second shift are trapped, or from a network newscaster telling you that hundreds of people have died following a chemical gas leak from your plant in India.

These are the disasters that chill the spine and turn the gut of any executive. These also are the events that turn an organization upside down. How quickly it rights itself will be determined as much by the media's coverage of the disaster as by the nature of the disaster itself. Many organizations have disaster plans, but few are realistic when it comes to anticipating how the news media will cover the story. Yet disasters happen. And then there are catastrophes like the Challenger accident that can occur in full view of the press and the very publics whose support will determine the future of your organization. You can't avoid them, but you can prepare for them. This chapter will show you how to be sure your organization is prepared for the media if the situation you dread most becomes a reality.

THE DOOMSDAY CALL

Most organizations that run the risk of an accident that may result in casualties and/or property damage have some kind of written plan for dealing with the crisis. Airlines are required by law to have emergency procedures and to practice them. Others—hospitals, for example—must have disaster plans to maintain their licenses or accreditation. Insurance companies often work with their large clients on accident prevention programs, which may include contingency planning.

The operational aspects of these plans are undoubtedly good. They may even have been tested in mock emergencies to ensure that employees are skilled in responding to the different situations that would be most likely to occur. But how workable is the plan for dealing with the news media, which undoubtedly will cover the situation from the moment the first notification goes out? That's the question you and your organization's other executives need to be asking because, when it's all over, what happened in a disaster won't have nearly as much impact on the organization as how it was reported in the news media. "A couple of things are very important for understanding what happened to us, but also for other people to think about when they make their plans," NASA's Shirley Green observed. "They always need to assume the worst scenario you can humanly imagine."[170]

Disaster plans and procedures often have a section on informing the press that indicates who is responsible and what they are supposed to do. But take a look at it. How well would it hold up if an accident occurred with a number of casualties? The organization suddenly would be deluged with calls from the local and national news media. Who would be the spokesperson? How would he or she come across in having to explain what happened? How comfortable would they be in responding to the barrage of questions from a mob of reporters with a phalanx of television cameras in the background? And where would all this take place?

You may think it could never happen to your organization, and I hope you are right. But why not check to see how much liability insurance you carry, and ask why you are spending that much money. And while you are at it, think about some of the newsworthy problems that have befallen other organizations in your field. What was your reaction when you first heard about their misfortunes? When Bhopal occurred the general feeling among the other companies in the chemical industry was "There, but for the grace of God, go I."

Let's take a hard look at your policy for dealing with a major accident and test its press relations potential. How would it apply if your organization and its employees were suddenly involved in an accident in the local area in which at least 23 people were killed or seriously injured, extensive property damage has occurred, and it will be 12 hours or longer before you'll know the exact toll?

If you do have a written policy and procedure for disasters, get it out and see how well it would apply to the situation I've outlined. If you don't have something in writing, start off by writing down what steps you would take if you just received that type of doomsday telephone call.

Now consider the news coverage which will start occurring in the next few minutes. Take a blank sheet of paper and list the news organizations that would be likely to cover the story.

Newspapers
    Local/Regional   National
Television
    Local/Regional   National
Radio
    Local/Regional   National
Wire services
News magazines and trade publications

This should give you a better idea of what you'll be up against. But before you throw the paper away, have somebody get the phone numbers for each news organizations on your list that has offices within 100 miles of your locality. That will make a good addendum for any procedure dealing with accidents or disasters, or just for your future reference.

Now let's see how well you think your procedure would hold up in dealing with the news media covering this accident. Start off by checking the appropriate space for each of these basic considerations.

	1 Don't know	2 Not sure	3 Fairly sure	4 Quite sure	5 Very sure
1. Who would be the spokespersons? What would be their limits of disclosure?					
2. Where would media calls be routed? Who would handle them? What would they be authorized to say?					
3. Where would briefings be held for 50–100 reporters and 6 or more TV cameras?					
4. What information would be provided? Who would decide what should be disclosed?					
5. What guidelines and policies for the news media would be in effect during the situation?					
6. How would media interviews be handled? Who would speak for the organization?					
Column Totals					

Total Score

Add up the checks in each column and multiply by the number at the top of the column. Then add the column totals to determine your total score.

How'd you do? Your score will be somewhere between 6 and 30. If it's anywhere above 21 you have reason to be pleased because that's the exception. If it's below 18, it would be a good idea to begin thinking about what can be done to change those checks in the left three columns.

Even if a media relations plan for contingencies does exist, will it work when a crisis actually occurs? You'll never know until the unthinkable happens, but some useful lessons can be learned from those who have had to contend with the media coverage of a disastrous situation. Consider what happened after the Challenger explosion, the crash of Delta Flight 191, and the Bhopal toxic gas leak.

CHALLENGER—A WELL-INTENTIONED PLAN THAT WOULDN'T WORK

We mentioned in Chapter 1 that NASA had formulated a plan to communicate with the news media if a disaster like the Challenger accident occurred. In 1983 it had developed its 19-page procedure, the Space Transportation System (STS) Public Affairs Contingency Plan, which provided detailed provisions for how the press relations would be handled if there was an accident on the launch pad, while the shuttle was in orbit, or during its reentry and landing. The plan had even been reviewed by members of the news media—and it reflected their suggestions—before it had been approved by the administration of NASA.

Shirley Green, NASA's director of public affairs, wasn't with the space agency when the plan was developed, but she believes it was an excellent plan based on the assumptions of what would be most likely to occur. The problem, she feels, was that "Almost all of the possible things that had been thought would happen didn't happen in the time frame." It turned out that no provisions had been made for an accident during the shuttle's lift-off and ascent, considered by most experts to be the most dangerous phase of the mission. That oversight wasn't mentioned by the news media. What they criticized was NASA's failure to live up to the provision in the plan that stipulated that an announcement on the status of the crew would be made in 20 minutes. "That was totally unrealistic, which was one thing we quickly discovered, " Green said. "That was just wrong. We couldn't have physically gotten out of the launch control building and back to the press site in 20 minutes."

NASA's inability to live up to the 20-minute time commitment immediately cast a pall on the space agency's reputation for integrity and openness with the press. It came at a critical time when rapport needed to be maintained and, if anything, reinforced. To make matters worse, a media briefing on the accident was scheduled and then delayed repeatedly, which conveyed the impression to the press and the public that the space agency was confused and didn't know what it was doing.

"There was very little that Jesse Moore [the associate administrator of spaceflight] was able to say at 4:30 that we couldn't have said at 1 or 1:30," Green added. "We could have said that the information is being impounded, teams are being put together in these areas to do these jobs, the ships and helicopters have gone out, surface debris is being found, there are no signs of any survivors. That could have been said much, much earlier, and I regret that we did not. Jess intended to—and wanted to—talk much earlier. He was shocked by how much time had gone by."

For five hours the NASA public affairs staffs at the Cape and in Houston, Huntsville, and Washington had to fend off frenzied journalists seeking information. They watched in helpless frustration as relationships with members of the news media that had been built and maintained over 25 years of spaceflight began to disintegrate because NASA could not provide any details on what had happened. That inability to supply even the most basic information set up the prism of hostile attitudes within the news media. It also started a negative chain reaction among reporters and their news organizations, which would grow in intensity in the ensuing days and weeks and spur the press to attack the space agency itself, not just its mismanagement of the shuttle program.

The STS Public Affairs Contingency Plan did not work because (1) the procedures didn't apply to what happened, (2) important provisions proved to be unrealistic, and (3) NASA's management was unable to carry out its responsibilities on a timely basis because of other priorities. Its major flaw was that it did not take into consideration what else would be going on. It also did not provide a person with authority to fill in gaps that became apparent when the plan had to be put into effect. "In the absence of a program person to come forward, public affairs will," Green added. "That's going to be one of my recommendations in the new contingency plan."

DELTA FLIGHT 191—THE STANDARD PRACTICES WERE IN DAILY USE

Delta Air Lines, on the other hand, responded to the crash of Flight 191 strictly by the book, both from an operational and a media relations standpoint, and received high marks from the press for the effectiveness of its media relations program in the aftermath of the tragedy. Mark Mayfield, the Atlanta bureau chief for *USA Today*, was able to compare Delta's media relations after the accident with NASA's after Challenger since he had been sent in to cover both stories. "Delta was as consistent in that bad time as they had been in the good times," Mayfield recalled. "They were ethical, and they were professional. They did what they could to provide me with information, which made my job as a reporter much easier. Other disaster stories I've covered were totally opposite, NASA being one of them.[171]

It's important to note that Delta's timely and forthright approach to the news media resulted in a positive prism being established in those critical first few hours. As a result the extensive media coverage of the tragedy, and the subsequent probable cause findings of the NTSB that the flight crew had erred in trying to land in the thunderstorm, have not affected the company's reputation for integrity. Nor has the accident affected Delta's business, profitability, or continued growth. Eighteen months after the accident, passenger volume had increased 5 percent and the company's net income was nearly $200 million. Delta had successfully entered four additional European markets and begun providing non-stop service to Tokyo. The company also had completed the acquisition of Western Airlines, which expanded its presence on the west coast of the United States from Mexico to Alaska and out to the Hawaiian Islands, making it the fourth largest airline in the United States.

Delta's success as a company and its ability to handle the media coverage of the Flight 191 accident so effectively can be traced directly to the company's management philosophy, which is built around adherence to the policies and procedures in its Standard Practices. Rather than being regarded as notebooks filled with dull, dry details, Delta's SPs are enthusiastically embraced by its public relations staff. "That's the Bible in doing the company's job," says Bill Berry, Delta's director of public relations. "It's the company's policy, it's the company's position, it's the company's way of doing things. It's set forth to be the most thorough and effective way of doing the job. So once you have a clear understanding of where you stand with the SP, then it's a rather simple process of carrying that practice into your own department's specialized procedures.[172]

One of the policies in the Delta Airlines Standard Practices is that the information in these manuals cannot be distributed outside the company. However, in the hope that it would help others in dealing with the news media, Berry could outline the general contents of

Delta's *Public Relations Emergency Incident Procedure Handbook*, which is based on relevant information from the Standard Practices for Emergencies. The 24-page handbook has the following sections:

Statement of Responsibility. This is a statement of the objectives and responsibilities of the public relations staff during emergencies.

Notification Process. The media relations responsibilities that will have to be staffed are outlined along with the procedures for contacting the appropriate people in public relations, and other areas of the company to help in responding to the news media. Staffing instructions include the steps to be taken if some public relations department employees are not available when the situation occurs because of travel, vacation, or illness. Procedures also are outlined for contacting other corporate departments so that sufficient personnel will be on hand 24 hours a day to respond to the media's information needs.

Staff Positioning. This section assigns specific people to responsibilities that range from answering the phones and compiling media background information to being the public relations contact in the Delta command center, serving as a Delta spokesperson for the news media, and providing on-site public relations support at the scene of the news story. The procedure takes into consideration that staffing may be required 24 hours a day so that work schedules will be established for the people assigned to the different areas of responsibility.

Staff Briefings. Instructions are provided for keeping everyone involved in the news situation up to date on the latest developments. Delta's Bill Berry indicated that may mean having people hold up on answering phones for a minute or two so they can be brought up to date, or pulling everyone together for a quick staff meeting to go over the latest developments. Delta's provisions emphasize keeping everyone appraised of the most recent information so that its people on the phones are working with the same facts as the company spokespersons at headquarters and at the scene of the news story.

Statements. Statements are prepared with blanks to be filled in for a variety of major or minor incidents. Rather than having to react under pressure and quickly come up with one or two paragraphs that are appropriate, the statements are already thought out and cover all of the necessary elements. Thus all that is needed is to fill in the flight number, the location, and basically what happened. These statements are used in the early information communicated throughout the company as well as in the initial releases to the press.

Satellite Public Relations Office Procedures.   Instructions are given for setting up and operating press relations facilities at locations other than the Atlanta headquarters when a major news story breaks. After the crash of Flight 191, these procedures were implemented immediately by the appropriate Delta personnel in Dallas-Fort Worth, but also in Fort Lauderdale, where the flight originated, and Los Angeles, its final destination.

Press Relations Policies and Procedures.   Sections are included from the Standard Practices, which set forth the general policies for dealing with the media and the procedures for contacting or responding to a member of the press from the headquarters public relations office or any of Delta's 150 locations in the United States and abroad. These basic policies and procedures apply to any situation, major or minor, that may be covered by the news media.

Company Contacts.   Information is provided on how to reach anyone in the Delta organization regarding a situation that may be covered by the news media. The list includes the home and office phone numbers of the public relations department as well as top management and the line and staff people in other divisions who might have to be contacted for specialized information or assistance, in accordance with the Standard Practices.

Major Media Contacts.   The phone numbers of important news organizations in the local area that might have to be contacted are listed. Space is provided for listing both the office and home phones of specific journalists who want to be called after business hours.

Critique.   Steps are included for assessing the effectiveness of the SP in dealing with specific emergency situations and noting areas where problems occurred so the procedures can be reviewed and improved for future use.

The nature of the airline business is that situations with news potential happen every day in the network of far-flung cities that each airline serves. An airplane has an engine failure in flight or blows a tire during a landing. A passenger has a heart attack while the plane is airborne. A dog gets out of its shipping kennel and has to be chased around the aircraft parking gates and taxiways. Those are all news items that Delta and the other airlines have to respond to, and that's what makes the *Public Relations Emergency Incident Handbook* work so well. It doesn't sit on the shelf waiting for an emergency. It's being used every day by people in Delta's public relations department and by its marketing managers in the United States and abroad.

Delta's public relations staff and its field managers learn what's in that handbook and how to use it when they move up into any job that will involve communicating with the news media. They become familiar with its procedures and how they fit into the other standard practices so they can respond to press calls regarding the newsworthy occurrences that frequently are a part of their jobs. Then when a major situation develops, there's no question what the procedure will be for dealing with the media. It's in the same handbook that they've referred to so often in the past.

When they were called about Flight 191, Bill Berry and Jim Ewing knew what had to be done at Delta's headquarters in Atlanta. And even though he'd only been the marketing manager in Dallas for three weeks, Matt Guilfoil knew what he'd be responsible for at DFW International Airport. Each had used the handbook many times. All that would change was the intensity of the media coverage which everyone would be facing.

UNION CARBIDE—WHEN THE SITUATION EXCEEDS THE PLAN

Like Delta Air Lines, the communications plan that Union Carbide put into effect after the Bhopal disaster is part of an overall contingency plan for dealing with emergency situations. It is much less structured, however, and focuses initially on pulling together the types of people who will be needed in responding to a chemical accident.

Carbide's plan is contained in a folder, along with names, phone numbers, and a "calling chain" procedure for contacting the executives in the line and staff functions who will be involved. "I carry that folder 365 days a year, 24 hours a day," said Carbide's Walter Goetz. "You always have to leave a phone number, and I've been called in some strange places. They know where they can get me on the golf course if they have to."[173]

The morning of the Bhopal accident, Goetz was called at home around 5 A.M. by the chairman of Carbide's eastern international region, which includes India. "By the time I got to my office, the communication had reached the president, the chief counsel, the president of the ag division," he said. "Our security and communications people already were in trying to bring together the ways and means to use one of our big conference rooms as a 'war room,' if you want to look at it that way."

Union Carbide's executives realized from the initial news reports that the magnitude of the Bhopal tragedy exceeded anything that Carbide had anticipated in its crisis planning. The company had experienced its share of industrial accidents, which were the basis of its contingency plan, and even one death was regarded as a major problem that would be reviewed at corporate headquarters. However, no executive at Carbide—or at any corporation—would be likely to have developed a realistic plan for dealing with an industrial accident in a foreign country that would have a death toll in the thousands. Jackson Browning still recalls driving through the darkness toward Union Carbide's headquarters, listening to the radio as the casualty figures steadily escalated with each news report on Bhopal.

The Carbide management team began meeting around 7 A.M. to assess the situation and implement the contingency plan for chemical accidents. They were hampered from the beginning by the inability to get information. "Trying to get a phone call through to India can be a five-hour exercise. To India—never mind Bhopal," Goetz added. "By the time we did get through, India's Central Bureau of Investigation had shut the plant off. They took it over! We couldn't talk to our people in the plant, so we were getting most of our information from the international news media, who were sending it out in various ways."

Another problem that quickly became apparent to the management team was that Carbide's Indian company didn't have anyone among its 9,000 employees with public relations responsibilities. "Public relations is not something you do in India," said Ron Wishart. "So we had nobody over there to work with, who could be our eyes and ears and communicate with their press."[174]

The switchboard at Carbide's headquarters was flooded with media calls from all over the world seeking more information as the magnitude of the Bhopal accident grew by the hour. Ed Van Den Ameele and the public relations staff responded with what little information could be confirmed, but after the first few hours they had more than 75 phone calls waiting to be returned. The decision was made to conduct a media briefing at the nearby Danbury Hilton hotel at 1 P.M. that afternoon to provide the news media with whatever information Carbide could confirm at the time.

Browning, as vice president of corporate safety and environmental control, seemed to be the logical spokesperson, although he had no previous experience with reporters. Browning wryly mentioned that speaking to the news media was not part of his job description. Alec Flamm, the president of Union Carbide, smiled and told him it would be.

Warren Anderson, bedridden with the flu, did not get involved until the second day. By then it was obvious that little could be done from the corporate offices in Danbury except to respond to the news media. "What I was thinking was when you have a natural disaster, people tend to coaslesce and work together, hand-in-hand with the establishment," Anderson said. "That's what I thought we could accomplish, but there was no way for UCIL [Union Carbide India, Ltd.] to do that. Therefore, we had to be involved."[175] At a media briefing on the second day, Anderson disclosed that he and a team of Union Carbide specialists were leaving immediately for Bhopal to determine what could be done to aid survivors of the chemical gas leak and the families of those who had been killed.

After his return from India, Anderson set up the Bhopal Team to resolve the problem, with Ron Wishart as its chief of staff. Wishart's first job was to draft a plan for resolving the Bhopal accident that defined Carbide's objectives and the specific responsibilities for those who would be involved in the Bhopal Team. The six-page plan was ready the following morning, and Anderson approved it that afternoon. The designated executives were notified, and the team began working over the weekend. Carbide made an internal announcement the following Monday to inform its employees worldwide of how the company was going to address the Bhopal problem and who would be involved.

Wishart's plan established Carbide's priorities and then laid out the organization of the groups that would address the diverse but related problem areas. "The task groups were necessary to cope with various types of problems, which were running parallel, yet they were interrelated," said Wishart. "The issues we'd have to deal with ran from the highly technical, chemical problems to legal considerations and legitimate questions on insurance and health and the politics here or abroad. The plan also brought in all the various persuasions, functions, knowledge, and professional skills that were necessary to orchestrate any response inside or outside."

"Objectives? Well, at that point in time, number one was to keep the company solid," Wishart continued. "Number two was to maintain a positive communications stance. We knew we'd have to be open. You can't sit in here because you don't know the answers to all the questions. The questions are infinite, and the knowledge is limited. The spokesman would either be Anderson or Browning. We agreed on what the standard answer was to anything. That was a committee job. It didn't matter how many media calls came in or what direction they took, there was only one answer and zero speculation."

The selection of Anderson and Browning was logical in that both had already had their baptisms by fire. Anderson's trip to Bhopal and subsequent arrest immediately made him the personification of Union Carbide and the center of attention for the news media. Browning, an executive with degrees in engineering and law, had conducted the initial news media briefing less than 12 hours after the first notification of the Bhopal accident and had been Carbide's chief spokesperson from that point on.

Anderson's and, to a lesser extent, Browning's responsibilities went beyond the news media. They were the principal spokespersons for Union Carbide during congressional hearings and in communications with stockholders, the financial community, and customers. Carbide's 100,000 employees heard from Anderson via a series of videotapes that were distributed to its facilities worldwide. "I tried with our employees to give them some rocks to throw back," he said. "I tried on TV to give them some facts so they could stand tall and feel that they had nothing to apologize for, and they could tell people they work for Carbide and not be embarrassed."

ELEMENTS OF A REALISTIC PRESS RELATIONS PLAN

So what should be done when the worst happens? You'll never know exactly how to deal with the news media when the crisis develops, any more than the participants will know how to handle the situation itself. However, a realistic plan will determine how effectively an organization works with the press in those critical first hours. That will get the relationship off on the right foot, regardless of whether the crisis is beyond the scope of normal contingency planning, as it was with the Bhopal catastrophe, or is something that has been anticipated, as with the Flight 191 crash or the Challenger accident.

A good press relations plan must be easily grasped by someone who has a limited understanding of the news media. That way it has the best chance of being used by those outside the public relations department who may have to work with the press. Like the Delta Air Lines handbook, it should contain information that will be referred to frequently. Then it will be kept current, and the contents of the important sections will be readily understood when a major situation breaks.

And it doesn't have to be dogmatic! Doggone it, if there's anything that people need to understand about press relations it's that it is basically common sense communications. Nobody has all the answers, especially during a crisis, and the news media knows that. The press relations plan that will work most effectively is one that encourages honesty and openness and helps the people who will have to work with the news media in disclosing the facts on a timely basis.

Here's what it should include:

Overview

The plan should begin with a short statement from top management regarding communications with the news media. The overview should be more than philosophical. It should be a straightforward, pragmatic expression of management's views, and it should define the corporate and field management responsible for ensuring that the organization's press relations convey the correct perceptions to its publics via the news media.

Goals and Objectives

The press relations plan should have realistic, achievable goals and objectives based on those in the organization's crisis contingency plan. When the crisis management team has a member who understands how the news media operates, its decisions will consider the information needs of the press. That's more likely to happen if the goals and objectives for the press relations plan and the crisis plan as a whole are interrelated.

Reporting Relationships

The crisis communications chain of command needs to be clearly defined, and it works best if there's only one link between the top person on the crisis team and whoever is in charge of press relations. If other facilities, operations, or divisions will be involved, as with Delta 191 and Bhopal, their line of command for dealing with the news media also should be defined in the plan. The reporting relationships may be temporary and only relate to the crisis, but the last thing anyone needs in an emergency situation is questions about who takes orders from whom and whether someone may be exceeding the limits of their authority.

Specific Responsibilities

What's expected of the public relations people? Are they supposed to handle employee and customer communications as well as the news media? Those responsibilities should be outlined in the communications plan. They may involve providing information to people in the organization responsible for communications with other important internal and external audiences and for receiving information, such as the names of those who were killed, injured, or are missing, for distribution to the news media. That needs to be clearly spelled out so the content and timing of those communications will be coordinated.

Press relations responsibilities during a crisis should be described in the plan in general terms so assignments can be made to the people who are available to help out. The different jobs, which range from answering telephones to developing relevant background material to serving as a spokesperson for the organization, are covered in Chapter 3 and can be adapted to the needs of any organization.

Spokespersons

The principal spokesperson for the organization if a crisis occurs should be established in advance, along with the designated public relations spokespersons. If specific divisions, locations, or facilities will be involved, their authorized spokespersons should be designated as they are in Delta's Standard Practices, which specifies that the marketing manager will be the Delta spokesperson in the locality where an accident occurs. Provisions also need to be made for alternates who will be authorized to speak for the organization if the designated spokesperson is not available. That will avoid the type of delay that occurred after the Challenger accident.

Some people will be inclined to speak to the press on their own, so the organization's position regarding unauthorized spokespersons needs to be clearly defined. The options range from dismissal on the spot to allowing anyone to say whatever they want to the news media without fear of reprisal. The designated spokespersons need to know what the organization's position is on unauthorized comments so their responses will reflect that policy.

Logistics

Considering the importance of telephones in a breaking news story, procedures need to be established so that adequate phone service is available to handle press calls and to maintain lines of communication with the crisis command center. The main switchboard also needs to know what the procedure is for responding to calls from the media, regardless of the hour or how many calls are coming in.

Provisions should be made for setting up media briefings, starting with a decision about where they will be held. Delta Air Lines used a large meeting room in its conference center across the street from the headquarters building because it was suitable and convenient. Union Carbide used the ballroom at the nearby Danbury Hilton so it wouldn't have to worry about reporters and camera crews wandering around its corporate headquarters. There will be several options, but the location for briefings should be worked out in advance so that potential source of confusion is minimized.

Additional Manpower

Even if everyone in public relations is in town and available when the crisis occurs, they won't number enough to handle all that has to be done 18 to 24 hours a day for who knows how long. The plan needs to have provisions for bringing in people who are qualified to help with the various assignments, and who can work the odd hours when the news coverage will be lighter so the principal people can rest and reload.

The procedures for contacting the people and securing the approval of their supervisors need not be complicated but should be defined, along with any accounting details for charging out their time. NASA routinely kept its media briefing center open 24 hours a day during shuttle missions, staffed with a cadre of retired public affairs people and former employees. They were invaluable in maintaining the overnight continuity of its press relations after the Challenger accident, but they also had to be paid out of someone's budget.

Disclosure Guidelines

The most important sections of the plan will be those dealing with the disclosures to the news media and the organization's other publics. The basic policies regarding public disclosures need to be established up front so there will be no questions, surprises, or misunderstandings later on. The Delta Air Lines Standard Practices, for example, made it clear that no information on the Flight 191 passengers would be made public until the company had confirmed that the next of kin of every person on the plane had been personally informed by a Delta employee.

The point at which disclosures will be made also needs to be established. At Union Carbide, the policy was not to provide information on the Bhopal situation until it had been confirmed and was considered factual. Details that will/will not be disclosed need to be clearly spelled out in the guidelines, as well as how they will be verified and who will be responsible for approving the information that is made public.

The Delta Air Lines command center kept both Matt Guilfoil in Dallas and Delta's public relations staff in Atlanta advised as more details on the Flight 191 accident became available. Therefore their statements to the press could be kept consistent. Bill Berry recalled that it sometimes was difficult to get the latest details to both locations simultaneously, because the phones were tied up. "Our big effort was to keep the information flow going and to be certain it was accurate on both ends," he said.

Timing

The procedures also should point out that the timing of disclosures is to be consistent, regardless of whether the information is good or bad. All too often the inclination is to delay or defer on negative developments in the hope that something positive may come up to offset it. The wiser approach is just the opposite. The news may be bad, but at least the integrity of the organization and its spokespersons will be maintained.

The procedures also should indicate when the verified information is to be made public, and who is to be advised before the details are disclosed to the news media. Anyone who is directly affected by the announcement, such as next of kin, should be contacted before any public disclosure. Provisions also should be made for alerting spokespersons at other locations so they have the latest details and can provide a consistent response.

In a related area, the guidelines for disclosures to the news media in the face of ominous legal concerns need to be clearly established. The inclination of some participants will be to hunker down and clam up as the news media rushes in, and many corporate attorneys will defend that stance. Union Carbide's Jackson Browning, who has a law degree, takes a different view. "The idea that you might be able to cover it up, sweep it under the rug, something of that sort, was preposterous—a fool's paradise to even think you could get something like that done," he said. "We decided to tell it like we saw it when we were sure of what we had. If the legal problems were there, you just had to hope in the long run the truth was going to help you. Whether it helped or hurt you, it was the truth and it was going to be on the table."[176]

WHAT MAKES THE DIFFERENCE WHEN THE UNTHINKABLE OCCURS

Why is it then that some press relations plans seem to work more effectively in a crisis than others? If you consider what happened with Bhopal, the Challenger, and Delta Flight 191, several conclusions can be drawn from how each organization handled the crisis to provide some answers to this important question.

Coordinated Contingency Planning

The press relations plan should be a direct spin-off of the operational plan for resolving the crisis, with the same goals, objectives, and priorities. In turn, the overall contingency plan of the organization needs to reflect the importance of maintaining open, credible lines of communication with its publics, all of which will be influenced by the news media's reports. Otherwise, like NASA, it may find the cause of the problem but suffer serious damage to its reputation and integrity as a result of the news coverage of what happened.

One basic flaw in the NASA public affairs contingency plan was that it was not an integral part of an overall STS accident plan, which deprived it of management participation in those critical first hours. Delta's incident emergency procedures handbook is an excellent example of how media relations activities can be tied into the overall contingency plan for an emergency, which is outlined in Delta's Standard Practices. Union Carbide's plan for addressing the Bhopal tragedy established forthright communications as its second most important objective, right behind maintaining Carbide's financial integrity.

The operations people in charge of resolving the situation may have a basic distrust of the news media. That's OK, but they and the organization's top management had better recognize that of all the groups who are closely following the course of what has happened, the most important by far are the members of the press. Sure, the owners are important, or maybe it's the investors, the customers, the Congress, or the consumer who will determine how well the organization survives the ordeal. But where will they get most of the information that influences their perceptions about what happened? It won't be from the organization. Somebody has to be authorized to communicate in those critical first hours, and top management has to be involved as the organization's principal spokesperson or right behind the scenes.

This is not the time for the "kill the messenger" management mentality, which frequently develops toward public relations people in the midst of a breaking news story. There had better be interaction if the organization is to maintain its reputation. Although technical specialists and lawyers will automatically be called in, the organization also needs someone who knows how to communicate, who understands how the media thinks, and who is actively involved in developing information that can be disclosed.

Having Someone at the Scene

An understanding of public relations will be needed in two places: where decisions are made and at the scene. If they are relatively close, it may be possible for the same person to cover both bases. During the Baby Fae coverage at Loma Linda Medical Center, the briefing center was a block from the hospital so Dick Schaefer, the hospital's spokesman, could easily get back and forth. It was even easier for John Dwan during the Barney Clark news coverage because the briefing area was in the hospital cafeteria.

When there are miles between the command center and the scene, the second public relations person becomes essential. Union Carbide badly needed someone in Bhopal who could provide its corporate management with factual information and also speak for the company in discussions with local officials and the news media the morning after the accident. However, that person probably would have been thrown in jail along with the rest of the Bhopal plant management, considering the Indian government's reaction to the tragedy.

Delta's designation of spokespersons is based on the premise that accidents are likely to happen anywhere in its 150-city system. The marketing manager therefore will be the spokesperson in any locality affected by the accident. The SP specifies that they are to be backed up by a representative from Delta's public relations department in Atlanta who provides whatever support and assistance is needed. He arrived in Dallas four hours after the accident on the same plane with Delta's president and the senior vice president who directed the company's response to the accident.

One of NASA's problems after the Challenger accident was that many of its public affairs people were not where they were needed. Several were on the West Coast at the Jet Propulsion Laboratories for the Voyager spacecraft flyby of the planet Uranus and for a public affairs audit at another NASA facility. "We were so short of personnel that it was really shocking," Green said. "Things like that nobody would write into a contingency plan."

Ongoing Management Support

The most important factor is this: An organization can have the best intentions for responding to the press, but if it doesn't have the firm support of its top management during those critical first hours, its plans will be meaningless.

The Challenger explosion came during an organizational upheaval within the space agency, which deprived NASA's public affairs efforts of vital management support in those early hours.

NASA's administrator, James Beggs, was on leave of absence after being indicted with the company he previously headed, which was accused of billing irregularities in defense contracts. The acting administrator, Dr. William R. Graham, had been on hand the day before the accident but had left for meetings in Washington after a faulty bolt in the crew cabin door forced a one-day postponement of the Challenger mission. With Jesse Moore tied up in meetings after the explosion and Dr. Graham flying back to the Cape, Shirley Green had no management support for implementing the STS Public Affairs Contingency Plan.

Top management was not at the Delta Air Lines headquarters on Friday at 7 P.M. when the Flight 191 crash occurred, but they didn't need to be. "Senior management's presence already was there in that detailed Standard Practice book," Bill Berry observed. "It's a very easy environment for a PR guy who's stressed to the limit when he knows all the machinery is in place so he can do the best job possible in informing the press."

Union Carbide's management support took a different form but it was equally effective—the CEO got directly involved. "It's not something that you seek out," Warren Anderson said. "It's not a battleground of your choosing, but I don't think anyone can do it as well as the chairman himself."

CHAPTER SIXTEEN

A Message for Management

It will never be a battleground of your choosing. It wasn't for Warren Anderson of Union Carbide after Bhopal, nor was it for any of the other principals in this book. All of them, physicians, presidents, administrators or executives, know they could have managed the situation far more easily and effectively if the news media was not present. They also know that was not a realistic consideration, as I am sure you do.

Even at the Loma Linda Medical Center, where the worst mishandling of the news media occurred, the institution anticipated that the press would cover the experimental transplant of a baboon heart into an infant. They held meetings several months prior to the operation to decide what provisions would be made for the press. But Loma Linda was not ready when Baby Fae was referred to the hospital and surgery was performed a week later. They compounded that error by not anticipating what questions reporters would ask, by giving out false information to protect the privacy of the baby's family, and by not having authoritative, well-informed spokespersons. As a result, Loma Linda created a negative impression in the first few hours, which continues to influence the news reports two years later. That coverage has conveyed a negative perception of that organization to its important publics, who cannot help but be influenced by what they see, hear, and read in the news media.

The same has been true of NASA since the Challenger accident. Here was the government's "Can Do" agency, which the public revered for being able to accomplish amazing feats in space. It also was an organization with a highly regarded public relations apparatus, which could provide virtually any information or visuals a journalist would need in covering aerospace stories. Yet its press relations system failed in those critical first few hours after the explosion, and NASA watched as the news media turned against it. In the ensuing weeks, the startling revelations and subsequent blunders by NASA's public affairs staff would be reported by news organizations that were already hostile, which drastically altered the favorable perceptions of the space agency that the public had developed over the preceding quarter century.

The problem is that Loma Linda and NASA are not the exceptions among organizations that may become the focus of significant news media attention. They are typical of most, be they publicly held corporations, private companies, nonprofit institutions, or government facilities. One had an effective public relations program in place; the other didn't. In both instances, top management was not involved when they were most needed. As a result, their organizations lost any chance they had for maintaining favorable working relationships with the news media.

THE NEWS MEDIA IS NO DIFFERENT THAN YOUR OTHER PUBLICS

The question I hear most often is, "How do I get our top management to understand the impact the news media can have on our organization if we're going to be in a major story?" While the question is legitimate, I also can understand your reluctance to get involved with the press, knowing you cannot control their news reports and that they can have a severe impact on you and your organization if they sense there has been mismanagement of your business. But isn't that also true of your competition? And what about your customers, your contributors, and your credit-line banks? Don't you make provisions for ensuring that each of these important publics will understand the strengths and accomplishments of your organization? Then why can't provisions also be made for conveying those same messages to the news media so you will be prepared if your organization should find itself in the midst of a major story?

You can't "wing it" with reporters, any more than you can with security analysts, legislators, or the members of your board. You know you have to prepare for each of these encounters if you expect them to accept what you say. In each instance it takes hours of preparation to ensure that your information is accurate, understandable, and will hold up under scrutiny. It's no different with the news media, although the majority of their questions will be far more benign than the ones you have to respond to in reviewing your financial results.

I am sure you can recall instances where how you communicated what you wanted to say, more than what you actually said, determined the support you received from the few people whose personal recommendations and written reports were critical to the future of your organization. You may have had a disastrous year, but if you can convey the perception that you know what is going on and are taking decisive steps to manage the situation, they'll often back you—the first time.

The same applies to the news media. They know what your management team will have to contend with when it's in the midst of a major news story and they were not assigned to attack you or your organization. As long as you're honest and open, and provide them with facts that can be disclosed on a timely basis, most will give you the benefit of the doubt in their news reports.

REALISTIC PLANNING

Planning your press relations is just as essential, as it is for any area of your organization's business, but a detailed contingency plan is not required for your organization to respond effectively when a news story breaks. NASA, in fact, had a detailed public affairs contingency plan for space shuttle accidents—and it didn't work. A more realistic approach is to define the basic communications resources that would be needed regardless of what has occurred, so they can be quickly adapted and put into effect in managing the specific situation. That approach, which is outlined in the preceding chapters, worked for Union Carbide in responding to the accident in Bhopal, which killed 2,000 people and injured 100,000. Where Carbide came up short was in not being able to communicate with the scene of the disaster and in not having anyone in Bhopal who could provide details and also respond to the news media as they moved in to cover the story. The inability of Carbide's management to assess the situation led to Warren Anderson's decision to travel to Bhopal with a team of company specialists to determine the cause of the accident and what could be done to rectify the situation.

THE ROLE OF TOP MANAGEMENT

As the CEO of Union Carbide, Anderson could easily have delegated the responsibility for resolving the Bhopal disaster to any one of several senior officers at Carbide rather than becoming personally involved in directing his company's response to the accident. While his decision has been applauded by leaders in the business community, it also is troubling to top executives in other organizations, large and small, who would prefer not to have to step out of their executive suites and into the glare of the public spotlight if their organization becomes involved in a news story.

Warren Anderson is no Lee Iacocca. Anderson had always been a strong executive but never a public figure and had shunned publicity for himself and his corporation. The decision to become personally involved was difficult. Anderson felt it was necessary for Union Carbide to resolve the situation but also to convey the perception of its corporate concern for the accident and its victims. He knew that perception could only be conveyed by the person in charge, not by a spokesperson, not by prepared statements.

The organization is yours. It exemplifies your personal ethics. Your professional priorities are interwoven throughout its management fabric, but it will need your leadership if it is to be prepared and responsive when a major news story breaks, just as it does when a change occurs in your business environment. It will need your personal involvement to convey to its internal and external publics the perception of being humanistic and concerned about the people who have been affected by what has happened. That may be through statements to the news media, or it may be through your actions. Warren Anderson went to Bhopal and became the personification of Union Carbide in speaking to the news media, Congress, Carbide's employees, and communities where its chemical facilities were located. James Burke, the chairman of Johnson & Johnson, did much the same thing after both Tylenol poisoning crises.

More and more members of top management are choosing to represent their organizations in public and with the news media. That's encouraging because it's the most effective and credible way for any organization to build support among its many internal and external publics which follow the organization and can be convinced most easily by its top management. Your employees, your customers, your creditors, will be looking for reassurance, which can only be provided by one or two individuals in the organization—its top management. You, better than anyone else, can provide the calming influence these publics will need in a crisis.

You probably are not a public figure and have no desire to be one. Very few executives are. And yet, if you stop to consider how often you have addressed meetings of employees, security analysts, or your peers at various conventions, you already are a public figure. If your organization is to grow, top management has no choice but to be visible. Providing information to the news media is an extension of what you've done already, and it can be effectively managed to allow the personality of the organization to be seen and understood, without you having to spend all of your time responding to questions and being interviewed by the press.

The Importance of Your Chief Spokesperson

Your success will be determined by the individual who's the chief spokesperson for your organization. Like the chief of staff for the president of the United States, he or she needs to be a member of your inner circle of advisers to understand how you think and the issues that are especially important or sensitive to the organization as it pursues its ongoing business and its strategic objectives.

He or she may be the "voice crying in the wilderness," but one of your chief spokesperson's essential functions should be in weighing the potential impact of your decisions, major or minor, on the perceptions of the publics who will determine whether you achieve your long-term goals. To be effecive your chief spokesperson has to understand how the news media thinks and operates because news organizations are the most important and influential of your publics. If you question that, consider where the people whose support you need most get a majority of the information that shapes their opinions.

Then consider how the course of recent history would have changed if one of President Reagan's closest advisors had thought through how the news media would react to a secret Iranian arms shipment, and had forcefully offered that perspective to the president before he accepted the recommendation of his national security advisors. Senator Edmund Muskie, a member of the Tower Commission which investigated the Iranian-Contras scandal, observed when the commission submitted its report, "The chief of staff, Donald T. Regan, also shares in this responsibility. . . . He, as much as anyone, should have insisted that an orderly process be observed. In addition, he especially should have insured that plans were made for handling any public disclosure for the initiative."[177]

More than anything else, that person has to have your trust. Are you willing to accept his advice regarding the news media and do what he says, even if it seems contrary to the course you'd otherwise take? Is he also respected by the other members of your management team so he can take whatever actions he believes are appropriate in responding to the news media? If you don't have that degree of confidence in the person who would be your chief spokesperson, you'd better make a change.

You need to be willing to accept and support the advice that comes from understanding and dealing with a foreign culture—the news media—just as you will listen to the advice of your attorneys, because the consequences often will be interrelated and can be equally profound in both instances. There also has to be mutual respect and a close working relationship between top management and the chief spokesperson, something that was evident at Union Carbide and the other organizations in which the media coverage has been generally balanced and accurate. Where that close working relationship was weak or lacking, as it was at NASA and Loma Linda, the institution is now viewed through the negative prism which the news media established at the time—and still maintains.

In the end, you and your chief spokesperson will determine the perceived value of the organization in a major news story. That's as true for you as it is for the president of the United States. Your organization may emerge with a few dents in its reputation. That has to be expected when you're the focus of national news. The important consideration is how the media coverage has affected your corporate goals and future prospects.

Working together, you and your chief spokesperson have the best chance of ensuring that the effects are negligible. They may even be enhanced through news reports when the media has been genuinely impressed with your organization, its management, and how you handled the difficult situation. Journalists are quick to mention Johnson & Johnson, Delta Air Lines, and Humana as examples of how an organization has effectively handled a major news story. Hopefully, with your involvement and leadership, the same will be true for your organization.

NOTES

INTRODUCTION

1. Personal interview with Ed Van Den Ameele, Union Carbide, Danbury, CT, September 3, 1986.

2. Personal interview with Warren Anderson, Union Carbide, Danbury, CT, September 30, 1986. Anderson, who had been chairman of the board and CEO of Union Carbide since 1982, retired in November 1986.

3. Personal interview with Shirley Green, NASA, Washington, DC, September 2, 1986. Ms. Green had been director of public affairs for NASA for less than a month at the time of the Challenger accident. She previously had been the press secretary for Vice President Bush.

4. Joani Nelson-Horchler, "Fallout from Bhopal, Industry Confronts the Long Term Consequences," *Industry Week*, August 13, 1985, p. 44.

5. Each patient determined the media exposure he received. Schroeder had been active in his community, his church, and his labor union, and he liked the publicity. Haydon, on the other hand, made it very clear to Dr. DeVries and to me before his operation that he didn't want the same type of worldwide media exposure that Schroeder had received. He was willing to allow photographs to be taken, but he wasn't interested in being interviewed by the press, and he never was. If there's a lesson here, it's that the participants in a major news story are *not* obligated to become public figures unless they want to.

6. In addition to the interviews with a variety of journalists, several chapters were distributed to a cross section of newspeople for their comments and suggestions. Some had a few comments over the phone; several wrote letters as long as three pages with their reactions and suggestions. A number of additions and changes were made to reflect the points they raised.

CHAPTER 1

7. A prominent public relations professional and the Public Relations Society of America demonstrated the same ostrich approach that PRSA members urge their organizations or clients to avoid. The month before he was to become PRSA president for 1986, Anthony Franco was questioned by the SEC about his involvement in a stock purchase that might represent an insider trading violation. The SEC later alleged that Franco, the president of a public relations counseling firm in Detroit, had purchased 3,000 shares of a client's stock when he learned the company was to be acquired, and then tried to cancel the trade when the American Stock Exchange contacted the company about the unusually large trade. Even though he knew he was under investigation by the SEC, Franco accepted the PRSA presidency in November 1985 without advising anyone in the organization.

   Franco served as president for seven months, spearheading a campaign to increase professionalism among the PRSA's 12,000 members while the SEC continued its investigation. He signed an SEC consent decree in June 1986 but still didn't advise the PRSA board or executive staff until August when the SEC findings were made public. Franco resigned two days later, but the PRSA board then compounded the problem by announcing the new president to its membership but not explaining why Franco had resigned. Many PRSA members, including a national director and members of its ethics committee, learned the details from *Jack O'Dwyer's Newsletter,* a widely read newsletter on public relations, or from newspaper reports, including a scathing article on Franco and the public relations profession in *The Wall Street Journal.*

8. Personal interview with Ed Yeates, KSL-TV, Salt Lake City, UT, November 21, 1985. Yeates had followed the development of the artificial heart at the University of Utah for 20 years before Barney Clark's operation. He subsequently covered Schroeder's artificial heart implant and the first few days of his recovery. Dr. DeVries regards him as one of the two best journalists in Utah who reported on the artificial heart.

9. Sandra Blakeslee, "Human Heart Replacement: New Challenges for Physicians and Reporters." p. 26. This 100-page booklet is an edited compilation of remarks at a symposium in Washington, DC in October 1985, which included prominent surgeons, medical journalists, and the public relations professionals who had been involved in heart transplants, the artificial heart implants, and the Baby Fae transplant.

   The purpose of the symposium, which was sponsored by The Foundation for American Communications and The Gannett Foundation, was to have an interchange of ideas between the participants so they might be able to relate more easily and effectively in the future. While there were some lively exchanges of views, especially in the morning session, the only area of general agreement seemed to be that guidelines should be developed so that the names of organ donors would not have to be disclosed to the news media.

10. Steven Fink, in his book "Crisis Management: Planning for the Inevitable," provides an extensive discussion of how Johnson & Johnson handled the two Tylenol crises. He also is highly critical of Union Carbide's actions in dealing with the Bhopal tragedy, although he never interviewed any of the Carbide executives who handled the problem. "Crisis Management" was published by AMACOM in 1986.

11. Lawrence K. Altman, M.D., "Confusion Surrounds Baby Fae," *New York Times*, November 5, 1984.

12. Loretta McLaughlin, "Loma Linda and Humana: Did PR Manage the News?" *ScienceWriter, The Newsletter of the National Association of Science Writers*, February 1985. The response of Richard Weismeyer and Dick Schaefer of Loma Linda to Ms. McLaughlin's article was published in the September 1985 issue of *ScienceWriter*. Among other things it stated:

> "The Humana story is a continuation of the Utah story. The artificial heart research had already been published in the scientific literature. The patient and family had agreed beforehand to meet the press. Animal rights were of no concern."

> "Loma Linda, on the other hand, had a request for confidentiality from the patient's parents. Under California law SB889 it would have been illegal to release some of the information Humana put into their press kit. Furthermore, the integrity of the Loma Linda research would have been compromised in scientific circles if it had been reported for the first time in the lay press. Science writers everywhere understand that scientists who are sensitive to the expectations of their peers prefer publishing the details of their research in the scientific literature before bringing it to the public. A press conference is not considered to be the best place to disseminate scientific discovery, especially while it is still in progress."

13. National Aeronautics and Space Administration, STS Public Affairs Contingency Plan, August 22, 1983, p. 1.

14. Report of the Presidential Commission on the Space Shuttle Challenger Accident, June 6, 1986, p. 1. What the Rogers Commission failed to mention in its preface was the close cooperation and extraordinary lengths which the management and employees of NASA went to in developing information for the Presidential Panel. In analyzing whether the right solid rocket booster might have been the cause of the

accident, NASA even documented exactly how long the suspected rocket section had been in transit from the Morton Thiokol plant and how far it had actually traveled. To come up with that detailed information NASA employees had gone through thousands of shipping documents to locate the orders and trace the railroad car which had carried the rocket booster from Utah to Cape Canaveral.

15. Candace Talmadge, "Delta Closed Ranks to Deal with the Dallas Passenger Disaster," *AdWeek*, August 12, 1985.

16. Personal interview with James Ewing, Delta Air Lines, Atlanta, GA, March 10, 1986. Ewing clearly conveyed a personal and professional sense of grief during our interview, partly because the co-pilot of Flight 191 had been a personal friend.

17. Ed Bean, "Damage Control: After 137 People Died in Its Texas Jet Crash, Delta Helped Families," *The Wall Street Journal*, November 7, 1986.

18. Associated Press, "Delta's Care Cuts Lawsuits from Crashes," *Chicago Sun-Times*, November 5, 1986.

19. Mark Whitaker, "Poison Gas Leak in India Kills 2,500 and Maims Up to 100,000 in the Worst Industrial Accident in History," *Newsweek*, December 17, 1984.

CHAPTER 2

20. Anderson interview, September 30, 1986.

CHAPTER 3

21. NEXIS and the Dow Jones News Retrieval systems were used extensively in the research for this book and provided important insights that subsequently became the basis for interview questions as well as specific recommendations in the following chapters.

22. Personal interview with Robert Henrie, Savage Industries, Oreham, UT, November 22, 1985. At the time of the Wilberg mine fire, Henrie was executive vice president of Savage Industries, a privately held corporation involved primarily in trucking and mining. Its Emery Mining subsidiary operated the Wilberg mine for Utah Power and Light, which used its coal to fuel one of its power plants several miles from the mine. Henrie's previous press relations experience was gained during eight years as a Congressional staffer and in working with the media in election campaigns. He has since established Henrie Group, a communications consulting firm in Salt Lake City.

23. The training was provided by Ammerman Enterprises, Houston, TX. Ammerman specializes in preparing spokespersons for news media

briefings and interviews, congressional testimony, regulatory hearings, and similar situations where tough questions are likely to be asked. Many public relations firms also can provide the same type of training as one of their client services.

24. Personal interview with Allan M. Lansing, M.D., Ph.D., Louisville, KY, December 22, 1986. Dr. Lansing is highly regarded by many of the journalists who covered the Bill Schroeder and Murray Haydon artificial heart operations for his detailed briefings and candor in responding to the media's questions. He was effective because he used basically the same approach during medical briefings that he uses so often in explaining to his open heart patients or their families what had been done during surgery and how the patient was progressing.

One of the primary reasons Humana's media relations efforts worked so well during the early months of the artificial heart program was that Dr. Lansing always went out of his way to accommodate the news media, even if it meant having one of his associates start a surgical case for him or giving up a quiet dinner at home to wait in a television station for a two-minute conversation with a camera that would be part of an intercity interview on one of the network news programs. Lansing was always articulate and even-tempered, no matter how unpleasant the situation or irritating the questions being asked by a reporter.

25. Personal interview with John Dwan, University of Utah Medical Center, Salt Lake City, UT, November 22, 1985. Dwan took a full month off during Barney Clark's 112 days with an artificial heart for Reserve duty with the Marines in Korea. His assistant, Anne Brillinger, filled in for him in his absence.

26. Anderson interview, September 30, 1986.

CHAPTER 4

27. Personal interview with Al Rossiter, Jr., United Press International, Washington. DC., October 23, 1985. Rossiter covers all aspects of science and medicine and has reported on the artificial heart as well as NASA's 25 years of manned spaceflight. He was one of several journalists interviewed for this book who had covered more than one of its case studies.

28. Personal interview with Denny Brisley, the White House, Washington, DC, April 14, 1986. Before joining the White House press office staff, Ms. Brisley had been press secretary for David Stockman, Director of the Office of Management and Budget. Her area of specialized media relations was in coordinating the television and radio coverage of the president. She left the press office staff the month after Larry Speakes' resignation became effective and is an associate editor of *Fairfax Magazine*.

The ability of the White House press office to prepare quickly for a breaking news story and the benefit of their three staff meetings a day was demonstrated the day of my first interview with Ms. Brisley. We met for three hours after the two morning staff meetings, taking time off for Larry Speakes' 11:00 A.M. briefing of the White House press corps and the Rose Garden ceremonies marking the conclusion of President Reagan's meetings with Japanese Prime Minister Nakasoni. Brisley was aware that something was up because of the presence of military staff people who usually were not seen at the White House. What she learned at the regular 5:00 P.M. staff meeting was that American bombers were enroute to Libya. The Tripoli raid was announced two hours later.

29. Personal interview with Peg Maloy, Director of Public Affairs, Federal Emergency Management Agency, Washington, DC, November 10, 1986. FEMA gets involved in providing assistance and financial aid when the governor of the state determines the situation cannot be effectively handled by the local and state agencies and asks the president to declare the situation a "major disaster" or an "emergency" according to the provisions of the Disaster Relief Act of 1974. The disasters can be natural phenomena like hurricanes, floods, and tornados or man-made crises like the Three Mile Island nuclear power plant accident or the riots of the Cuban boat people after they were interned. Assistance is coordinated through the nearest of 10 regional FEMA offices, with the Washington headquarters providing whatever support is required in specialized areas such as media relations.

   FEMA has an excellent pamphlet, "When Disaster Strikes: A Handbook for the Media" which can be obtained from the Office of Public Affairs, Federal Emergency Management Agency, 500 C Street SW, Washington, DC 20472.

30. Henrie interview, November 22, 1985.

31. Dwan interview, November 22, 1985. Even though the University of Utah Medical Center was only one component of the University of Utah, it had autonomy in its media relations activities relating to the artificial heart. The president of the university had given Dr. Peterson responsibility for all aspects of the clinical trial, which meant that he and Dwan did not have to be concerned about being overruled at the "corporate" level. Some members of the university's public relations staff were brought in to help Dwan, but they served in a supplemental capacity.

32. Henrie interview, November 22, 1985.

33. Union Carbide initially offered to pay as much as $350 million to the families of the Bhopal victims. The American lawyers representing the

families filed suit in U.S. courts seeking $150 billion in damages for the victims. The Indian government initially sued Union Carbide for damages which they said could not be calculated at the time. In November 1986, nearly two years after the accident, the government finally determined the amount sought was $3.15 billion in damages.

CHAPTER 5

34. One of the ironies of the "Ingelfinger Rule" is that *The New England Journal of Medicine* maintains its reputation in part by disclosing newsworthy articles and editorials to the news media several days before the new issue is distributed to subscribers. Disclosures are made with the understanding that news reports will be embargoed until the publication date. The problem is that organizations like Humana, which are mentioned in an article or editorial, find themselves having to respond to calls from the national news media about the latest issue of *The New England Journal of Medicine* without knowing what has been said because the magazine will not arrive in the mail for several days.

35. Personal interview with George Strait, ABC News, Washington, DC, May 24, 1985. One of Strait's first medical stories for ABC involved research at the National Institutes of Health to develop a new acne medication in which he had volunteered to be a participant. His story aired the night before an article was published on the research in *The New England Journal of Medicine*. Strait recalled that the resulting anger of Dr. Arnold Relman, the journal's editor, caused one of the co-authors of the paper, who had done the biochemical laboratory analysis, to withdraw from subsequent work on the project, fearing that his involvement would jeopardize any future chances to have articles published in *The Journal*.

36. Telephone interview with Lawrence K. Altman, M.D., *New York Times*, October 28, 1986. Dr. Altman has written and spoken extensively on the dilemma facing scientists who are reluctant to disclose their work to science writers employed by the general news media for fear of compromising the chances of their work being published in a medical or scientific journal. In an article entitled "Medical Journals' Muzzling Policies Threaten Quality" in the September 1986 issue of *ScienceWriter*, the newsletter of the National Association of Science Writers, Dr. Altman stated "In many ways, peer review is a self-serving phrase that is often misused to provide a more scientific appearance to what in other forms of journalism is considered to be part of the normal editing process."

37. Personal interview with Bill McAda, Federal Emergency Management

Agency, November 10, 1986. McAda is a veteran public affairs officer for FEMA who handled a variety of disasters while assigned to a regional office and has since been involved in natural disasters as well as major problems like Three Mile Island and the Cuban refugee riots.

38. News Media Briefing Book, Humana Heart Institute International, prepared by the Humana Public Relations Department, 1984, p. 56.

39. Personal interview with Michael Isikoff, *Washington Post*, Washington, DC, September 4, 1986. Isikoff's article on the media coverage of the Wilberg mine fire triggered the idea of expanding the scope of this book beyond the artificial heart program. Like many of the journalists I interviewed, Isikoff covered a curious diversity of the news stories in this book. In addition to the Wilberg fire, he reported on the Challenger crew recovery, the Bhopal aftermath, and Union Carbide's difficulties after the subsequent chemical gas leak at its plant in Institute, WV.

40. Dwan interview, November 22, 1985.

41. Dr. William R. Graham, the acting administrator, was flying to the Kennedy Space Center with Vice President Bush aboard Air Force Two. The plane's radio telephone was busy at the time Green placed the call.

   Within a few minutes after the accident, Green had the only outside phone functioning in The Launch Control building. All other lines had been cut off as part of the information impoundment procedures after the accident. The only reason Green's phone still worked was that she had placed the initial call to Dr. Graham in Washington seconds after the accident and never hung up. Subsequent calls had to be routed through the administrator's office to the White House and other locations in Washington, which had to be called on an emergency basis.

42. Arie W. Kruglanski, "Freeze-Think and the Challenger," *Psychology Today*, August 1986, p. 48.

43. Personal interview with William C. DeVries, M.D., Humana Heart Institute International, Louisville, KY, September 18, 1985. In spite of the worldwide publicity and considerable criticism within the medical profession, DeVries has not lost his down-to-earth personality that comes across when he has briefed the news media or been interviewed. According to medical journalists who have known him since his early involvement with the artificial heart, he has evolved from a medical researcher to a media-wise physician.

44. An interesting divergence of opinion is found in "Town Squirms Under Glare of Spotlight: Mine-Fire Coverage Labeled Intrusion," Michael Isikoff's article on the media coverage of the Wilberg fire in the December 31, 1984, *Washington Post*. The story described the

Sunday morning mass at the tiny San Rafael Mission near Huntington, UT, after the announcement that there was no hope for the 27 miners.

> "Now as the churchgoers clutched their hands in prayer and wept for their dead neighbors, bright hand-held television lights glared into their faces. Cameramen moved in for closeup shots, knocking over a Christmas crèche.
>
> 'It was a difficult situation to try and pray when somebody's got a camera poking in your face,' said the Rev. Gerald P. Lynch, the church's pastor. 'This community is not used to being in the public eye and having their tears broadcast all over the nation.'
>
> The shots of the bereaved parishioners of San Rafael and other local churches presented striking images on network newscasts that night. CBS correspondent David Dick, who didn't attend the services but narrated that network's account, called the images, 'beautiful . . . one of the stories I did we were most proud of.'
>
> But some residents were outraged. One member of the San Rafael congregation watched in disgust as cameramen tramped down the aisles. 'I hope you will forgive the hate I feel for you people right now,' he said to two photographers."

45. Personal interview with David Cohen, ABC-TV, Louisville, KY, February 12, 1986. Cohen at the time was a field producer for ABC News, based in Chicago. He has since been named chief of the recently established ABC News bureau in St. Louis.

46. Personal interview with Mark Mayfield, *USA Today*, Atlanta, GA, March 10, 1986. Mayfield, bureau chief for *USA Today* in Atlanta, was their primary journalist in covering the artificial heart program at Louisville and Tucson. He also was sent in immediately to cover the Challenger accident, as well as the crash of Flight 191 where he was aboard one of the Delta flights bringing in passengers' families. Mayfield recalls passing by the burnt-out hulk of the L-1011 as they landed in Dallas and hearing the agonized crying of passengers around him.

CHAPTER 6

47. Personal interview with Allan Biegel, M.D., University of Arizona, Tucson, AZ, August 30, 1985. Dr. Biegel, vice president of university relations at the University of Arizona, became the medical spokesperson when the emergency artificial heart implant was performed on Thomas Creighton. By the time the university's public relations office, which reported to Dr. Biegel, was advised of the emergency and he reached the hospital, the press had known about the problem for more

than one hour. The media had the airport staked out waiting for the artificial heart to arrive, and two dozen members of the press were in the hospital lobby looking for someone to brief them on the situation.

Dr. Biegel initially got off on the wrong foot with the press. Wanting to be as open as he could, he held the first briefing while the operation was still in progress and before he had enough of the facts to handle the questions and details adequately. He also was forced to conduct the briefing in the dean's conference room, the only meeting room available at the time but much too cramped for two dozen newsmen and television cameras.

48. Henrie interview, November 22, 1985.

49. Personal interview with members of the Loma Linda University Medical Center community relations staff, Loma Linda, CA, August 13, 1986. Participating in the discussion were Dick Schaefer, director of community relations, Richard Weismeyer, director of university relations, Joyce McClintock, editor of community relations publications, Anita Rockwell, assistant director of community relations, and Waldena Gaede, associate director of university relations.

Eavesdropping also may occur within the news media itself and is one of the techniques that journalists sometimes use to get a competitive edge on the fellow members of their profession. Three days after Bill Schroeder's artificial heart operation, I was confronted by a producer for one of the TV networks angrily demanding to know why we had given NBC an exclusive interview with Schroeder. I was baffled since Schroeder was still in isolation in the Coronary Care Unit. It turned out that NBC had noticed the producer lurking around the door of their editing room at the Convention Center, trying to determine what they were planning to feed to New York for the Nightly News. During a subsequent lull, Bob Bazell, NBC's medical correspondent, concocted an interview with "Bill Schroeder" with the answers to Bazell's questions coming from the old videotape of Barney Clark telling about how he felt with an artificial heart. From outside the door the producer didn't know the difference when she heard the playback of the completed interview (with the volume turned up a notch or two), but she soon found out to her anger and embarrassment.

50. Sandra Blakeslee, ed., "Human Heart Replacement," p. 34.

CHAPTER 7

51. Personal interview with Mark Knoller, Associated Press Radio, Washington, DC, October 22, 1985.

52. Telephone interview with Tom Noland, Humana Inc., Louisville, KY, July 31, 1986.

53. Brisley interview, April 14, 1986.

CHAPTER 8

54. Personal interview with Hugh Harris, NASA, Kennedy Space Center, FL, July 7, 1986.

55. Robert Bazell, "Hearts of Gold," *The New Republic*, February 18, 1985, p. 17.

56. Personal interview with George Atkins, Humana Inc., Louisville, KY, April 25, 1985.

57. Personal interview with Stephen Lyons, Louisville *Times*, Louisville, KY, October 19, 1985. Lyons has since joined the staff of WGBH, the PBS station in Boston, as a recipient of a Macy Fellowship in Science Broadcast Journalism.

58. Green interview, September 2, 1986.

59. Personal interview with Ira J. Furman, National Transportation Safety Board, Washington, DC, April 14, 1986. Furman has since left the NTSB to become an attorney with the firm of Schneider, Harris & Harris in Woodmere, NY.

60. Dwan interview, November 22, 1985.

61. Personal interview with Jackson Browning, Mamaroneck, NY, September 30, 1986. Browning retired in September 1986.

62. Telephone interview with Morton Kondracke, *The New Republic*, Washington, DC, January 3, 1987. Kondracke is probably best known as a panelist on the "McLaughlin Group" and "This Week with David Brinkley" television programs.

63. George J. Church, "What He Needs to Know: With Reagan Unwilling to Force Out the Facts, Oliver North's Web Spreads Even Wider." *Time*, December 22, 1986, p. 14.

64. Brisley interview, April 14, 1986.

65. Rossiter interview, October 22, 1985.

66. Telephone interview with Barbara Dolan, *Time*, Chicago, IL, December 13, 1986.

67. DeVries interview, September 18, 1985.

68. Personal interview with Gary Schwitzer, CNN, Atlanta GA, March 10, 1986.

69. Strait interview, May 24, 1985.

CHAPTER 9

70. Loma Linda discussions, August 13, 1986.

71. Personal interview with Benjamin J. Chapnick, Black Star, New York, NY, June 5, 1986.

72. In addition to its own staff of photographers, NASA contracts out to have photographic and video services during major launches like the space shuttles. These photographers were also used throughout the Challenger investigation while the documentation work was undertaken during the recovery and analysis of wreckage from the orbiter and solid rocket boosters.

73. Brisley interview, April 14, 1987.

74. Personal interview with C. Thomas Hardin, Louisville *Courier-Journal*, Louisville, KY, August 28, 1986. When we were planning for the press coverage of the first artificial heart patient, Hardin talked to me about having a member of his photographic staff serve as the pool photographer for the media. The photographer would have been available whenever needed, and we would not have had any of the costs or problems involved in the photographic processing and distribution. Hardin had several excellent photographers on his staff who were well qualified for the assignment; however, we would have had no say in the selection of pictures that would be made available to the media. I therefore opted to hire Bill Strode on a free-lance basis and in retrospect believe that was the right decision. Those pictures would have been available to any news organization, and there were several frames among the thousands that could have been used by certain publications to convey the wrong impression about Schroeder and his family, especially during the long post-stroke recovery periods.

   Humana distributed every picture that was newsworthy and in good taste, but we also could check with the physicians and families if there was any question about whether they would want the shot released. The picture of a nurse placing Schroeder's diseased heart beside the JARVIK-7 before the artificial heart was implanted had excellent news value and was used by *Time* and other publications, but we showed it to the Schroeders before it was released.

75. Personal interview with Ed Harrison, NASA, Kennedy Space Center, FL, July 17, 1986.

76. Photo credit caption on photography released by the National Aeronautics and Space Administration.

77. *Special Patient Consent for the Implantation of the Total Artificial Heart and Related Procedures*, Humana Heart Institute International News Media Briefing Book, p. 33. This is an unpublished work of authorship of Dr. W. C. DeVries and Symbion Inc., 1983. All rights reserved.

78. Chapnick interview, June 5, 1986.

79. Personal interview with Dale Minor, Medstar Communications, Allentown, PA, June 4, 1986. Minor is a former CBS News producer.

CHAPTER 10

80. Speech by Jody Powell, former White House Press Secretary, Public Relations Society of America National Conference, Detroit, MI, November 11, 1985.

81. The observations of Shirley Green of NASA were echoed by every spokesperson interviewed for this book. Even at Loma Linda, Dick Schaefer observed, "There were many good and bad things that happened. We found most of the news people to be very professional. It was only a few who were obnoxious and hard to work with."

82. Personal interview with Paul Raeburn, Associated Press, New York, NY, September 4, 1985.

83. Yeates interview, November 21, 1985. There's an interesting irony if you compare Ed Yeates's statement with comment number seven from the Hill and Knowlton interviews with journalists on pages 35–36. As Yeates said himself, "Somebody's going to be grumped."

84. Hardin interview, August 28, 1986.

85. Browning interview, September 30, 1986.

86. Strait interview, May 24, 1986.

87. "Informing the People: A Public Affairs Handbook" contains several chapters that describe the genesis of the freedom of Information Act and its evolution since it was signed into law by President Johnson in 1966. Chapter 6 is a description of the Freedom of Information Act which concludes with a statement by Russell M. Roberts, "In the dozen or so years that the Freedom of Information Act has been on the books there has been a notable change throughout government. From a disposition to conceal there has been a swing to an impulse to reveal. This is not, of course, all-embracing; and there undoubtedly have been acts of nullification which have surfaced. Nevertheless, changes there have been."

   "Informing the People: A Public Affairs Handbook" was edited by Lewis M. Helm, Ray Eldon Hiebert, Michael R. Naver, and Kenneth Rabin. It was published by Longman in 1981.

88. Knoller interview, October 22, 1985.

89. Personal interview with Chuck Zehnder, Price *Sun Advocate*, Price UT, November 23, 1985. A former Minneapolis-St. Paul newspaper man, Zehnder maintains an Associated Press affiliation for his twice-weekly newspaper, which proved invaluable for the national media when they moved in to cover the Wilberg fire. Zehnder also had studied the history of coal mining in central Utah and had written a pamphlet on the coal mines of Carbon County, so he was able to assist many of the journalists who had been sent in to report the story but who knew little or nothing about mining terminology.

90. Jan Quarles, "An Analysis of News Coverage of an Artificial Heart Implant and Related Public Relations Activities," unpublished doctoral thesis, University of Kentucky, July 1986. Dr. Quarles analyzed the coverage of CBS, ABC, and NBC for their respective evening news programs as well as the newspaper coverage of the story by the Louisville *Courier-Journal* and the *New York Times*.

91. Personal interview with Mike King, the *Courier-Journal*, Louisville, KY, October 17, 1985. King had returned from Washington the previous year to take over the medical news beat for the *Courier-Journal*. He had no formal training in medical journalism but quickly developed a unique style by combining medical news with his previous general and investigative reporting experience. The *Courier-Journal* brought in Gideon Gil who had a degree in biochemical sciences from Harvard to work with King after Dr. DeVries announced he was coming to Louisville. At the height of the story, the *Courier-Journal* had King and Gil working full time on the coverage, along with Judy Bryant. The Louisville *Times*, the *C-J*'s afternoon rival under the same ownership, had three reporters, Steve Lyons, Martha Barnett, and Larry Bleiberg, assigned to the artificial heart story. Ms. Barnett left the paper to write "The Bill Schroeder Story," an authorized biography published by William Morrow & Company in June 1987.

92. Sandra Blakeslee, ed., "Human Heart Replacement," p. 39.

93. Lansing interview, January 2, 1987.

94. Personal interview with Father Gerald Lynch, Notre Dame Church, Price, UT, November 23, 1986. Father Lynch maintains the San Rafael Mission, a small church on the outskirts of Huntington, for Catholic families in the area who cannot make the 26-mile trip to his parish in Price. He travels to Huntington several times a week and was there daily during the fire.

95. Strait interview, May 24, 1985.

96. Telephone interview and followup letter from Jon Meyersohn, CBS News, Chicago, IL, January 12, 1987.

97. Telephone interview and followup letter from Roger Brown, NBC News, Chicago, IL, January 15, 1987.

98. Personal interview with Tom Becherer, WLKY-TV, Louisville, KY, January 7, 1987.

99. Producers for the network interview programs have separate responsibilities from the field producers in that most of their work involves lining up the guests and coordinating segments of the show from remote locations. The field producer's primary job is coordinating the production of the live and videotaped news reports that will be used on the evening news and on the news segments of the morning shows. Field and show producers by necessity will work closely on a major news story, as they did on the artificial heart coverage, and they will cover for each other when the need arises.

100. Personal interview with Rich Gimmel and Carol Grady, WAVE-TV, Louisville, KY, December 30, 1986. Gimmel was news director for WAVE-TV at the time of Schroeder's implant. After 20 years in journalism, he resigned to manage his family's business—a machine shop. Gimmel says he wasn't sure when he left television news whether there was life after deadlines, but he now is certain there is.

101. Knoller interview, October 22, 1985.

102. Personal interview with Al Rossiter, Jr., United Press International, Washington, DC, October 22, 1985.

103. Kondracke interview, January 3, 1987. Kondracke was Washington Bureau Chief for *Newsweek* for 18 months in 1985–86, before returning to *The New Republic* as a senior editor.

104. Telephone interview with George Raine, *Newsweek*, San Francisco, CA, December 8, 1986. Prior to joining the magazine's San Francisco Bureau, Raine had been a newspaper reporter in Salt Lake City and had covered the development of the artificial heart as well as the Barney Clark story.

105. Although *Time* did not have a cover photo on the Iranian-Contras scandal in December, it shouldn't be concluded that they missed the boat. The two previous issues of the magazine had the scandal as the cover story.

106. Lucille DeView, "An Aftermath of Restraint, Recklessness," 1986–87 Journalism Ethics Report, Society of Professional Journalists, Sigma Delta Chi, p. 40.

107. Stuart Diamond, "$350 Million Pact Reported in Suits Over Bhopal Leak," *New York Times*, March 23, 1986, p. 1.

108. Zehnder had made an editorial decision that his paper would not interview any family members of the trapped miners because they were in emotional shock and knew very little about mining. David Dick, the CBS News correspondent, was quoted in Mike Isikoff's *Washington Post* article on the media coverage as saying, "I think that's preposterous. . . . We had the wife of one of the miners on and she believed there was a direct causal relationship between the deaths in that mine and the effort to set a production record. Are you not going to show that?"

The Mine Safety and Health Administration of the U.S. government concluded after an 18-month investigation that the most probable cause of the Wilberg tragedy was that an air compressor in another part of the mine, which was not being used by the miners, had been left running and had overheated, igniting the fire. David Dick has since retired from CBS and is now teaching at the University of Kentucky School of Journalism.

109. Dolan interview, December 13, 1986.

CHAPTER 11

110. Bazell, "Hearts of Gold," p. 19.

111. Editorial, "Nobility and Knowledge in Space," *New York Times*, July 30, 1986.

112. Lawrence K. Altman, M.D., "Confusion Surrounds Baby Fae," *New York Times*, November 5, 1984. (Copyright 1984 with permission of the *New York Times*.)

113. Yeates interview, November 21, 1985.

114. Raeburn interview, September 4, 1985.

115. Henrie interview, November 22, 1985.

116. James B. Stewart and David B. Hilder, "Union Carbide Could Face Staggering Gas-Leak Damage Claims, Experts Say," *The Wall Street Journal*, December 6, 1984.

117. Brisley interview, April 14, 1986.

118. National Aeronautics and Space Administration Transcript, January 28, 1986.

119. National Aeronautics and Space Administration Transcript, January 29, 1986.

120. Bazell, "Hearts of Gold." p. 18.

121. Editorial, "The Chemical Industry's Canaries," *New York Times*, April 3, 1986, Sec. A, p. 26.

122. Anderson interview, September 30, 1986.

123. McAda interview, November 10, 1986.

124. Kondracke interview, January 3, 1987.

125. Barry Meier and Joanne Lipman, "Carbide Chairman Says GAF 'Can Win' If It Boosts Its $68-a-Share Tender Offer," *The Wall Street Journal*, December 20, 1985.

126. Dolan interview, December 13, 1986.

127. Hardin interview, August 28, 1986.

128. Brisley interview, April 14, 1986.

129. George J. Church, "The Tower of Babel," *Time*, December 1, 1986, p. 18.

130. Jonathan Alter, "Will There Be a Backlash?: The Media Play It Carefully but Love the Chase," *Newsweek*, December 15, 1986, p. 40.

CHAPTER 12

131. Anderson interview, September 30, 1986.

132. Biegel interview, August 30, 1985. Dr. Biegel, a psychiatrist as well as a college administrator, was well thought of by the media because of his candor and willingness to provide as much general information as he had without getting into the technical details. Dr. Jack Copeland, the cardiac surgeon who had implanted the artificial heart in Thomas Creighton, made himself available once a day to the press, which relieved considerable pressure from Dr. Biegel.

133. Lansing interview, December 22, 1986.

134. DeVries interview, September 18, 1985. A member of Dr. Lansing's staff frequently accompanied him when he conducted medical briefings. She would often bring him a cup of water in the midst of the briefings to be seen on television, which would prompt hand signals from the correspondents to their camera crews to go tight on Lansing's face whenever they saw her coming. On one occasion one TV crew placed a glass of water on the podium before a briefing and had bets, using a stopwatch, to see if, and how quickly, she would take Lansing a second glass of water. She did, in less than three minutes.

135. Personal interview with Ronald Wishart, Union Carbide, Danbury, CT, September 4, 1986.

136. Dwan interview, November 22, 1985.

137. Bazell, "Hearts of Gold," p. 18.
138. Green interview, September 2, 1986.
139. Yeates interview, November 21, 1985.
140. Dolan interview, December 13, 1986.
141. Strait interview, May 24, 1985.
142. Raeburn interview, September 4, 1985.
143. Isikoff interview, September 4, 1985.
144. Kondracke interview, January 3, 1987.
145. Brisley interview, September 4, 1986.
146. Lyons interview, October 19, 1985.
147. Schwitzer interview, March 10, 1986.
148. Strait interview, May 24, 1985.
149. Thomas J. Lueck, "Crisis Management at Carbide," *New York Times*, December 14, 1984, Sect. D, p. 1.
150. Browning interview, September 30, 1986.
151. Zehnder, interview, November 23, 1986.
152. Telephone interview with Bill Berry, Delta Air Lines, Atlanta, GA, October 8, 1986. Berry indicated that while the Standard Procedure for accidents worked well after the Flight 191 accident, they had difficulty handling the number of phone calls on a round-the-clock basis. Changes have been made in their procedures to provide more people to handle the phones in the future.
153. Yeates interview, November 21, 1985.
154. Atkins and I are both 6'6" which made it easy to have discussions in the briefing center without being overheard. We also saw eye to eye with Dr. DeVries, who's 6'5", on most questions regarding the news media.

CHAPTER 13

155. Sandra Blakeslee, ed., "Human Heart Replacement," p. 8.
156. DeVries interview, September 18, 1985.
157. Personal interview with Ron Wishart and Walter Goetz, Union Carbide, Danbury, CT, September 3, 1986.
158. Henrie interview, November 22, 1985.
159. Telephone interview with David Dick, University of Kentucky, Lexington, KY, October 27, 1986.
160. Cohen interview, October 10, 1985.
161. Dolan interview, December 13, 1986.

162. Telephone interview with Lawrence Altman, M.D., *New York Times*, October 28, 1986.

163. Anderson interview, September 30, 1986.

CHAPTER 14

164. Yeates interview, November 21, 1985.

165. Dr. Altman's book, *Who Goes First? The Story of Self Experimentation in Medicine*, deals with medical experiments in which the first subjects have been the medical researchers themselves. The book is being published by Random House in the summer of 1987.

166. Wishart/Goetz interview, September 3, 1986.

167. Anderson interview, September 30, 1986.

168. Berry interview, October 10, 1986.

169. Joani Nelson-Horchler, "Fallout from Bhopal," p. 44.

CHAPTER 15

170. Green interview, September 2, 1986.

171. Mayfield interview, March 10, 1986.

172. Berry interview, October 8, 1986.

173. Wishart/Goetz interview, September 3, 1986.

174. Wishart/Goetz interview, September 3, 1986.

175. Anderson interview, September 30, 1986.

176. Browning interview, September 30, 1986

CHAPTER 16

177. John Tower, Edmund Muskie, Brent Scowcroft, "The Tower Commission Report," Bantam Books, Inc./Times Books Inc., 1987, pp. xviii–xix.

CONTRIBUTORS

Lawrence K. Altman, M.D.
Medical Writer
New York Times
New York, New York

Warren M. Anderson
Chairman of the Board
Union Carbide Corporation
Danbury, Connecticut

George L. Atkins
Vice President, Public Affairs
Humana Inc.
Louisville, Kentucky

Tom Becherer
News Director
WLKY-TV
Louisville, Kentucky

William Berry
Director of Public Relations
Delta Air Lines
Atlanta, Georgia

Allan Biegel, M.D.
Vice President, University Relations
University of Arizona at Tucson
Tucson, Arizona

Janet Bingham
Editorial Coordinator
University of Arizona at Tucson
Tucson, Arizona

Denny Brisley
Assistant Press Secretary
  to the President
The White House
Washington, D.C.

Linda Broadus
Public Relations Manager
Humana Inc.
Louisville, Kentucky

Roger Brown
Field Producer
NBC News
Chicago, Illinois

Jackson Browning
Director of Safety and
  Environmental Affairs
Union Carbide Corporation
Danbury, Connecticut

Mrs. Jack Burcham
Bloomington, Illinois

Benjamin J. Chapnick
Executive Vice President
Black Star Publishing Company
New York, New York

David H. Cohen
St. Louis Bureau Chief
ABC News Inc.
St. Louis, Missouri

William C. DeVries, M.D.
Principal Investigator
Humana Heart Institute International
Louisville, Kentucky

Barbara Dolan
Correspondent
Time
Chicago, Illinois

David Duarte
Public Information Officer
Food and Drug Administration
Washington, D.C.

John Dwan
Director of Community Relations & Development
University of Utah Medical Center
Salt Lake City, Utah

James Ewing
Director of National Media Relations
Delta Air Lines
Atlanta, Georgia

Ira J. Furman
Deputy Director for Public Affairs
National Transportation Safety Board
Washington, D.C.

Gideon Gil
Reporter
The *Courier-Journal*
Louisville, Kentucky

Rich Gimmel
Assistant News Director
WAVE-TV
Louisville, Kentucky

J. Walter Goetz
Director, Corporate Communications
Union Carbide Corporation
Danbury, Connecticut

Carol Grady
Health Reporter
WAVE-TV
Louisville, Kentucky

Shirley Green
Director of Public Affairs
National Aeronautics & Space Administration
Washington, D.C.

C. Thomas Hardin
Director of Photography
The *Courier-Journal & Louisville Times*
Louisville, Kentucky

Hugh Harris
Chief, Public Information Office
National Aeronautics & Space Administration
Kennedy Space Center, Florida

Mrs. Murray Haydon
Louisville, Kentucky

Robert Henrie
Executive Vice President
Savage Industries
Orem, Utah

Mike Isikoff
Correspondent
The Washington Post
Washington, D.C.

Rick Jones
Reporter
WAVE Radio
Louisville, Kentucky

Sharon Khy
Director of the Office of Public Relations
University of Arizona at Tucson
Tucson, Arizona

Mike King
Medical Writer
The *Courier-Journal*
Louisville, Kentucky

Mark Knoller
Correspondent
Associated Press Network Radio
Washington, D.C.

Morton Kondracke
Senior Editor
The New Republic
Washington, D.C.

Allan Lansing, M.D., Ph.D.
Medical Director
Humana Heart Institute International
Louisville, Kentucky

Father Gerald Lynch
Pastor
Notre Dame Church
Price, Utah

Steve Lyons
Medical Writer
The Louisville Times
Louisville, Kentucky

Peg Maloy
Assistant Director of Public &
Intergovernmental Affairs
Federal Emergency Management Agency
Washington, D.C.

Mark Mayfield
Bureau Chief
USA Today
Atlanta, Georgia

Bill McAda
Public Affairs Specialist
Federal Emergency Management Agency
Washington, D.C.

Jon Meyersohn
Producer
CBS News
Chicago, Illinois

Dale Minor
Producer
MedStar Communications
Allentown, Pennsylvania

Thomas Noland
Senior Public Affairs Manager
Humana Inc.
Louisville, Kentucky

Gil Owen
Reporter
Associated Press
Louisville, Kentucky

Paul Raeburn
Science Editor
Associated Press
New York, New York

George Raine
Correspondent
Newsweek
San Francisco, California

Al Rossiter, Jr.
Science Editor
United Press International
Washington, D.C.

Richard Schaefer
Director of Community Relations
Loma Linda University Medical Center
Loma Linda, California

Mrs. William Schroeder
Jasper, Indiana

Gary Schwitzer
Medical Correspondent
Cable News Network
Atlanta, Georgia

Earl J. Slack
Manager, Media Relations
 and Key Issues
Union Carbide Corporation
Danbury, Connecticut

Ed Staats
Chief of Bureau
Associated Press
Louisville, Kentucky

George Strait
Medical Correspondent
ABC News
Washington, D.C

Steve Swift
Reporter
Associated Press
Louisville, Kentucky

Edward W. Van Den Ameele
Manager, Media Relations
Union Carbide Corporation
Danbury, Connecticut

Twyla Van Leer
Reporter
Deseret News
Salt Lake City, Utah

Richard W. Weismeyer
Director of University Relations
Loma Linda University
Loma Linda, California

Ronald S. Wishart
Vice President, Public Relations
Union Carbide Corporation
Danbury, Connecticut

Ed Yeates
Science Specialist
KSL-TV
Salt Lake City, Utah

Chuck Zehnder
Editor
Price Utah Sun Advocate
Salt Lake City, Utah

Research and Transcribing:
Linda Pearman, Suzanne Dunckley,
Debbie Mason, Lisa Wade

Note: The positions held by several of those who contributed to the writing of this book have changed since the interviews were completed. Their new positions are listed in the footnotes.

INDEX